XML in Action

William J. Pardi

PUBLISHED BY
Microsoft Press
A Division of Microsoft Corporation
One Microsoft Way
Redmond, Washington 98052-6399

Library of Congress Cataloging-in-Publication Data
Pardi, William J.
    XML in Action / William J. Pardi.
        p.   cm.
    ISBN 0-7356-0562-9
    1. XML (Document markup language)   I. Title.
    QA76.76.H94P374   1999
    005.7'2--dc21   98-52991
                                                              CIP

Printed and bound in the United States of America.

  2 3 4 5 6 7 8 9   QMQM   4 3 2 1 0 9

Distributed in Canada by ITP Nelson, a division of Thomson Canada Limited.

A CIP catalogue record for this book is available from the British Library.

Microsoft Press books are available through booksellers and distributors worldwide. For further
information about international editions, contact your local Microsoft Corporation office or
contact Microsoft Press International directly at fax (425) 936-7329. Visit our Web site at
mspress.microsoft.com.

Acquisitions Editor: Juliana Aldous
Project Editor: Thom Votteler
Technical Editor: Linda Harmony

For my family—Jodie, Cody, and Ryan.
I love you.

Contents

Acknowledgments

Something I never really thought about as a *reader*, but that becomes very clear as an *author*, is that while writing a book, life often gets in the way. Fortunately, books are not produced by just one person. It takes a lot of hard work by a lot of talented people to see a project like this completed. And I have many people to thank for helping to get this book into your hands. First I would like to thank Juliana Aldous, acquisitions editor, for catching the vision for this book and helping to make it happen. Thanks to Thom Votteler, project editor extraordinaire, for managing the endless headaches, filling in wherever needed, and safeguarding the quality all along the way. Thanks to Lisa Theobald, manuscript editor, for all her work improving my writing while maintaining my voice. Special thanks to Linda Harmony, technical editor, whose scrutiny of and persistence with the code and technical aspects of this book have been invaluable. Thanks also to Kurt Meyer, Bill Teel, Paula Gorelick, Gina Cassill, Alton Lawson, Roger LeBlanc, Julie Miller, Valerie Woolley, and all the talented editorial and production people at Microsoft Press. They're the best in the biz!

I would also like to thank the folks on the XML development team, especially John Murray, for their help and input. Special thanks also to my wife, Jodie, and our two boys, Cody and little Ryan. Writing this book has meant many late nights and long weekends, and I couldn't have done it without their encouragement and support.

Introduction

HTML (Hypertext Markup Language) has been called the foundation of the World Wide Web. It provides a standardized way to create pages of formatted information that can be delivered to an ever-increasing global audience by means of the Internet. In a very real way, HTML—combined with HTTP (Hypertext Transport Protocol)—has revolutionized how people send and receive information. But HTML was designed primarily for data *display*. As a result, HTML focuses almost entirely on how information looks, not on what the information is or how it is structured. This is where Extensible Markup Language (XML) comes in.

XML is an open, text-based markup language that provides structural and semantic information to data. This "data about data," or *metadata*, provides additional meaning and context to the application using the data and allows for a new level of management and manipulation of Web-based information. XML, a subset of the popular Standard Generalized Markup Language (SGML), has been optimized for the Web. This helps make XML a powerful, standards-based complement to HTML that could be as important to the future of information delivery on the Web as HTML was to its beginning.

XML is intended to be used by content creators as well as by programmers. Since XML is text-based, it can be read and worked with easily in relatively nontechnical situations, but its ability to organize, describe, and structure data also makes it ideal for use in highly technical applications. XML thus provides common ground for creating structured data and making it available for manipulation and display.

Although XML is often called a language, it is, strictly speaking, a *metalanguage*. This means that XML can be used to create other languages. Thereby, vocabularies, which are language applications of XML, can be created to address targeted needs or solve specific problems. Some examples of XML vocabularies include:

- ♦ **XSL**   A style sheet–based formatting language that can take XML data and produce a wide range of output results.

- ♦ **XLL**   An extended linking specification that takes the hyperlinking mechanism of HTML to new levels.

- ♦ **SMIL**   A standardized multimedia authoring language that allows sophisticated multimedia authoring on the Web.

- ♦ **XSL Patterns**   An XML query language that provides advanced searching capabilities on XML data.

About This Book

As a dedicated observer of XML development and a participant in its implementation almost since its creation, I have been amazed to witness the degree to which the software industry has come to support this technology. It has become rare to pick up a computer magazine or look at an industry Web site without seeing something about XML. As you might imagine, I believe in the need for and benefits of XML, and I want it to succeed. The developers of XML and its many applications and vocabularies realize that for XML to be used and adopted widely, it not only must be easy to understand, it must be supported by resources that help make it easy to use. In my own work with XML, I have seen the need for practical XML resources. My hope is that this book contributes to the pool of effective tools that help developers and authors work successfully with XML.

The Focus of This Book

There are several implementations of XML, and there are many XML processors. This book focuses on the implementation of XML in Microsoft Internet Explorer 5 and on the Microsoft XML processor, called Msxml. I point this out because there are special features regarding the use of XML in Internet Explorer 5 that are distinct from the functionality of the Msxml processor. These special Internet Explorer features are addressed in Chapter 11, and I do not focus on them throughout most of the book. Rather, I attempt to deal directly with the XML language itself and the Msxml processor. This should afford you, the XML author, the most flexibility in the event that Microsoft decides to make the processor available outside of the browser. While all the examples in this book and on the companion CD will work in Internet Explorer 5, they will also work in earlier versions of Internet Explorer or in other applications (such as Microsoft Visual Basic or C++ applications) that use the current version of Msxml. (Note that at the time of this writing, Microsoft does not support the use of Msxml outside of Internet Explorer 5, but it's possible that policy will be reevaluated in the future.) The only exception to my focus on the Msxml processor is Chapter 7, "Linking with XML." XLink and XPointer—two vocabularies focused on linking with XML—are not currently supported by Msxml in Internet Explorer 5. Nevertheless, I included a chapter on this topic because it is an important part of XML and will eventually be part of many XML solutions.

What You Should Know

This book is targeted at intermediate computer users. It is expected that readers will have a working knowledge of the World Wide Web and some level of familiarity with HTML. Knowledge of markup languages such as SGML is helpful but not necessary. While programming experience also is not necessary, scripting is used throughout the book, and so some familiarity with programming concepts would be helpful. This book most likely will benefit:

- ◆ Web developers who want to get started with XML and incorporate it into their Web development work

- ◆ Technology executives or other professionals who want to gain an understanding of the XML language and how it might be applied to their businesses

- Programmers who want information on how to begin incorporating XML into their code

- Content developers who want to learn to use XML to create and manage structured data

- Computer hobbyists who want to understand XML and how it works

Conventions

Code samples appear in monospaced courier font as shown here:

```
<?xml version="1.0"?>
<MEMO>
  <TO>Jodie</TO>
  <FROM>Bill</FROM>
  <CC>Philip</CC>
  <SUBJECT>My first XML document</SUBJECT>
  <BODY>Hello, World!</BODY>
</MEMO>
```

Code samples that are included on the companion CD appear in the book with a shaded background. (Most code samples are contained on the companion CD, as noted in each chapter.) JScript, Microsoft's implementation of JavaScript, is used for all code samples in the book.

CASE SENSITIVITY

Markup tags appear in uppercase letters—for example, <TITLE></TITLE>—in code and in text. Object properties, attributes, methods, and events are case sensitive and appear with the proper case applied. One such case is the XML declaration. It should always appear in lower case, as shown here: <?xml version="1.0"?>. While the XML specification does not specify case in most instances, it is important that *consistency* be maintained when coding. For example, if you define an element name with a certain case, you should use that case when referencing that element. While this is not always required, it is the safest way to go. Another thing to keep in mind is that vocabularies defined in XML are often case sensitive. These are noted throughout the book, but a general rule is to use the vocabulary as it is defined in its specification.

Web Links

Most chapters contain relevant Web addresses where appropriate. While these were accurate and active at the time this book was written, please remember that URLs change and might no longer be active in some cases.

Appendix C contains a list of relevant topics available on the Microsoft Site Builder Network (SBN) and the Microsoft Developer Network (MSDN). These topics can be accessed on the companion CD or on the Internet. To access a topic on the CD, open the file *Workshop XML Reference.htm* to reach the SBN XML Table of Contents (XML TOC), and then navigate as described to the link for that particular topic. These topics are also available on the Internet. To get to the online versions of these topics, visit the MSDN Online Resource page at *http://msdn.microsoft.com/resources/pardixml.htm* (or open the file named *MSDN_OL.htm* on the companion CD). This page will direct you to the appropriate location on the MSDN Web site. (You can also access the SBN home page on the CD by opening the file *SBNSetup.exe*.)

Using the Msxml Parser from the Command Line

From the *Tools\Command Line XML* folder on the companion CD, copy *Msxml.exe* to your computer and launch from a DOS command prompt, pointing to an XML file to parse. This tool tells you whether the specified XML code is valid and can also be used to convert the XML to a different encoding. See the *Command Line XML_readme.htm* file for information on how to use this tool.

What's on the Companion CD

The companion CD contains:

◆ All the code samples in the book, organized by chapter name in subfolders of the *Samples* folder (You can install these samples by double-clicking *Setup.exe*.)

◆ An electronic version of the book in HTML format, in the *Ebook* folder

◆ A snapshot of the SBN Workshop Web site

◆ Tools to help you create and test XML files, in the *Tools* folder

◆ A copy of the XML 1.0 specification in HTML format, in the *XML1Spec* folder

Part 1
Introducing XML

Chapter 1
Understanding
Markup Languages

It's a good guess that you're reading this book because you want to learn how to use XML (Extensible Markup Language). If you are like me, you want to pick up a computer book and start writing code by at least the second or third page. You've probably heard all the hype about how XML will change the Web and bridge gaps among the world's various types of digital information. You're convinced that XML is something you need to learn, and you might be anxious to jump right in and start coding. If you are that type of person, you won't have to wait too long. We'll get into some XML code before the end of the second chapter. But to really understand XML—and after all, that is the goal—you could probably benefit from some background information. These first few chapters provide a framework for the rest of the book—in addition to getting us into a little code. After reading these chapters, you should have a better understanding of and appreciation for XML. Establishing a framework is especially important with XML for a couple of reasons:

♦ You might not be familiar with some concepts utilized by markup languages. The information in these chapters will help get you up to speed on the basics of these languages and how they work.

♦ You might have experience using HTML (Hypertext Markup Language) or SGML (Standard Generalized Markup Language). You should understand how XML differs from these two languages and what makes it such a powerful alternative (or complement, depending on how you use it).

In many ways, XML represents a fundamental shift in the way information is delivered on the Web. While XML might not be as "flashy" as some of the other new Web technologies, it has the potential to have as much impact on Web delivery as HTML did several years ago. In this chapter, you'll begin to see why an extensible language like XML is necessary. We'll look at a brief background of text markup and how it works. We'll also examine differences between some of the more common markup languages.

A Brief History of Markup Languages

Markup has its roots in the print-based world, and even the term *markup* is a concatenation of the words *mark up,* which refer to the traditional way of marking up a document in the print and design worlds. The term *markup* specifically refers to tagging electronic documents for one of two purposes: to modify the look and formatting of text or to establish the structure and meaning of a document for output to some medium, such as a printer or the World Wide Web.

If you have worked with an HTML editor such as Microsoft FrontPage or a word processing program such as Microsoft Word, you are familiar with the idea of changing the formatting of text in a document. What you might not know is that those editing programs use markup to accomplish that formatting. We will look at how this works later in this chapter.

In addition to formatting text, markup can work to determine the structure and meaning (or context) of textual elements. For example, markup can establish that a document can contain only the elements Name, Birthday, and Age. It can further state that the document cannot contain Birthday and Age elements unless it contains a Name element. Markup can then state that the Name element must be text, the Birthday element must be a date, and the Age element must be a number. In this way, markup sets up the structure of the document and defines the semantic meaning of the elements. Later chapters will cover this subject in much more detail.

The Way Things Were

Before the advent of electronic publishing, a typed (or handwritten) document would be edited and marked up by hand on a draft copy. The draft would then go through several more rounds of revisions and reviews. Sometimes the document would be retyped, and sometimes it would end up with several layers of handwritten editorial marks. Based on a list of specifications for that type of document, formatting and style preferences for various parts of the document would be included as part of the handwritten notes. The document would then go to a typesetter, where the final typeset proof would be formatted and laid out. Then the finished document would be sent to the printer.

Enter Electronic Publishing

Electronic document preparation made a lot of this manual work unnecessary. It also made it much easier to change elements in a document at various points throughout the process before the document ever went to the printer. With traditional typesetting, such text formatting options as fonts, leading, margins, and justification were all established by the typesetter. The typesetter would use the typeface that was identified in the document mark up or in the specification sheet, perform copy-fitting calculations to make sure the page was readable, and then set the page in type. To accomplish this same level of control in the electronic world, a way to code the text was needed so that the output device would know how the document was supposed to be structured and how the text was supposed to look. The answer was electronic markup.

How Markup Works

Markup consists basically of codes, or *tags* (also called *tokens*), that are added to text to change the look or meaning of the tagged text. The tagged text for a document is usually called the *source code,* or just *code,* for that document. Most word processors, desktop publishing systems, and even simple text editors that can produce formatted text use some sort of markup language. For example, this book was written using Microsoft Word, which supports the markup language RTF (Rich Text Format).

Markup is commonly used to change the look of text by adding formatting, such as bold or italic fonts, text indents, font sizes, and font weights. Markup tags typically work by turning these attributes on when they are needed and off when they are not. Let's look at an example.

A Look at RTF Markup

As I mentioned, Word supports the RTF markup language. The WordPad applet that comes with Microsoft Windows also supports RTF. Following is a short memo document formatted in RTF using WordPad:

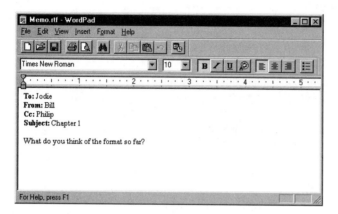

This text looks like any other text you might see when using a word processor or desktop publishing program or even while viewing a Web page. But as already stated, this text has been formatted with RTF and saved as an RTF file. Here is how the tagged text, or code, for this document looks:

```
{\rtf1\ansi\ansicpg1252\deff0\deftab720{\fonttbl
  {\f0\fswiss MS Sans Serif;}
  {\f1\froman\fcharset2 Symbol;}
  {\f2\froman Times New Roman;}}
{\colortbl\red0\green0\blue0;}
\deflang1033\pard\plain\f2\fs20\b To: \plain\f2\fs20 Jodie
\par \plain\f2\fs20\b From: \plain\f2\fs20 Bill
\par \plain\f2\fs20\b Cc: \plain\f2\fs20 Philip
\par \plain\f2\fs20\b Subject: \plain\f2\fs20 Chapter 1
\par
\par What do you think of the format so far?
\par }
```

The tagged text looks much different than the displayed text, doesn't it! This code tells the application that processes it (called a *processor*) just about everything the application needs to know about the text in the document. The markup tags throughout the document tell the application everything, from the markup language used (see the *\rtf1* tag at the beginning) to the color of the text (*\colortbl\red0\green0\blue0*) to where each new line begins (*\par*). One visible feature of the displayed text in the screen shot above is that some text is bold and other text is not. This is indicated in the code as well. In the code, notice the *\b* tag that appears just before the word *To:* on the sixth line. That tag "turns on" the bold attribute for that line of text. Just after the word *To:*, you'll see the *\plain* tag. This tag effectively "turns off" bold and "turns on" plain, which is really the same as no formatting at all.

As you can see, after you know a little about what each of the tags means, the RTF code is actually quite readable. However, this is not always true with other markup languages. If you try to look at a document saved in Word Document format, for example, it will not look like much. Here is our memo document saved in Word Document format and viewed as plain text.

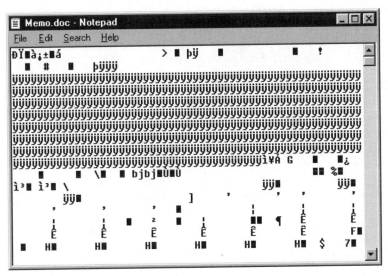

Word adds some extra "stuff" to the RTF markup tags and saves the entire document as a binary file, which isn't readable as text. Word Document format is also *closed*, which means that it is not publicly available. The implication is that vendors do not have access to the rules for the markup language and therefore cannot create their own processors for the language. The specification for an *open* language, on the other hand, is publicly available—allowing any vendor to create a processor for it. Some vendors are looking for ways to package HTML documents, which are in open formats, into compressed or binary formats to make their code more secure. In fact, Microsoft Internet Explorer 5 provides a way to package all the elements on an HTML page into a single binary file, allowing an author to deliver a single file instead of having to deliver separate HTML files, graphic files, and so on for every page. This "packaging" does not mean that the HTML language itself would be closed; it means that the code for some documents would not be viewable, as it is today.

You might be wondering how the RTF code was retrieved from the WordPad display in the first screen graphic. Here's a simple explanation: I created the document in WordPad and saved it. I then opened the document in Notepad, a plain-text application. Since Notepad cannot interpret the RTF tags, it simply displays everything in the document without applying any formatting to the text, so human eyes can easily read all the code in the document.

This illustrates an important notion about markup. For markup to work properly, it requires that a processor read the markup codes, interpret how they affect the text, and display the results. WordPad acts as the processor for RTF, but WordPad cannot process any other markup language, such as HTML. So if you were to open an HTML document in WordPad, you would see the plain text *and* markup tags, not the formatted text.

Document Structure

If you look closely at the RTF markup code in the example on page 6, you will notice that it is impossible for you to derive the *structure* of the document simply from the code shown. Nothing within the markup tells you whether rules exist to govern how the document should be put together. The author of the document can place words and formatting anywhere in the document and in any order. While this kind of freedom might seem desirable, it can actually create a lot of problems. For one thing, it makes it difficult for human readers to interpret the markup code of a complex document. While you might be able to decipher a specific section of the markup, you would not be able to determine why it is located there or whether it is related to other markup. This loose structure also makes it almost impossible for someone else to author a document of exactly the same type. For example, if someone wanted to make another memo similar to ours, they would have to make an exact copy of all the code we used and then replace only those parts that needed to be changed in the new memo. While that might be possible with small documents, it would be extremely difficult with long and complex documents. Yet another problem is that this particular document is not necessarily portable to other platforms or devices. Since no rules exist for how this document is structured, it would be difficult for someone else to create a processor that will interpret the document accurately. And the document would certainly not be extensible beyond the markup already coded into it. In other words, without the ability to set rules for a document, it is impossible to create other types of reusable document structures from the original document.

A Look at HTML Markup

As you might have guessed, the problems described above are not new ones. And of the efforts to fix the problems, some are more complex than others. One of the most popular solutions is HTML. Let's look at this same document using the HTML markup language.

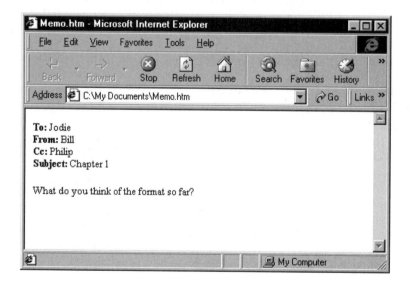

As you can see, the HTML document looks pretty much the same as the RTF document, even though the markup is completely different. Let's look at the HTML markup code:

```
<!DOCTYPE HTML PUBLIC "-//W3C//DTD HTML 3.2 FINAL//EN">
<HTML>

  <HEAD>
    <TITLE>Memo</TITLE>
  </HEAD>

  <BODY>
    <FONT FACE="Times New Roman" SIZE="2">

      <P>
        <B>To: </B>
        Jodie<BR>
        <B>From: </B>
        Bill<BR>
        <B>Cc: </B>
        Philip<BR>
        <B>Subject: </B>
        Chapter 1
      </P>

      <P>
        What do you think of the format so far?
      </P>

    </FONT>
  </BODY>

</HTML>
```

If you closely examine this document's markup, you can see that an implicit structure has been applied to the document. Notice that the <HTML> tag appears at the beginning and a similar tag, </HTML>, appears at the end. Everything else within the document is contained between these tags. Also notice the Head element, the Title element, and the Body element. Each of these pieces of code has a specific place and purpose in the document. Now look at some of the formatting tags. The markup includes bold formatting, as does the RTF document, but notice that two bold tags are used—one to turn bold on (<B>) and another to turn it off (</B>).

HTML's structure is not accidental. HTML documents are supposed to conform to a specific set of rules that identify exactly how a document should be put together. These rules tell the processor which elements are available in HTML markup. They identify which elements can and cannot be contained "inside" other elements, and they identify what types of external files are allowed in a document. They even set the rules for linking to other documents or files, a process called *hyperlinking*. All of the rules are included in the *Document Type Definition* (DTD). You might have noticed the line at the beginning of the HTML code that included the letters *DTD*. This line is called a *document type declaration,* and it tells the processor which DTD to use. DTDs will be discussed in Chapter 4, but if you are not familiar with them, all you need to know at this point is that each DTD works as a blueprint that defines a document structure.

Although each HTML document is *supposed* to conform to a DTD, in real-world applications, HTML processors (most often Web browsers) do not check a document against the DTD, nor do they even read the DTD. Because of this, most browsers let HTML authors break the rules a bit. For example, in the Memo.htm file shown previously, you could break the rules by putting the Title element outside the Head element or the Body element outside the HTML element. (You really shouldn't write code in this way, but the point is that you *could* do it and most browsers would still be able to read it.) As you come to understand XML, however, you will see that this casual approach to markup rules does not work when writing XML code.

> **NOTE**
>
> An *element* in many markup languages is simply a pair of opening and closing tags. For example, <TITLE> and </TITLE> are tags, but if you put them together, as in <TITLE></TITLE>, you have created a Title element. Most elements also contain some content between the opening and closing tags, as does the example on the previous page: *<TITLE>Memo</TITLE>*. However, not all markup languages require an opening tag and a closing tag to make up a valid element. In some cases, a single tag (usually the opening tag) is all that is needed.

Specific and Generalized Markup Languages

Two types of markup languages are in use today: *specific* markup and *generalized* markup. Specific markup languages are used to generate code that is specific to a particular application or device. These markup languages are often built to serve a particular need. Generalized markup describes the structure and meaning of the text in a document, but it does not define how the text should be used. In other words, the language itself is not made for any specific application and is generic enough to be used in many different applications. Documents described with a generalized markup language are usually portable to more applications than those described with a specific markup language. Let's examine these concepts in more detail.

Specific Markup Languages

The examples of markup shown so far in this chapter have demonstrated specific markup—that is, the HTML and RTF languages were developed for specific purposes. HTML has the specific purpose of formatting documents for the Web. And RTF has a similar purpose—that of text formatting. As you saw in the previous examples, however, the markup code for HTML and RTF look different, even though both were created for similar purposes. As you might have guessed, the two languages are not interchangeable. A processor that understands RTF will not understand HTML, and vice versa.

Even though markup languages are not interchangeable, a single application might still be able to read and display several different kinds of markup. For example, with the correct filters installed, Word can read and display RTF, HTML, Plain Text, Word-Perfect, Microsoft Works, and other types of documents. Note that different processing software is required for each markup language. Also, the markup codes are not interchangeable within a document. An RTF document, for example, must contain only RTF markup or the text will not display as intended.

Many markup languages have served quite well as document formatting tools for printing or for the Web. However, they do not perform as well at describing the data they contain or at providing contextual information for the data. Let's look at the markup for our RTF memo example again.

```
{\rtf1\ansi\ansicpg1252\deff0\deftab720{\fonttbl
  {\f0\fswiss MS Sans Serif;}
  {\f1\froman\fcharset2 Symbol;}
  {\f2\froman Times New Roman;}}
{\colortbl\red0\green0\blue0;}
\deflang1033\pard\plain\f2\fs20\b To: \plain\f2\fs20 Jodie
\par \plain\f2\fs20\b From: \plain\f2\fs20 Bill
\par \plain\f2\fs20\b Cc: \plain\f2\fs20 Philip
\par \plain\f2\fs20\b Subject: \plain\f2\fs20 Chapter 1
\par
\par What do you think of the format so far?
\par }
```

Notice that every tag describes how the text should be formatted but tells us nothing about the *kind* of text data included in the document. We could easily change all the text in the document and completely lose the fact that this was originally a memo document. We can do this because many markup languages are created for the specific purpose of describing text formatting and layout but not for any other purposes, such as defining a certain structure of data or providing a way to interchange incompatible data formats. Such specificity results in several limitations common to specific markup languages:

◆ Authors are limited to a particular set of tags. If this set of tags does not meet a need, authors must find a workaround or live with the limitation.

◆ A document might not be portable to other applications. Because the data is not self-describing, it cannot be used for any other purpose than that for which it was intended.

◆ The language probably has a proprietary way of marking up text that is not compatible with other markup languages. This can create confusion and extra work for authors who must use several languages to accommodate different applications.

Self-describing documents, examined in later chapters, basically provide data about data (also called *metadata*) so that the data in the documents can stand apart from the formatting that describes how the documents are displayed. For example, a document might contain information in the form of a number. A self-describing document might identify the number as an age, the age as that of a tree, the tree as part of a reforestation project, and so on.

Back when electronic documents were starting to make a big impact on information delivery, it was obvious that these kinds of limitations would cause a lot of problems down the road. This encouraged the use of generalized markup languages.

Generalized Markup Languages

In the 1970s, Dr. C. F. Goldfarb (an attorney who eventually went to work for IBM) and two of his colleagues proposed a method of describing text that was not specific to an application or a device. The method had two basic parts:

♦ The markup should describe the structure of a document and not its formatting or style characteristics.

♦ The syntax of the markup should be strictly enforced so that the code can clearly be read by a software program or by a human.

The result of these suggestions was the Document Composition Facility Generalized Markup Language (DCF GML, or GML for short) developed for IBM. GML was the precursor to the Standard Generalized Markup Language (SGML) that was adopted as a standard by the International Organization for Standardization (ISO) in 1986.

The ISO was founded in 1947 and comprises some 130 member countries. The ISO exists to "promote the development of standardization and related activities in the world with a view to facilitating the international exchange of goods and services, and to developing cooperation in the spheres of intellectual, scientific, technological and economic activity." The ISO's work results in a set of published standards that are used throughout the world. ISO standards affect fields ranging from telecommunications to agriculture to entertainment. You will often see a published standard referenced by its ISO number. (ISO 8879, for example, is the SGML standard.) For more information on the ISO, see *http://www.iso.ch/welcome.html.*

The SGML standard brought some important changes to text markup. In addition to providing a way to lay out the structure of a document, SGML added provisions for:

♦ Identifying the characters to be used in a document. This makes it easier to ensure that a processor can understand everything in a document by allowing a document to specify which character set it is using (ISO 646 or ISO 8859, for example).

- Providing a way to identify objects that will be used throughout a document. These objects, called *entities,* are convenient to use when pieces of text or other data appear in several places in a document. By *declaring* an entity in one place in the document, any changes to that declaration will be reflected in all occurrences of the entity throughout the document. (Entities will be discussed in Chapters 3 and 4.)

- Providing a way to incorporate external data into a document. This allows data that might not be text to be used in the document.

Now let's look at how our memo document might appear as an SGML document:

```
<!DOCTYPE MEMO PUBLIC "-//BJP//DTD MEMO//EN">
<MEMO>
  <TO>Jodie
  <FROM>Bill
  <CC>Philip
  <SUBJECT>Chapter 1
  <BODY>What do you think of the format so far?
</MEMO>
```

If you take a close look at this code, you'll see some elements that look similar to those in the markup we have already covered—and you'll see some differences as well. First let's look at the similarities.

This document should appear similar to the HTML version of our memo document on page 9. If you look back at that version, you will see a similar DTD declaration at the top of the document and you'll notice a similar tagging format. For example, the Memo element includes both opening and closing tags. For the most part, the content (text between tags) is also the same as that of the HTML document—for good reason. These similarities exist because HTML is an *application* of SGML. That is, HTML was created using the SGML standard. Because of this, many of the details of SGML are carried through to HTML, but not all details. Now let's look at how the two versions differ.

First of all, notice that many of the SGML elements do not include closing tags. These tags are optional and could easily have been included for any of the elements. For example, I can add a closing tag to the Body element without changing the meaning of the SGML code:

```
<!DOCTYPE MEMO PUBLIC "-//BJP//DTD MEMO//EN">
<MEMO>
  <TO>Jodie
  <FROM>Bill
  <CC>Philip
  <SUBJECT>Chapter 1
  <BODY>What do you think of the format so far?</BODY>
</MEMO>
```

HTML also supports this type of *minimization technique.* While this might not seem important to you now, you'll see its relevance later when we discuss XML.

The biggest difference between SGML and HTML is that nothing in the SGML document indicates how the data should look. The markup does, however, identify the structure of the document. Notice that some content has been removed, specifically the address information

(To:, From:, and so on). This could be done safely because that information is now part of the document structure. In fact, the DTD outlines all the rules for what types of elements can exist in this type of document, where they can appear, and what kinds of data they can contain. The processor can read the document and, based on the structure and context, output the data in an appropriate way.

The Big Markup Picture

If you are new to some of these concepts, this discussion might have seemed a bit confusing, so here's the bottom line. The tags in the SGML version of our memo were created *specifically* for a memo document. That is possible because SGML is *extensible,* which means that it allows an author to define a particular structure (such as a memo document structure) by defining the parts (tags) that fit that structure. You know that HTML is an application of SGML. That means that a group of people sat down and, using SGML, came up with a whole new language to be used specifically for formatting documents on the World Wide Web. The HTML language, however, is not extensible, which means that HTML cannot be used as a basis to create another markup language with its own rules and purposes. Because SGML allows for the creation of other languages, calling SGML a markup language is a bit misleading. Instead, it's actually a *metalanguage* that allows for the creation of other languages.

At this point, you might be wondering what SGML has to do with the purpose of this book, which is to teach XML. Well, XML is a direct descendant of SGML. But unlike HTML, XML is not really a *new* language. It is actually a subset of SGML and also qualifies as a metalanguage. In fact, SGML can do everything that XML can do, and more. But if this is true, why do we need XML? The next chapter answers that question.

Chapter 2
Enter XML

You learned about markup languages in general in Chapter 1. In this chapter, you'll learn why XML was developed. You'll discover how XML fits in with SGML and HTML. This chapter also discusses the goals of the XML language and surveys some of the work being done in the standards groups. And, as promised, you'll work with actual XML code before the end of the chapter.

What Is XML?

As noted in Chapter 1, XML is derived from SGML. But unlike HTML, XML is not an application of SGML but is a subset, or *profile,* of it. That being the case, XML is a metalanguage in much the same way as SGML. That is, other languages, or *vocabularies,* can be developed in XML (more on vocabularies in Chapter 5). As mentioned in Chapter 1, anything that can be done in XML can also be done in SGML. So why is XML needed?

The Case for XML

Because XML is optimized for use on the World Wide Web, the XML initiative brings to the table some benefits that are not found in SGML. XML has the ability to work *with* HTML for data display and presentation, so XML provides several advantages over SGML for Web-delivered data:

◆ XML is a smaller language than SGML. The designers of XML tried to cut out everything in SGML that was not needed for Web delivery. The result is a much simpler and slimmed down language. (The specification proves this: the basic SGML specification is about 155 pages long, while the XML specification is only about 35 pages long.)

◆ XML includes a specification for a hyperlinking scheme, which is described as a separate language called *Extensible Linking Language* (XLL). Not only does XML support the basic hyperlinking found in HTML, but it takes the concept further with extended linking. (Extended linking is covered in detail in Chapter 8.) While SGML allows a hyperlinking mechanism to be defined, it does not include hyperlinking as part of its original specification.

◆ XML includes a specification for a style language called *Extensible Stylesheet Language* (XSL). This language provides support for a style-sheet mechanism, also something that is not found in SGML. Style sheets allow an author to create a template of various styles (such as bold, italic, and so on) or combinations of styles and apply them to elements in a document.

NOTE

XLL and XSL are two powerful additions to the XML family of languages. XLL is discussed in Chapter 7, and XSL is covered in Chapter 8.

To put it simply, XML provides 80 percent of the features and functionality of SGML with 20 percent of the complexity.

XML Is About Data

If HTML is about *displaying* information, XML is about *describing* information. XML is a standard language used to structure and describe data that can be understood by different applications. The power of XML is its ability to separate the user interface from the data. Let's rewrite the memo document from Chapter 1 and see how this works. The XML code for the new document is shown here:

```
<?xml version="1.0"?>
<MEMO>
  <TO>Jodie</TO>
  <FROM>Bill</FROM>
  <CC>Philip</CC>
  <SUBJECT>Chapter 2</SUBJECT>
  <BODY>This is where we start getting into some XML code!</BODY>
</MEMO>
```

You'll notice that the code above looks similar to the SGML version of the document in Chapter 1, with the exception that every element has a closing tag—but more on that later. Notice here that nothing inherent in the document indicates how the data should look. In other words, no formatting information (such as bold or italic fonts, text indent, and font size) is included. However, much of the document code describes what the data *is*. A human reader could easily look at this code and understand what the document is about and how it is structured.

XML documents are also known as *self-describing*. That is, each document contains the set of rules to which its data must conform. Because any set of rules can be reused in another document, other authors can easily create the same *class* of document, if necessary.

NOTE

Document classes are discussed in Chapter 4. The class concept was borrowed from object-oriented programming, in which each class is used to describe a group of objects that have a common set of characteristics. Classing documents is a powerful way to group documents based on the kind of content they contain.

Some other ways that XML can be used to work with data include the following:

◆ Using XML as a data interchange format. Many systems that have been in use for a while, called *legacy systems,* can contain data in disparate formats, and developers are doing a lot of work to connect these systems using the Internet. One of their challenges is to be able to exchange data between systems that ordinarily are not compatible. XML might be the answer. Since the XML text format is *standards based* (implying that many applications can understand it), data can be converted to XML and then easily read by another system or application.

◆ Using XML for Web data. Imagine having an HTML page in which none of the content is located on the page itself. Instead, the content is stored in an XML file, and the HTML page is used simply for formatting and display. The content can be updated, translated into another language, or otherwise modified without an author ever having to touch the HTML code.

◆ Using XML to create a common data store for information that might get used in many different ways. Suppose, for example, that you are writing an article for a magazine. The publisher also wants to include the article on a Web site and then submit it for inclusion in a book or journal. If the original article was authored in a proprietary format, such as RTF, the article would have to be reworked for the Web posting and then probably reworked again for the book or journal. If the article was written in XML, however, it could be published to the three different environments simultaneously because the data of the article is independent of how it is being displayed. The formatting, layout, and so on are dependent upon the application using the data and are not attached to the content itself. Furthermore, the application code that displays the data needs to be written only once, and it then can be used to display any number of articles.

As you will see, XML can be an extremely powerful way to author and store data, not only for use on the Web but for use in other applications as well.

Where Does XML Fit In?

You already know that XML is a subset of SGML. And you know that XML is not intended to replace HTML but rather to complement it. In this section, we'll take a closer look at where the XML markup language fits between these two closely related languages.

How XML Relates to SGML

SGML had been used for many years in sophisticated and highly complex publishing applications. Despite the fact that HTML, an application of SGML, is the standard for Web publishing, SGML itself never got any traction with the Web development community. This was primarily due to the complexity of SGML and the resulting overhead required to use it.

In August 1996, a group called the SGML Editorial Review Board (SGML ERB) formed within the World Wide Web Consortium (W3C). This group eventually became the XML Working Group. The group's goal was to create a generalized markup language that would be easy to implement on the Web. The SGML ERB worked with a larger group called the

SGML Working Group, which later became the XML Special Interest Group. Together, these groups decided what parts of SGML would make up the XML language.

The focus of the XML Working Group was to include in XML only the parts of SGML that were needed for use in Web publishing. As a result, XML did away with much of the complexity and *all* of the optional features that have proved burdensome in SGML. Even with all that cutting, XML retains the primary benefits of SGML:

- XML is a generalized markup language; authors can define their own tag sets.

- Documents are self-describing. A valid document contains all of the rules for that particular class of document.

- Documents can be validated. By using the rules found in the Document Type Definition (DTD), the processor can verify that the document is authored according to the rules.

NOTE

You might wonder why it's beneficial to remove all of the optional features from SGML. Generally, the use of options increases the likelihood that a document will be incompatible with an application. That is, an application designed to process an SGML document with a particular set of options might not be able to process another SGML document with a different set of options. The designers of XML wanted to reduce, and preferably eliminate, incompatibility problems caused by options.

It is important to emphasize again that XML is a subset of SGML. Any valid XML document is also a valid SGML document. You might think of XML as "SGML Lite."

How XML Relates to HTML

Many people think of XML as a replacement for HTML. Although this might be partly true, the two languages are more likely to be complementary to one another than in competition. In reality, the two languages operate at different levels with regard to how they treat data. For cases in which XML is used to structure and describe data on the Web, HTML will likely be used to format that data. Because most HTML pages store the data as well as the formatting for that data in the HTML code, any replacement of HTML will likely occur in the area of data storage. In many cases, XML might take over the job of data storage (in addition to retaining its job of data description), and HTML would be used just for formatting and scripting.

Looking at Some XML Code

I promised that we would work with some XML code before the end of this chapter, so here we go. To help you get a picture of how XML and HTML can work together, let's take a look at how to use them to display data on a Web page. This sample will involve two documents: an XML document for the data and an HTML document for the formatting and display. Let's start by modifying the memo document created earlier in this chapter. As in all good programming books, our first code sample will display the words "Hello World!" The XML document, which you can find in the Chap02\Lst2_1.xml file on the companion CD, is shown in Code Listing 2-1.

```xml
<?xml version="1.0"?>
<MEMO>
  <TO>Jodie</TO>
  <FROM>Bill</FROM>
  <CC>Philip</CC>
  <SUBJECT>My first XML document</SUBJECT>
  <BODY>Hello, World!</BODY>
</MEMO>
```

Code Listing 2-1.

Next we'll create an HTML page to display the data in the memo. To do this, we'll need to add the XML processor to the page and use some script code to extract the data and put it in the format we want. The HTML code, which you don't need to understand in depth at this point, can be found in the Chap02\Lst2_2.htm file on the companion CD and is shown in Code Listing 2-2.

```html
<!DOCTYPE HTML PUBLIC "-//W3C//DTD HTML 3.2 Final//EN">
<HTML>

  <HEAD>
    <SCRIPT LANGUAGE="JavaScript" FOR=window EVENT=onload>
      loadDoc();
    </SCRIPT>

    <SCRIPT LANGUAGE="JavaScript">
      var rootElem;
      var xmlDoc = new ActiveXObject("microsoft.xmldom");
      xmlDoc.load("Lst2_1.xml");

      function loadDoc()
        {
        if (xmlDoc.readyState == "4")
          start();
        else
          window.setTimeout("loadDoc()", 4000)
        }
```

Code Listing 2-2.

```
    function start()
      {
      rootElem = xmlDoc.documentElement;
      todata.innerText = rootElem.childNodes.item(0).text;
      fromdata.innerText=rootElem.childNodes.item(1).text;
      ccdata.innerText=rootElem.childNodes.item(2).text;
      subjectdata.innerText=rootElem.childNodes.item(3).text;
      bodydata.innerText=rootElem.childNodes.item(4).text;
      }
  </SCRIPT>

  <TITLE>Code Listing 2-2</TITLE>
</HEAD>

<BODY>
  <DIV ID="to" STYLE="font-weight:bold;font-size:16">
    To:
    <SPAN ID="todata" STYLE="font-weight:normal"></SPAN>
  </DIV>
  <BR>

  <DIV ID="from" STYLE="font-weight:bold;font-size:16">
    From:
    <SPAN ID="fromdata" STYLE="font-weight:normal"></SPAN>
  </DIV>
  <BR>

  <DIV ID="cc" STYLE="font-weight:bold;font-size:16">
    Cc:
    <SPAN ID="ccdata" STYLE="font-weight:normal"></SPAN>
  </DIV>
  <BR>

  <DIV ID="subject" STYLE="font-weight:bold;font-size:16">
    Subject:
    <SPAN ID="subjectdata" STYLE="font-weight:normal"></SPAN>
  </DIV>
  <BR>

  <HR>
  <SPAN ID="bodydata" STYLE="font-weight:normal"></SPAN>
</BODY>

</HTML>
```

Keeping Data Separate from the Display

You might be thinking that it takes a lot of code just to display that little memo. Although using XML is probably overkill in this case, the intent of this sample is to show how the content, or data, is kept separate from the formatting. So if you want to change the information in the memo, you only have to make changes to the XML code, and you don't have to wade through the HTML code to find what you need to change. I won't go through this code in depth at this point, since more in-depth information is covered in later chapters, but you can easily see how XML can be a powerful data storage mechanism, even without understanding any of the HTML code. To make changes to the memo, you follow these steps:

1. Open the Lst2_1.xml file in a text editor such as Notepad, and change the *content* of the XML elements, taking care not to change the tags. For example, the To element could be changed to *<TO>Yoko</TO>*. You can change the content of these elements in any way you'd like.

2. Save the XML document with your changes, and close the document.

3. Open the Lst2_2.htm file.

> **NOTE**
>
> If you copy Lst2_1.xml and Lst2_2.htm from the companion CD rather than running Setup, you need to turn off the Read-only attribute for the XML file so that you can make changes to it. To do this, right-click the Lst2_1.xml file in Windows Explorer and select Properties from the context menu. In the Lst2_1.xml Properties dialog box, clear the Read-only check box.

Your changes will be reflected in the display of the HTML document. Notice that the formatting is exactly the same as that of the original XML document, even though the data is different. You could even type the XML content in another language, such as German, and still it would display just as you intended, without your changing the HTML code. This is a simple example of how XML can be used to structure and store data. As you will see in later chapters, this is just the tip of the iceberg!

XML and HTML Working Together

As you can see from the preceding sample, HTML and XML can work well together. Since all the content for the memo was kept separate from the HTML code, the content is easy to change and work with. And the HTML document can be used as a template to create many memo documents containing different data. In one sense, XML replaced portions of the HTML code because the HTML code no longer stored any of the data for the document. But the XML code did not constitute a total replacement of the HTML code.

In later chapters, you'll see more of this collaboration between XML and HTML. You can even embed XML data fragments inside an HTML document as "XML data islands." As usual, the formatting is handled by HTML, but the data is kept to the strict structure and processing rules of XML.

Since it should now be obvious that the intent of XML is not to create a replacement for HTML, let's look at what the creators of XML did intend as they were developing the language.

The Goals of XML

XML is designed to work well on the Web. While that goal is certainly a primary factor in the design of the language, XML is intended to work in many environments outside the Web as well, including publishing, data interchange, and commercial applications. For XML to be adopted in such a wide variety of applications, its designers knew that it would have to be simple, powerful, and easy to implement for many different kinds of users.

Defining the Goals for XML

To help you better understand what XML is intended to do, let's look at the goals for the language as defined by the creators of XML.

GOAL 1: XML SHALL BE STRAIGHTFORWARDLY USABLE OVER THE INTERNET. First XML should work well on the Internet and take into account the needs of applications running in a distributed networked environment. This does not mean that XML should be able to instantly plug into current Web applications, but working well on the Internet should be of primary importance.

The next point regarding this goal focuses on the word *straightforwardly*. SGML has proven to be too complex for some authors to work with and its structure too sophisticated for clients to process efficiently in networked environments. Because XML leaves out all the extras and leaves in only what is necessary, most of the complexity and overhead that was problematic with SGML is removed as well. Note that this goal does not mean that XML should be limited to Internet applications, and this brings us to the next goal.

GOAL 2: XML SHALL SUPPORT A WIDE VARIETY OF APPLICATIONS. This goal stipulates that XML should be utilized by a wide range of applications, such as authoring tools, content display engines, translation tools, and even database applications. The creators of XML realized that the rapid adoption of XML would depend on the availability of software applications that use it.

NOTE

Quite a few freestanding software products now support XML. Check out *http://www.gca.org/conf/xml/xml_what.htm#xmlsoft* for a list of some of them. Eventually, most popular applications that work with text or other data will support XML.

GOAL 3: XML SHALL BE COMPATIBLE WITH SGML.   This goal is a crucial aspect of the XML design, but it is also one of the most troublesome goals. The idea is that any valid XML document must also be a valid SGML document. This goal was established so that existing SGML tools would also work with and *parse* XML code. Note that while valid XML is also valid SGML, the reverse is not true. Remember, XML was built by removing all the inessential pieces from SGML, so SGML contains a lot more that would cause a failure when using an XML processor.

NOTE

What is *parsing*? To parse an XML or SGML document, a processor must break down the document into its constituent parts and understand the structure of the document and the relationship of its parts. XML (and SGML) are considered parsable because they are required to follow strict rules (usually in the form of a DTD) that allow any processor that understands those rules to interpret the document correctly. HTML, even though it is an application of SGML, is usually not truly parsable, since most processors don't strictly enforce the rules and most authors don't strictly follow the rules.

GOAL 4: IT SHALL BE EASY TO WRITE PROGRAMS WHICH PROCESS XML DOCUMENTS. The idea behind this goal is that the adoption of the language would be proportional to the availability of tools. The definition of what is "easy" is, of course, relative, but the original idea was that someone with a computer science degree should be able to write a basic XML processor in a week or two. While the "two-week" benchmark of this goal has all but been abandoned, the proliferation of XML tools, many of them freeware, is testament that the goal has been reached.

GOAL 5: THE NUMBER OF OPTIONAL FEATURES IN XML IS TO BE KEPT TO THE ABSOLUTE MINIMUM, IDEALLY ZERO.   This goal comes from another problem users had with SGML. The SGML specification comes with a lot of options—many of which are never used. This adds excess overhead to SGML processors and often makes document/processor compatibility difficult, if not impossible. If, for example, an application was designed to read and process SGML documents with specific options, the application might not correctly understand documents that used different options. XML avoids this potential for incompatibility by reducing the number of options to zero. This means that any XML processor should be able to parse any XML document, no matter what data or structure the document contains.

GOAL 6: XML DOCUMENTS SHOULD BE HUMAN-LEGIBLE AND REASONABLY CLEAR. This goal is included for both philosophical and practical purposes. Since XML uses plain text to describe data and relationships among that data, it has the inherent advantage of being easier to work with and read than a binary format that accomplishes the same thing.

Since the code is formatted in a straightforward way, it makes sense for XML to be easily readable by humans as well as machines. From a practical standpoint, if XML is easy to understand and use, you don't need complex tools and procedures to work with it. So no matter how sophisticated some tools get, any author can sit down with a simple text editor and write XML code.

GOAL 7: THE XML DESIGN SHOULD BE PREPARED QUICKLY. As already mentioned, XML was conceived because an extensible language for the Web was needed. This goal was included out of concern that if XML was not made available quickly as a way to extend HTML, another organization might come up with a proprietary solution, a binary solution, or both. The SGML ERB believed that the solution for extensibility needed to come from the SGML community—the same group responsible for HTML. The board also determined that the solution had to be open and extensible and could not be owned by any single vendor. An ad hoc group was formed to work on XML, and eventually, the XML Working Group was formed and operated within the guidelines of the W3C to formalize XML.

GOAL 8: THE DESIGN OF XML SHALL BE FORMAL AND CONCISE. This goal focuses on the XML specification. The goal was to make it as concise as possible by formalizing the wording of the specification. To help accomplish this, the specification uses Extended Backus-Naur Form (EBNF), a standard form used to describe programming languages that include declarations. Prose is avoided and EBNF is used throughout to keep it as formal and concise as possible. As with Goal 4, the idea with this goal is that the language will be adopted more readily if it is easy to understand and use.

GOAL 9: XML DOCUMENTS SHALL BE EASY TO CREATE. Just as an XML document should be easily understood by human readers as stated in Goal 6, creating an XML document should be easy as well. And while XML documents *can* be authored in something as simple as a plain text editor, the reality is that complex documents sometimes prove to be too cumbersome to work with in that environment. It will be up to the market to decide ultimately if this goal has been met, but many tools (both commercial and freeware) are already available for creating and using XML, which indicates that the W3C has succeeded so far in meeting this goal.

GOAL 10: TERSENESS IN XML MARKUP IS OF MINIMAL IMPORTANCE. This is another goal that grew out of the need to remedy implementation problems in SGML. SGML supports *minimization techniques,* which simply means that SGML allows some shortcuts in the interest of reducing the amount of typing the author has to do. One well-known SGML minimization that is also part of HTML is the ability to omit the closing tag for many elements. In these languages, the beginning of the next opening tag is enough to signal that the previous element should be closed. Although this reduces some work for the author, it can be a source of confusion for the reader. In XML, clarity always takes precedence over brevity.

Implementing the Goals

These 10 goals were used to drive the development of the XML specification. As you get to know XML, you will see that the "flavor" and many of the features of the language are direct results of decisions that were made based on these goals. I think you will find that XML is a simple yet extremely powerful and flexible markup language.

XML, Recommendations, and Standards

This section looks at the current state of the XML specification and discusses other XML-related specifications that are being developed and reviewed by the W3C.

XML 1.0

The XML 1.0 specification is currently approved as a recommendation by the W3C, which means that the members of the W3C have reached a consensus and the specification is stable enough to be widely used. However, this does *not* mean that the specification has been adopted as a standard. According to the W3C, "The process...for creating a Recommendation is an alternative to, and not a replacement for, or modification of, the standards process in the W3C Member agreement. In the event that there is a need to revise a Recommendation, the same process will apply to the creation of the revised Recommendation." Although W3C recommendations might be submitted to a standards body such as the ISO, this process is not a requirement.

> **NOTE**
>
> For more information about how the W3C administers its activities, check out *http://www.w3.org/Consortium/Process/*. This Web page outlines the entire W3C activity process, from proposal to official recommendation.

The XML specification is not the only work being done on XML by the W3C. Several other initiatives, which are either applications of XML or enhancements to the language itself, are under consideration.

Mathematical Markup Language

As I write this, Mathematical Markup Language (MathML) 1.0 has just been released as a W3C recommendation. MathML is an XML application designed to make it easier to use mathematical formulae and scientific content on the Web. This metalanguage will have applications in the scientific, mathematical, engineering, and medical communities. For more information, visit the MathML 1.0 specification Web site at *http://www.w3.org/TR/REC-MathML/* and the W3C math activity page at *http://www.w3.org/Math/Activity.html*.

Resource Description Framework

Resource Description Framework (RDF) is a data modeling framework that serves as a foundation for processing metadata. RDF uses XML as its encoding syntax, although other ways exist to represent the RDF model. The RDF model and syntax specification is, as of this writing, in the working draft stage of the W3C recommendation process. For more information, visit the Web page containing the current specification at *http://www.w3.org/TR/WD-rdf-syntax/*. For a description of RDF, check out the introduction to RDF on the W3C Web site at *http://www.w3.org/RDF/*.

XML Linking Language

XML Linking Language (XLink) is an application of XML that defines powerful mechanisms for linking in XML documents. In addition to providing a way to use the simple links that we have become accustomed to with HTML, XLink includes an extended linking mechanism that:

♦ Enables links to have more than one target resource

♦ Enables linking in documents that cannot include traditional links inline with the text

♦ Facilitates "smart" links that can be dynamically applied and that can filter links based on content and context

♦ Enables links in data formats that do not natively support linking, such as images

For more information, see the XLink working draft at *http://www.w3.org/TR/WD-xlink*.

Synchronized Multimedia Integration Language

Synchronized Multimedia Integration Language (SMIL) is an XML application that is intended to enable the use of TV-like multimedia on the Web. The strength of SMIL is that it will allow authors to create sophisticated, synchronized multimedia without having to convert content to another format such as video and without using a complex scripting language. SMIL will be covered in depth in Chapter 8. As I write this, SMIL 1.0 has just been released as a recommendation by the W3C. You can look at the current SMIL specification at *http://www.w3.org/TR/REC-smil/*.

Extensible Stylesheet Language

Extensible Stylesheet Language (XSL) is a text-formatting language that is designed to be flexible and extensible. XSL picks up where Cascading Style Sheets (CSS) leaves off and adds such features as allowing code to be included in style sheets to accomplish complex formatting tasks. The XSL specification is, as of this writing, a working draft with the W3C. For more information and to view a copy of the current proposal, visit the W3C XSL Web page at *http://www.w3.org/TR/NOTE-XSL.html*.

Part 2
XML Basics

Chapter 3
XML Structure
and Syntax

As you learned in the last chapter, the designers of XML had particular goals in mind as they developed the specification for the language. To help meet those goals, they designed XML with some rather strict structure and syntax rules. Although at first glance these rules might seem to make the language more cumbersome than, for example, HTML, you will see that XML includes a level of extensibility and aids in interoperability in a way that cannot be accomplished with HTML.

In this chapter, we'll examine the logical and physical structures of an XML document and how the XML language is used to create these structures. We'll also look at the basic syntax of the XML language and compare it to HTML syntax. During the course of this chapter, we'll construct and discuss a simple XML document to demonstrate these principles.

XML Structure

One of XML's best qualities is its ability to provide structure to a document. Every XML document includes both a *logical structure* and a *physical structure*. The logical structure is like a template that tells you what elements to include in a document and in what order. The physical structure contains the actual data used in a document. This data might include text stored in your computer's memory, an image file stored on the World Wide Web, and so on. To get an idea of how an XML document is structured, examine the document model shown in Figure 3-1.

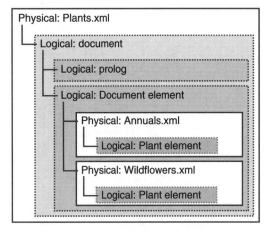

Figure 3-1. *An XML document has a logical structure and a physical structure.*

Logical Structure in XML

If you are familiar with HTML, you are probably familiar with the concept of logical structure. Logical structure refers to the organization of the different parts of a document. Put another way, logical structure indicates *how* a document is built, as opposed to *what* a document contains. The logical structure of an HTML document, for example, is indicated by the elements that make it up, as shown in the following code:

```
<HTML>

  <HEAD>
    <TITLE>Title content goes here</TITLE>
    Other Head content goes here
  </HEAD>

  <BODY>
    Body content goes here
  </BODY>

</HTML>
```

This code indicates that the Head, Title, and Body elements are all contained within the Html element; that the Title element is located inside the Head element; and so on. The HTML 3.2 Document Type Definition (DTD), found at *http://www.w3.org/TR/REC-html32 .html#dtd*, provides the complete rules for how an HTML document should be built.

> **NOTE**
>
> An XML document is made up of declarations, elements, processing instructions, and comments. Some components are optional and some are required. This section examines the basic declarations and elements of an XML document as a sample document is built. The other components will be discussed in the next chapter.

THE PROLOG

The first structural element in an XML document is an optional *prolog*. The prolog consists of two basic components, also optional: the *XML declaration* and the *document type declaration*.

THE XML DECLARATION   The XML declaration identifies the version of the XML specification to which the document conforms. Although the XML declaration is an optional element, you should always include one in your XML document. The sample document begins with a basic XML declaration:

```
<?xml version="1.0"?>
```

> **NOTE**
>
> The above line of code must use lowercase letters.

An XML declaration can also contain an *encoding declaration* and a *stand-alone document declaration.* The encoding declaration identifies the character encoding scheme, such as UTF-8 or EUC-JP. Different encoding schemes map to different character formats or languages. For example, UTF-8, the default scheme, includes representations for most of the characters in the English language. XML parsers are required to support certain Unicode schemes, enabling support for most human languages.

The stand-alone document declaration identifies whether any markup declarations exist that are external to the document (more on this later). The stand-alone document declaration can have the value *yes* or *no.*

NOTE

For more information on the specifics of the encoding declaration or the stand-alone document declaration, see sections 2.8, 2.9, and 4.3.3 in the XML 1.0 specification included on the companion CD.

THE DOCUMENT TYPE DECLARATION   The document type declaration consists of markup code that indicates the grammar rules, or Document Type Definition (DTD), for the particular class of document. The document type declaration can also point to an external file that contains all or part of the DTD. The document type declaration must appear following the XML declaration and preceding the Document element. This code adds a document type declaration to the sample document:

```
<?xml version="1.0"?>
<!DOCTYPE Wildflowers SYSTEM "Wldflr.dtd">
```

This statement tells the XML processor that the document is of the class *Wildflowers* and conforms to the rules set forth in the DTD file named *Wldflr.dtd.* (Chapter 4 discusses the idea of document classes and the details of the DTD.)

So ends the prolog. Following the prolog is the *Document element*, the heart of an XML document, where the actual content lives.

THE DOCUMENT ELEMENT

It might seem strange that a single element—the Document element—contains all the data in an XML document. However, this single element can comprise any number of nested subelements and external entities. It's similar to the C: drive on your computer. All the data on your computer is stored on that single drive. But any number of folders and subfolders keep the individual pieces of data in a (hopefully) logical and easy-to-manage structure.

This code adds a Document element (in this case, the Plant element) to the sample document:

```
<?xml version="1.0"?>
<!DOCTYPE Wildflowers SYSTEM "Wldflr.dtd">

<PLANT>
  <COMMON>Columbine</COMMON>
  <BOTANICAL>Aquilegia canadensis</BOTANICAL>
</PLANT>
```

Nesting

Nesting is the process of embedding one object or construct within another. For example, an XML document can contain nested elements and even other documents. Element nesting sets up *parent/child relationships*. Every child element (an element that is not the Document element) resides *completely* within its parent element. This can be represented as follows:

```
<DOCUMENT>
  <PARENT1>
    <CHILD1></CHILD1>
    <CHILD2></CHILD2>
  </PARENT1>
</DOCUMENT>
```

The following code, however, does not contain properly nested elements and will cause an error:

```
<DOCUMENT>
  <PARENT1>
    <CHILD1></CHILD1>
    <CHILD2></CHILD2>
</DOCUMENT>
  </PARENT1>
```

Physical Structure in XML

The physical structure of an XML document is composed of all the content used in that document. If you think of the logical structure as the blueprint for a parking garage, you can think of the physical structure as all the actual parking spaces within the garage. These parking spaces or storage units, called *entities,* can be part of the document or external to the document (like offsite parking for the airport). Each entity is identified by a unique name and contains its own content, from a single character inside the document to a large file that exists outside the document. In terms of the logical structure of an XML document, entities are *declared* in the prolog and *referenced* in the Document element.

An entity declaration tells the processor what to fill the "parking space" with. Once declared in the DTD, an entity can be used anywhere in the document. An entity reference tells the processor to retrieve the content of the entity, as declared in the entity declaration, and use it in the document.

PARSED AND UNPARSED ENTITIES

An entity can be either *parsed* or *unparsed*. A parsed entity, sometimes called a text entity, contains text data that becomes part of the XML document once that data is processed. An unparsed entity is a container whose contents might or might not be text. If text, the content is not parsable XML.

PARSED ENTITIES   A parsed entity is intended to be read by the XML processor, so its content will be extracted. After it's extracted, a parsed entity's content appears as part of the text of the document at the location of the entity reference. For example, in our Wildflowers document, a light requirement (LR1) entity can be declared as

```
<!ENTITY LR1 "light requirement: mostly shade">
```

This declaration means "I am declaring an entity with the name *LR1* that contains the content *light requirement: mostly shade."* Whenever this entity is referenced in the document, it will be replaced by its content. You might now begin to see a benefit to using entities—if you want to change the content of the entity, you need to change it in only one place, the declaration, and the change will be reflected *everywhere* that the entity is used in the document.

ENTITY REFERENCES   As described above, the content of each entity is added to the document at each entity reference. The entity reference acts as a placeholder for the content author, and the XML processor places the actual content at each reference site. To include an entity reference, you first insert an ampersand (&) and then enter the entity name followed by a semicolon (;). So, to use our LR1 example above, we would insert *&LR1;.* Here's how it might look in a document:

```
<TERM>Wild Ginger has the following &LR1;</TERM>
```

When that line is processed, the entity *&LR1;* will be replaced with the entity's content, so the line would read, "Wild Ginger has the following light requirement: mostly shade."

PARAMETER ENTITY REFERENCES   Another kind of entity reference is the parameter entity reference. A parameter entity reference uses a modulus (%) instead of an ampersand but otherwise looks identical to any other entity reference. *%CDF;* is an example of a parameter entity reference. The next chapter discusses parameter entities in detail.

UNPARSED ENTITIES   An unparsed entity is sometimes referred to as a *binary* entity because its content is often a binary file (such as an image) that is not directly interpreted by the XML processor. Even so, an unparsed entity could contain plain text, so the term *binary* is a bit misleading. An unparsed entity requires different information from that included in a parsed entity: it requires a *notation*. A notation identifies the format, or type, of resource to which the entity is declared. Let's look at an example:

```
<!ENTITY MyImage SYSTEM "Image001.gif" NDATA GIF>
```

This entity declaration literally means, "The entity *MyImage* is a binary file in the GIF notation"—a rather complex way of saying, "This is a GIF image." To make matters even more complicated, for these entity declarations to be valid, the notation must be declared as well. The *notation declaration* helps the XML application deal with these external, binary files. So for the GIF notation we used above, a notation declaration like this can be used:

```
<!NOTATION GIF SYSTEM "/Utils/Gifview.exe">
```

This tells the XML processor that whenever it encounters an entity of type *GIF*, it should use Gifview.exe to process it. As with other declarations, once declared, the notation declaration can be used throughout the document. We will examine this topic more closely in the next chapter.

An entity reference should not contain unparsed entity names. Unparsed entities should be referred to only in attribute values of type ENTITY or ENTITIES. See the section "Opening and Closing Tags" later in this chapter for information about attributes and attribute values. See Chapter 4 for more information about attribute types.

PREDEFINED ENTITIES

In XML, certain characters are used specifically for marking up the document. For example, in the following element, the angle brackets (<>) and forward slash (/) are interpreted as markup and not as actual character data:

```
<PLANT>Bloodroot</PLANT>
```

These and other characters are reserved for markup and cannot be used as content. If you want these characters to be displayed as data, they must be *escaped*. To escape a character, you must use an entity reference to insert the character into a document. So, for example, if you want to insert the text *<PLANT>* into a document, you would use this sequence:

```
&lt;PLANT&gt;
```

In this example, the sequence *<* is the entity reference for the opening angle bracket (<), and the sequence *>* is the entity reference for the closing angle bracket (>).

Following are the entity references for all the predefined entities:

Entity Reference	Character
<	< (opening angle bracket)
>	> (closing angle bracket)
&	& (ampersand)
'	' (apostrophe)
"	" (double quotation mark)

According to the W3C, all XML processors must recognize predefined entity references even if these entities are not declared. Even so, it is required that the entities be declared in the DTD for the document to be considered *valid* XML.

INTERNAL AND EXTERNAL ENTITIES

The preceding examples have demonstrated the difference between internal and external entities. An internal entity is one in which no separate physical storage unit exists; the content of the entity is provided in its declaration, as shown below:

```
<!ENTITY LR1 "light requirement: mostly shade">
```

An external entity refers to a storage unit in its declaration by using a system or public identifier. The system identifier provides a pointer to a location at which the entity content can be found, such as a URI (Uniform Resource Identifier), as shown here:

```
<!ENTITY MyImage
    SYSTEM "http://www.wildflowers.com/Images/Image001.gif"
    NDATA GIF>
```

In this case, the XML processor must read the file Image001.gif to retrieve the content of this entity.

In addition to the system identifier, an entity can include a public identifier. The public identifier provides an additional, alternative way for the XML processor to retrieve the content of an entity. This identifier can be used if the application is connected to a publicly available document library, for example. If the processor is not able to generate an appropriate location from the public identifier, it must then check the URI specified by the system identifier.

NOTE

When discussing XML, the acronym URI is often used instead of the more familiar acronym URL (Uniform Resource Locator). In XML, a URI can be a Uniform Resource Name (URN) or a URL. The term URI is generally used to describe Web resources and is included in the XML specification as a matter of W3C (World Wide Web Consortium) policy. The W3C has the goal of generalizing pointers to Web resources and making URIs more common. For more information on URIs, please see *http://www.w3.org/Addressing*.

The following code shows the use of a public identifier:

```
<!ENTITY MyImage
    PUBLIC "-//Wildflowers//TEXT Standard images//EN"
    "http://www.wildflowers.com/images/image001.gif"
    NDATA GIF>
```

A public identifier can be useful when working with an entity that is publicly available. The XML processor can check the public identifier against a list of resources to which it is connected and determine that it does not need to get a new copy of the entity because it is already available locally. However, until such public information storage mechanisms become more widely available, the system identifier will be more commonly used.

It might be helpful to summarize the different entity types. Here are the four types of entities we have covered:

◆ Internal Entity—An entity defined within its declaration and declared within the prolog. (An internal entity is always text.)

◆ External Entity—An entity that refers to an external storage unit, such as a binary file. (An external entity might or might not be text.)

◆ Parsed Entity—An entity made up of parsable text. (Once parsed, the text becomes part of the XML document.)

- ◆ Unparsed Entity—An entity that cannot be parsed by the XML processor. (An unparsed entity might or might not be text. If text, it is not parsable text.)

From these, there are four possible combinations:

- ◆ Internal, Parsed Entity—An internal entity composed of parsable text.

- ◆ Internal, Unparsed Entity—An internal entity composed of unparsable text.

- ◆ External, Parsed Entity—An external entity reference that points to parsable text. (Once parsed, the text becomes part of the XML document.)

- ◆ External, Unparsed Entity—An entity reference that points to a binary file or to unparsable text.

XML Syntax

XML's structural rules are reflected in its linguistic rules, or *syntax*, and this section looks at how some of the structural rules play out in writing the language components. Since most readers will probably be more familiar with HTML than with SGML, HTML is used here as a reference to the XML included in this section. As you know, HTML and XML are both applications of SGML. Because HTML and XML have the same parent language, the similarities in the syntax of both are obvious. But these similarities do not go very deep.

Opening and Closing Tags

In HTML code, an element usually contains both opening and closing tags. XML, unlike HTML, *requires* that a closing tag be used for every element. Consider, for example, the HTML Paragraph element, which would normally include an opening tag, some content, and a closing tag as shown here:

```
<P>This is an HTML Paragraph element.</P>
```

If you have written much code in HTML, you might be thinking, "Wait a minute, I never use the closing Paragraph tag in my pages!" You might not be aware that a closing Paragraph tag even exists because HTML (and its parent, SGML) allow tagging shortcuts. That is, you can omit closing tags and the code is still valid.

HTML is based on a predefined structure that allows processors to assume where certain tags should be located in a document. Because a paragraph in HTML cannot be nested inside another paragraph, the processor can read an opening Paragraph tag and assume that it also marks the end of the preceding paragraph. Such minimization techniques are not allowed in XML, and this represents the most obvious syntactical difference between the two languages.

THE EMPTY-ELEMENT TAG

Even though XML requires that closing tags be used, it does support a shortcut for empty elements called, well, the *empty-element tag*. The empty-element tag effectively combines the opening and closing tags for an element containing no content. It uses a special format: <TAGNAME/>. Notice that the forward slash follows the tag name—this is not supported in HTML. Suppose, for example, that we created a tag called <GENUS>. If the Genus element contained no data, we could write it using opening and closing tags, as shown below:

```
<GENUS></GENUS>
```

Or we could write it using an empty-element tag:

```
<GENUS/>
```

Attributes

Attributes provide a method of associating values to an element without making the attributes a part of the content of that element. For example, let's look at a common HTML element and how it uses an attribute:

```
<A HREF="http://www.microsoft.com">Microsoft Home Page</A>
```

Here, the Anchor element indicated by the <A> tag contains an attribute with the name *HREF*. The value for the attribute is *http://www.microsoft.com*. While the value of this attribute is never displayed to the user, it contains important information about the element and provides the destination for the anchor. This name/value format demonstrates the way attributes are used in XML.

This example adds an attribute to one of the elements in the sample document:

```
<?xml version="1.0"?>
<!DOCTYPE Wildflowers SYSTEM "Wldflr.dtd">

<PLANT ZONE=3>
  <COMMON>Columbine</COMMON>
  <BOTANICAL>Aquilegia canadensis</BOTANICAL>
</PLANT>
```

Notice that the *ZONE* attribute in the opening <PLANT> tag follows the name/value format.

> **NOTE**
>
> Although not demonstrated in the example above, an important aspect of attribute values is that they can contain any ASCII characters, including those normally reserved for markup. Because of this, attribute values were not designed to be parsable by an XML processor—meaning that attribute values cannot be validated. The processor will check to determine that an attribute name and value match the type that was declared in the DTD, but it will not care what the value is. (For more information about writing attribute declarations, see Chapter 4.)

Valid Versus Well-Formed XML

Two of XML's most valuable features are its ability to provide structure to documents and to make data self-describing. These features would not be of much use if you could not enforce the structural and grammatical rules. If you have created SGML documents, you should understand the idea of a valid document. If you're familiar with HTML, you should understand the concept of a well-formed document. The next two sections discuss these terms.

Valid Documents

As you learned earlier in the chapter, the DTD specified in the prolog outlines all the rules for the document. A *valid* XML document strictly obeys all these rules. (The next chapter looks at the parts of a DTD in detail.) A valid document also obeys all the validity constraints identified in the XML specification.

Here is an example of a validity constraint for attribute defaults from section 3.3.2 of the XML specification:

Validity Constraint: Required Attribute

If the default declaration is the keyword #REQUIRED, then the attribute must be specified for all elements of the type in the attribute-list declaration.

The processor must understand the validity constraints of the XML specification and check the document for possible violations. If the processor finds any errors, it must report them to the XML application. The processor must also read the DTD, validate the document against it, and again report any violations to the XML application. Because all of this processing and checking can take time (not to mention bandwidth) and because validation might not always be necessary, XML supports the notion of the well-formed document.

Well-Formed Documents

Even though being *well formed* means that some rules must be obeyed, these rules are not nearly as strict as those constraints required for validity. The XML specification addresses the concept of a well-formed document that is not validated. Fortunately, only XML processors have to deal with the rules for well-formedness. If you, as an XML document author, don't follow the rules, the processor will let you know!

NOTE

Although a well-formed document isn't required to adhere to validity constraints, a valid document must adhere to all the rules for well-formedness as well as to all the validity constraints.

Why does XML allow an author to simply follow the syntax rules and create content without worrying about a DTD? While this might seem like an invitation to chaos, that is not the intention. Remember from Chapter 2 that one of XML's goals is to make XML documents easy to create. Well-formedness helps meet that goal by not requiring additional work to create a DTD. Following are some other ways that well-formedness provides a benefit:

◆ Well-formedness can reduce the amount of work a client has to do. For example, if the server has already validated a document, it is not necessary to burden the client with validating it again. As a result, well-formedness can save download time because the client does not need to download the DTD, and it can save processing time because the XML processor does not need to process the DTD.

- In many cases, authoring a DTD or validating a document is unnecessary. For example, someone in a small company might want to use XML to provide structure to a departmental Web site, but all the features that validation provides are not needed for the site.

- Rules for a document can be provided in ways other than using a DTD, as you will see in Chapter 10. In these cases, a DTD is unnecessary.

According to the XML specification, a well-formed document must meet the following criteria:

1. It matches the definition of a *document* (as described below).

2. It observes the constraints for a well-formed document as defined by the XML specification.

3. All of the parsed entities referenced in the document are well formed.

IT MATCHES THE DEFINITION OF A DOCUMENT.   Matching the definition of a document means that:

1. It contains one or more elements.

2. It contains exactly one root element, also called the Document element, and any other elements are properly nested.

Let's look again at the sample document created earlier in the chapter:

```
<?xml version="1.0"?>
<!DOCTYPE Wildflowers SYSTEM "Wldflr.dtd">

<PLANT>
  <COMMON>Columbine</COMMON>
  <BOTANICAL>Aquilegia canadensis</BOTANICAL>
</PLANT>
```

This document contains the Plant element as the single Document element, and the Common and Botanical elements are nested inside the Document element. To illustrate this concept, the following example is *not* well-formed XML because it contains two elements at the root:

```
<?xml version="1.0"?>
<!DOCTYPE Wildflowers SYSTEM "Wldflr.dtd">

<COMMON>Columbine</COMMON>
<BOTANICAL>Aquilegia canadensis</BOTANICAL>
```

The Common and Botanical elements are both located at the root level of the document—in other words, these two complete elements immediately follow the prolog. Each element has opening and closing tags, but neither element is nested within the other.

IT OBSERVES THE CONSTRAINTS FOR A WELL-FORMED DOCUMENT AS DEFINED BY THE XML SPECIFICATION. The XML specification identifies certain constraints by which a document must abide to be considered well formed. Anyone creating a processor needs to understand these constraints and enforce them in the processor. Following is a sample constraint from the XML specification:

Well-Formedness Constraint: Legal Character

Characters referred to using character references must be legal according to the nonterminal Char.

If the character begins with "&#x", the digits and letters up to the terminating ";" provide a hexadecimal representation of the character's value in ISO/IEC 10646. If it begins just with "&#", the digits up to the terminating ";" provide a decimal representation of the character's value.

ALL OF THE PARSED ENTITIES REFERENCED IN THE DOCUMENT ARE WELL FORMED. Since parsed entities become part of the document once they are parsed by the XML processor, they must also be well formed for the document to be considered well formed. This is important to note if you are using external entities created by someone else. If the creator of the external entity you are using did not meet the well-formedness constraints, the entity might cause errors in your document.

Chapter 4
Playing by the
Rules—The DTD

n Chapter 3, you learned about the physical and logical structure of an XML document, including the prolog that contains the XML declaration and the document type declaration. This chapter focuses on the prolog's document type declaration, which identifies the specific type of document being processed and the rules that govern the overall document. These rules are called the Document Type Definition, or DTD—by far the most involved part of the document type declaration.

Before getting into the details of creating a DTD, let's examine the document type declaration.

Document Classes

By declaring that a document matches a specific type, authors are able to create documents that fall into a certain category, or *class*. The concept of classing is drawn from the programming world—specifically, object-oriented programming. You need to take a look at some of the concepts and features of object-oriented design before you'll see how they apply to XML documents.

> **NOTE**
>
> You don't need to be familiar with object-oriented programming languages to create XML documents. This section is included specifically to provide some background on the design of XML.

Objects: Reusable Program Code

Reusable objects are self-contained items that can be used independently but are usually employed in conjunction with other objects or programs. Most objects are designed to be used for a specific purpose; they have their own properties and perform particular actions (called *methods*). Objects also have some common features and characteristics that make them especially powerful and flexible programming aids. If you're familiar with object-oriented programming, you might have heard of the terms *inheritance, polymorphism,* and *encapsulation.* With regard to XML document classes, the concepts of inheritance and polymorphism are particularly important.

Maintaining Relationships with Inheritance

Inheritance in programming is based loosely on the idea of familial inheritance: via familial genetic inheritance, a person carries some of the same family traits as a parent. Object-oriented programming works in a similar way. A programmer can create an object that contains all of the characteristics and properties of a "parent" object. The new "child" object *inherits* these characteristics from the parent object. The programmer can then modify some of the new object's characteristics or even add to them to create a completely separate object with individual characteristics.

At this point, the concept of *classes* enters the picture. The original parent object is called the *base class*—the object upon which other objects will be based. Subsequent child objects are called *subclasses* of the base class. Programmers can create as many subclasses as they want and can even subclass a subclass! This beneficial approach allows the programmer to use most or all of the necessary features and functions of an object and then modify them to suit particular needs. Using object classes not only saves programmers a tremendous amount of repetitive programming, but it makes programs more consistent and saves testing time because the base object never changes.

Here's an example. Let's say you wrote a program object called *Book*. This object had the properties *NumberOfChapters* and *CoverColor*. The *Book* object represents the base class upon which you will base all subsequent *Book* subclasses. Now you are going to create two subclasses: *CookBook* and *TextBook*. In the new *CookBook* object, you specify that the *NumberOfChapters* property equals 10, and in the new *TextBook* object, the *NumberOfChapters* property equals 21. The *CoverColor* property for *CookBook* is *Red*, and the *CoverColor* property for *TextBook* is *Blue*. Next you add a property to *CookBook* called *Recipe* and a property to *TextBook* called *Glossary*. You now have created two objects based on a single base class, and each contains additional properties to suit specific purposes. The *NumberOfChapters* and *CoverColor* properties are inherited directly from the base class *Book* and are available to any subclassed object. The class hierarchy for this example is shown in Figure 4-1.

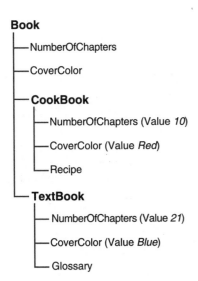

Book
- NumberOfChapters
- CoverColor
- **CookBook**
  - NumberOfChapters (Value *10*)
  - CoverColor (Value *Red*)
  - Recipe
- **TextBook**
  - NumberOfChapters (Value *21*)
  - CoverColor (Value *Blue*)
  - Glossary

Figure 4-1. *The* Book *base class and its subclasses.*

As you might have guessed, you could take this example even further by subclassing one of the *derivative objects* (subclassing a subclass). For example, you could create an object called *VegetableCookBook* based on the *CookBook* class that contains all the properties from the *CookBook* class, including properties inherited from the base class *Book*.

Polymorphism—Making a Good Object Better

Through polymorphism, the characteristics of a derivative object can be modified to perform different functions, thereby overriding the characteristics of the base class. Consider the *Book* example. Suppose you want to create a subclass called *ArtBook*. But instead of the *CoverColor* property being able to accept only colors, you want the property to be able to specify the names of patterns—you want your *ArtBook* object's *CoverColor* property to be equal to *PolkaDots*. In this case, the *CoverColor* property from the base class is overridden with a modified property of the same name. This explains the concept of polymorphism.

Making Document Classes with XML

Inheritance and polymorphism carry over into the XML world as well—but in concept only, as you'll see. Consider the XML code example used in the last chapter:

```
<?xml version="1.0"?>
<!DOCTYPE Wildflowers SYSTEM "Wldflr.dtd">

<PLANT>
  <COMMON>Columbine</COMMON>
  <BOTANICAL>Aquilegia canadensis</BOTANICAL>
</PLANT>
```

This code declares the document type as *Wildflowers* and tells the XML processor that the document should follow the rules found in the file Wldflr.dtd. In XML programming, as in object-oriented programming, you can create child documents that inherit the rules of the parent document, even though the children might include completely different content. You can also modify the rules in a child XML document to suit particular needs; this concept corresponds to the notion of polymorphism. The piece that makes all of this possible is the second part of the document type declaration, the DTD.

The Document Type Definition

The remainder of this chapter focuses on the DTD—how to structure a DTD and how to create a DTD for your documents. As mentioned previously, the DTD acts as a rule book that allows authors to create new documents of the same type and with the same characteristics as a base document. For example, suppose a DTD was created for use by the medical community. Documents created with this DTD could contain items such as a patient's name, medications, medical history, and so on. The information could easily be read by any medical institution that used an XML-based document system. This system would not only provide a standardized document format for all organizations, but it would provide a format to be used within departments of a single organization. The same document format can be used by doctors, nurses, administrative staff, pharmacists, specialists, and others. Another DTD advantage, which will be discussed shortly, is that a DTD can be modified to suit the needs of a particular application. This is where the notion of subclassing comes in.

DTD Structure

A DTD can comprise two parts: an *external DTD subset* and an *internal DTD subset*. An external DTD subset is a DTD that exists outside the content of the document, which is usually the case when a common DTD is used, as in the medical example above. An internal DTD subset is a DTD that is included within the XML document. A document can contain one or both types of subsets. If a document contains both, the internal subset is processed first and takes precedence over any external subset. This is beneficial when an author is using an external DTD but wants to customize some parts of the DTD for a specific application. We'll look at an example of this in the section Class DTDs.

If you want to include an internal DTD subset in your document, you simply write it directly in the document type declaration. An external DTD subset, however, must be included via a *DTD reference,* which tells the processor where to find the external subset by specifying the name of the DTD file. The DTD reference also contains information about the creator of the DTD, about the purpose of the DTD, and about the language used. This is demonstrated in the declaration below:

```
<!DOCTYPE catalog PUBLIC "-//flowers//DTD Standard //EN"
    "http://www.wildflowers.com/dtd/Wldflr.dtd">
```

Creating a Simple DTD

Before we get into too much detail, let's create a document with a simple DTD to see what one looks like. We'll modify the Memo document created in Chapter 2 so that it is an Email document with an internal DTD subset. The new document, which you can find in the Chap04\Lst4_1.xml file on the companion CD, is shown in Code Listing 4-1.

```
<?xml version="1.0"?>

<!DOCTYPE EMAIL [
  <!ELEMENT EMAIL (TO, FROM, CC, SUBJECT, BODY)>
  <!ELEMENT TO (#PCDATA)>
  <!ELEMENT FROM (#PCDATA)>
  <!ELEMENT CC (#PCDATA)>
  <!ELEMENT SUBJECT (#PCDATA)>
  <!ELEMENT BODY (#PCDATA)>
]>
```

Code Listing 4-1.   *(continued)*

```
<EMAIL>
  <TO>Jodie@msn.com</TO>
  <FROM>Bill@msn.com</FROM>
  <CC>Philip@msn.com</CC>
  <SUBJECT>My First DTD</SUBJECT>
  <BODY>Hello, World!</BODY>
</EMAIL>
```

Notice that the code contains additional information in the document type declaration. This is the internal DTD subset, and it identifies the elements that are allowed in the document and the type of data they can contain. If you run this document by displaying the HTML page found in the Chap04\Lst4_1.htm file on the companion CD, and then clicking the Start button, the document looks similar to the one that was created in Chapter 2 (without the DTD), as shown in Figure 4-2.

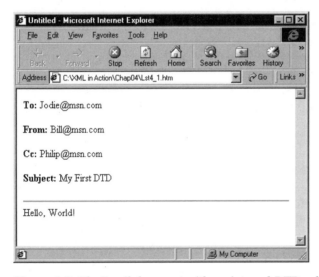

Figure 4-2. *The Email document with an internal DTD subset.*

NOTE

The HTML page that displays the XML document is not discussed in detail here, but it is similar to the HTML page we created in Chapter 2. You can use the Lst4_1.htm page to view all the sample XML documents in this chapter. Simply change the filename in the *xmlDoc.load* statement from *Lst4_1.xml* to the filename of the XML document you want to display.

This document differs from the document created in Chapter 2 because in this case the XML processor is *validating* the document against the DTD. In other words, the HTML page that displays the document is parsing the page using a validating processor. This simply means that the processor is checking the document against the DTD to make sure that all the code used in the document is allowable.

To see how validation works, let's add an element to the document that is not part of the DTD. We'll add a Signature element near the end of the document, as shown below.

```
<?xml version="1.0"?>

<!DOCTYPE EMAIL [
  <!ELEMENT EMAIL (TO, FROM, CC, SUBJECT, BODY)>
  <!ELEMENT TO (#PCDATA)>
  <!ELEMENT FROM (#PCDATA)>
  <!ELEMENT CC (#PCDATA)>
  <!ELEMENT SUBJECT (#PCDATA)>
  <!ELEMENT BODY (#PCDATA)>
]>

<EMAIL>
  <TO>Jodie@msn.com</TO>
  <FROM>Bill@msn.com</FROM>
  <CC>Philip@msn.com</CC>
  <SUBJECT>My First DTD</SUBJECT>
  <BODY>Hello, World!</BODY>
  <SIGNATURE>Bill</SIGNATURE>
</EMAIL>
```

If you try to run this document, you will see an error message similar to the following because the processor does not find a declaration for the Signature element in the DTD:

```
Element content is invalid according to the DTD/Schema.
```

Back to the original XML file. This time, we'll change part of the DTD. Notice the first element declaration concerns the Email element:

```
<!ELEMENT EMAIL (TO, FROM, CC, SUBJECT, BODY)>
```

Within this line of code, in parentheses, is a list of the other content elements that the document can contain. This list is called a *content model*, and it identifies the child elements that the Email element must contain and the order of those child elements. (For more details on the content model, see the next section.) If you remove the Subject element from the content model, the DTD looks like this:

```
<!DOCTYPE EMAIL [
  <!ELEMENT EMAIL (TO, FROM, CC, BODY)>
  <!ELEMENT TO (#PCDATA)>
  <!ELEMENT FROM (#PCDATA)>
  <!ELEMENT CC (#PCDATA)>
  <!ELEMENT SUBJECT (#PCDATA)>
  <!ELEMENT BODY (#PCDATA)>
]>
```

As you might expect, running the document causes the processor to return an error because the document did not follow the specified content model. Let's go back to the original document to change the order of the From element and the Cc element so that the bottom portion of the document looks like this:

```
<EMAIL>
  <TO>Jodie@msn.com</TO>
  <CC>Philip@msn.com</CC>
  <FROM>Bill@msn.com</FROM>
  <SUBJECT>My First DTD</SUBJECT>
  <BODY>Hello, World!</BODY>
  <SIGNATURE>Bill</SIGNATURE>
</MEMO>
```

Again, when you try to run the document, an error is returned because the processor got one element when it was expecting another.

By now it should be clear to you that the DTD acts as a strict rule book for the XML document. Because the rules are strict, it is important that you take care while authoring your DTDs if you plan to use them. The DTD shown in this chapter has been simple, not to mention rigid. The rest of this chapter looks at the other pieces that can be added to a DTD to make it more robust and flexible.

Element Declarations

Each element declaration contains the element name and the type of data the element contains, called its *content specification*, which consists of one of four types:

◆ A list of other elements, called the content model

◆ The keyword *EMPTY*

◆ The keyword *ANY*

◆ Mixed content

MORE ON THE CONTENT MODEL

The DTD in the previous example started with an element declaration that contained the document's content model, as shown in parentheses below:

```
<!ELEMENT EMAIL (TO, FROM, CC, SUBJECT, BODY)>
```

The Email element contains only subelements, or child elements. For each of the elements in the content model, a corresponding element declaration must appear in the remainder of the DTD that follows.

THE EMPTY-ELEMENT DECLARATION

To declare that an element cannot contain any content, you can use the keyword *EMPTY* in the element declaration, as shown here:

```
<!ELEMENT TEST EMPTY>
```

A Test element in a document containing the above declaration could never contain content and would be required to be an empty element, such as <TEST/>. Although it might seem that empty elements would not be useful, they can contain attributes that provide meaningful content or they can provide specific functions in a document. The <BR> tag in HTML is an example of an empty-element tag. The <BR> tag tells an HTML processor to insert a line break in a document, but the element never contains content.

THE ANY-ELEMENT DECLARATION

At the opposite end of the scale is the *ANY* content specification. If an element declaration uses the keyword *ANY* for the content specification, that type of element can contain any content allowed by the DTD in any order. The any-element declaration looks like this:

```
<!ELEMENT TEST ANY>
```

MIXED CONTENT

The content specification can also be a single set of alternatives in which the alternatives are separated by pipe symbols (|). For example:

```
<!ELEMENT EXAMPLE (#PCDATA|x|y|z)*>
```

The use of *#PCDATA*; character data such as *x, y,* and *z*; the pipe symbol (|); and the asterisk (∗) are discussed in detail below.

Data Types

XML stays relatively simple when it comes to including data types, but some tricky issues are worth a look. In document content, XML allows for parsed character data (declared with the keyword *#PCDATA*, as shown above) and character data (declared with the keyword *CDATA*). Parsed character data is marked up character data—that is, it contains markup tags. Character data is ordinary text that can include characters normally reserved for markup. XML processors assume that content in an XML file is parsed character data by default. (The exception to this is attribute data, which is generally character data. This is covered in detail later in this chapter.)

While parsed character data is usually used in the content of an XML document, character data can be used when an author wants to include data that does not get parsed. For example, examine the usage of a character data section in the following document:

```
<?xml version="1.0"?>

<LESSON>
  <TITLE>Working with XML Markup</TITLE>
  <EXAMPLE>
    <![CDATA[<ELEMENT>A sample element</ELEMENT>]]>
  </EXAMPLE>
</LESSON>
```

The data in the Example element will be displayed as *<ELEMENT>A sample element </ELEMENT>*, and the markup tags will not be parsed. As shown here, to declare a section as character data, you must mark the beginning of the section with the sequence *<![CDATA[* and mark the end with two closing brackets: *]]*. Any data that resides inside this set of markers will be interpreted as straight unparsed data.

Structure Symbols

XML uses a set of symbols for specifying the structure of an element declaration. You have already seen some of these symbols, such as the pipe and the comma. Table 4-1 identifies each of the available symbols, the purpose of each symbol, an example of how each is used, and what each symbol means.

TABLE 4-1
Element Declaration Symbols

Symbol	Purpose	Example	Meaning
Parentheses	Encloses a sequence, a group of elements, or a set of alternatives	*(content1, content2)*	Element must contain the sequence *content1* and *content2*.
Comma	Separates items in a sequence and identifies the order in which they must appear	*(content1, content2, content3)*	Element must contain *content1*, *content2*, and *content3* in the specified order.
Pipe	Separates items in a group of alternatives	*(content1| content2| content3)*	Element must contain either *content1*, *content2*, or *content3*.
Question mark	Indicates that an item must appear one time or not at all	*content1?*	Element might contain *content1*. If *content1* does appear, it must appear only once.

Symbol	Purpose	Example	Meaning
Asterisk	Indicates that the item can appear as many times as the author wants	*content1**	Element can contain *content1*. If it appears, it can appear once or more.
Plus sign	Indicates that an item must appear once or more	*content1+*	Element must contain *content1* at least once, but it can appear more than once.
No symbol	Indicates that exactly one item must appear	*content1*	Element must contain *content1*.

Let's look at a simple example by adding to the content model from our example document.

```
<!ELEMENT EMAIL (TO+, FROM, CC*, SUBJECT?, BODY?)>
```

This declaration indicates that:

- The To element is required and can appear more than once.

- The From element must appear exactly once.

- The Cc element is optional, but it can appear one or more times.

- The Subject element is optional, but it can appear only once if included.

- The Body element is optional, but it can appear only once if included.

Attributes

In addition to defining the structure of an element and the kind of content it contains, you can associate *attributes* with an element. Attributes provide additional information about the element or the content of that element. If you work with HTML, you are familiar with attributes. Take, for example, the following HTML code:

```
<HTML>

<HEAD>
  <TITLE>Database Web Site</TITLE>
</HEAD>

<BODY>
  <A HREF="http://mspress.microsoft.com">
    Click here for a Web link
  </A>
  <BR>
  <IMG SRC="Schemas2.gif" BORDER=0 ALT="A Schema Map">
</BODY>

</HTML>
```

The Anchor element (indicated by the <A> tag) and the Image element (indicated by the <IMG> tag) both contain attributes: the Anchor element contains the *HREF* attribute, and the Image element contains the attributes *SRC*, *BORDER*, and *ALT*. These attributes provide additional information of use mostly to the browser. Notice that the Anchor element contains the content, *Click here for a Web link*, but the Image element appears to be an empty element—it contains no visible content. In reality, however, this is not entirely true. While the element does not contain content, the *SRC* attribute is a filename that tells the processor which file to display. So in this case, a graphic file is displayed on the Web page. This example presents an important aspect about attributes. Attributes can, and usually do, contain important information that is not part of the content of the element. This means that, while the results of the attribute are usually visible, often the attribute itself is more important to the XML processor than it is to the person viewing the content.

ATTRIBUTE DECLARATIONS

In XML, attributes are declared in the DTD using the following syntax:

```
<!ATTLIST ElementName AttributeName Type Default>
```

Here <!ATTLIST> is the tag that identifies an attribute declaration. The *ElementName* entry is the name of the element to which the attribute(s) apply. The *AttributeName* entry, obviously, is the name of the attribute. The *Type* entry identifies the type of attribute being declared. The *Default* entry specifies the default for the attribute.

NOTE

The attribute declaration can be located anywhere in the DTD, but keeping the attribute declaration close to the corresponding element declaration can make the DTD easier for humans to read. You can also include multiple attribute declarations for a single element. In this case, the processor will combine all the declarations into one big list. If the processor encounters more than one declaration for the same attribute, only the first one will be counted.

Table 4-2 lists the types of attributes that are available in XML.

TABLE 4-2
Attribute Types in XML

Attribute Type	Usage
CDATA	Only character data can be used in the attribute.
ENTITY	Attribute value must refer to an external binary entity declared in the DTD.
ENTITIES	Same as *ENTITY*, but allows multiple values separated by white space.
ID	Attribute value must be a unique identifier. If a document contains *ID* attributes with the same value, the processor should generate an error.

Attribute Type	Usage
IDREF	Value must be a reference to an *ID* declared elsewhere in the document. If the attribute does not match the referenced *ID* value, the processor should generate an error.
IDREFS	Same as *IDREF*, but allows multiple values separated by white space.
NMTOKEN	Attribute value is any mixture of name token characters, which must be letters, numbers, periods, dashes, colons, or underscores.
NMTOKENS	Same as *NMTOKEN*, but allows multiple values separated by white space.
NOTATION	Attribute value must refer to a notation declared elsewhere in the DTD. Declaration can also be a list of notations. The value must be one of the notations in the list. Each notation must have its own declaration in the DTD.
Enumerated	Attribute value must match one of the included values. For example: *<!ATTLIST MyAttribute (content1|content2)>*.

The final part of the attribute declaration is the default for the attribute value. The default can come in one of four types. Table 4-3 shows the available attribute defaults.

TABLE 4-3
Attribute Defaults

Default	Usage
#REQUIRED	Every element containing this attribute must specify a value for that attribute. A missing value results in an error.
#IMPLIED	This attribute is optional. The processor can ignore this attribute if no value is found.
#FIXED fixedvalue	This attribute must have the value *fixedvalue*. If the attribute is not included in the element, *fixedvalue* is assumed.
default	Identifies a default value for an attribute. If the element does not include the attribute, the value *default* is assumed.

Let's take a look at how attributes are used by adding some attribute declarations to the DTD of the sample document:

```
<?xml version="1.0"?>

<!DOCTYPE EMAIL [
  <!ELEMENT EMAIL (TO+, FROM, CC*, BCC*, SUBJECT?, BODY?)>
  <!ATTLIST EMAIL
    LANGUAGE (Western|Greek|Latin|Universal) "Western"
```

(continued)

```
      ENCRYPTED CDATA #IMPLIED
      PRIORITY (NORMAL|LOW|HIGH) "NORMAL">

   <!ELEMENT TO (#PCDATA)>
   <!ELEMENT FROM (#PCDATA)>
   <!ELEMENT CC (#PCDATA)>

   <!ELEMENT BCC (#PCDATA)>
   <!ATTLIST BCC
     HIDDEN CDATA #FIXED "TRUE">

   <!ELEMENT SUBJECT (#PCDATA)>
   <!ELEMENT BODY (#PCDATA)>
   ]>
```

In this example, attributes have been added to two elements, Email and the new element Bcc. The first attribute added to the Email element is *LANGUAGE*. The *LANGUAGE* attribute can contain one of several options. The attribute will contain the default value, *Western*, if none other is specified. The next attribute in the Email element is *ENCRYPTED*. This element must contain character data, and since the default is *#IMPLIED*, the processor will simply ignore this attribute if no value is specified. The last attribute in the Email element is *PRIORITY*. The *PRIORITY* attribute can have any one of the three values *NORMAL*, *LOW*, and *HIGH*. The default value is *NORMAL*.

The *HIDDEN* attribute has been included for the Bcc element. The *HIDDEN* attribute is a *CDATA* type, and since it has a default of *#FIXED*, the default value is specified following the keyword *#FIXED*. This attribute must always have the value specified in the DTD, in this case *TRUE*.

NOTE

Even though the attribute name is *HIDDEN* and the value is *TRUE*, the XML processor does not actually know what that means. In other words, the word "HIDDEN" has no special meaning in XML; it simply happens to be the attribute name used. It will be up to the application to know what to do with the attribute and its value.

HOW ATTRIBUTES WORK IN AN XML DOCUMENT

Let's put the DTD together with the rest of the document to see how the attributes look in the document. The code, which you can find in the Chap04\Lst4_2.xml file on the companion CD, is shown in Code Listing 4-2.

```
<?xml version="1.0"?>

<!DOCTYPE EMAIL [
  <!ELEMENT EMAIL (TO+, FROM, CC*, BCC*, SUBJECT?, BODY?)>
  <!ATTLIST EMAIL
```

Code Listing 4-2.

```
     LANGUAGE (Western|Greek|Latin|Universal) "Western"
     ENCRYPTED CDATA #IMPLIED
     PRIORITY (NORMAL|LOW|HIGH) "NORMAL">

  <!ELEMENT TO (#PCDATA)>
  <!ELEMENT FROM (#PCDATA)>
  <!ELEMENT CC (#PCDATA)>

  <!ELEMENT BCC (#PCDATA)>
  <!ATTLIST BCC
    HIDDEN CDATA #FIXED "TRUE">

  <!ELEMENT SUBJECT (#PCDATA)>
  <!ELEMENT BODY (#PCDATA)>
]>

<EMAIL LANGUAGE="Western" ENCRYPTED="128" PRIORITY="HIGH">
  <TO>Jodie@msn.com</TO>
  <FROM>Bill@msn.com</FROM>
  <CC>Philip@msn.com</CC>
  <BCC>Naomi@msn.com</BCC>
  <SUBJECT>My First DTD</SUBJECT>
  <BODY>Hello, World!</BODY>
</EMAIL>
```

Note that the Email element in the code listing includes all of the attributes and specifies a value for each one. In this code listing, the Bcc element includes no attribute. Since the *HIDDEN* attribute has a default of *#FIXED*, the processor will assume the value from the DTD. When the document is displayed, it appears as shown in Figure 4-3.

Figure 4-3. *An XML document with attributes.*

If you've noticed that this document looks the same as the document without attributes, you've been paying attention! This figure illustrates the idea that attributes often provide more information to the processor and the application than they provide to the user. Although the attributes in this document can affect how the content appears (such as inserting a different value for the *LANGUAGE* attribute, for example), it is up to the application to make use of the information that's provided by the document. Since none of the attributes used in our example changed the appearance of the content, there was no visible difference.

Entities

Recall from Chapter 3 the concepts of physical structure and entities. In addition to the general entity discussed in that chapter, another kind of entity exists called the *parameter entity*. This section covers both types of entities in detail and describes how you declare entities in a DTD. First let's review general entities.

GENERAL ENTITIES: A REVIEW

You know that entities are used as containers for content and that the content can reside in the XML document (as an internal entity) or outside the document in an external file (an external entity). Most entities must be declared in the DTD. (You'll recall that some predefined entities are already built into XML and are used to display characters normally used for markup.) Entity declarations follow the same basic syntax used by other declarations:

```
<!ENTITY EntityName EntityDefinition>
```

Entities in the DTD can be parsed or unparsed. Parsed entities, or text entities, contain text that becomes part of the XML document. Unparsed entities, or binary entities, are usually references to an external binary file. Unparsed entities can also be text that is not parsable, so it is best to think of unparsed entities as items that are not intended to be treated as XML.

INTERNAL ENTITIES

Internal entities are declared in the DTD and contain the content that will be used in the document. This line adds an internal entity called *SIGNATURE* to the example XML document:

```
<!ENTITY SIGNATURE "Bill">
```

This entity will be added to the DTD, and (as you will see in the "Entity References" section later in this chapter) whenever that entity is referenced in the document, it will be replaced with the content of the entity (*Bill*).

EXTERNAL ENTITIES: *SYSTEM* AND *PUBLIC* KEYWORDS

Here's an external entity declaration you can add to the DTD. This entity references an external GIF file and will appear in the body of the XML document:

```
<!ENTITY IMAGE1 SYSTEM "Xmlquot.gif" NDATA GIF>
```

Notice that the external entity declaration differs from the internal entity declaration: it uses an additional keyword (*SYSTEM*) following the entity name (*IMAGE1*).

An external entity declaration can include the *SYSTEM* keyword or the *PUBLIC* keyword. Many DTDs are developed *locally*—that is, they are developed for a specific organization or business or they are used only for a specific Web site. In this case, the *SYSTEM* keyword should be used. The *SYSTEM* keyword is followed by a URI (Uniform Resource Identifier) that tells the processor where to find the object referenced in the declaration. In the example above, the filename was used because the code is for local use. In the following declaration, the URI is a Web address that points to the location of the referenced file:

```
<!ENTITY IMAGE1 SYSTEM
    "http://www.XMLCo.com/Images/Xmlquot.gif" NDATA GIF>
```

Some DTDs are established standards that are available to a wide range of users. The *PUBLIC* keyword should be used, followed by the public identifier that the processor can use if a standards library is available. Following the public identifier is a URI, similar to the URI used with the *SYSTEM* keyword in the preceding example. A declaration that uses the *PUBLIC* keyword might look like this:

```
<!ENTITY IMAGE1 PUBLIC "-//XMLCo//TEXT Standard images//EN"
    "http://www.XMLCo.com/Images/Xmlquot.gif" NDATA GIF>
```

EXTERNAL ENTITIES: NOTATIONS AND NOTATION DECLARATIONS

Again, consider the entity declaration:

```
<!ENTITY IMAGE1 SYSTEM "Xmlquot.gif" NDATA GIF>
```

A *notation* (*NDATA GIF*) appears at the end of the declaration. This notation tells the processor what type of object is being referenced. At this point, if you simply added the entity declaration to the DTD and ran it through a processor, you'd get an error like the following:

```
Declaration 'IMAGE1' contains reference to undefined notation 'GIF'.
```

The error results because the entity declaration is referencing a binary file type and the processor has not been told what to do with the binary file. Remember that this is an unparsed entity that the processor cannot "understand." In this case, the notation must be declared as a *notation declaration*. A notation declaration tells the processor how to deal with a specific binary file type.

Although the information in a notation declaration will usually identify a "helper" application, the XML specification does not require this. The processor passes this information on to the processing application; it doesn't care whether the application can understand it or not. The information in the declaration could also be used for other purposes, such as to provide a message to the application that could then be displayed to the user.

Notation declarations follow this format:

```
<!NOTATION GIF SYSTEM "Iexplore.exe">
```

This declaration tells the processor that whenever it encounters a GIF file in the DTD, it should use the Iexplore.exe program to process the file.

We'll add a simple entity declaration to the sample DTD:

```
<?xml version="1.0"?>

<!DOCTYPE EMAIL [
  <!ELEMENT EMAIL (TO+, FROM, CC*, BCC*, SUBJECT?, BODY?)>
  <!ATTLIST EMAIL
    LANGUAGE (Western|Greek|Latin|Universal) "Western"
    ENCRYPTED CDATA #IMPLIED
    PRIORITY (NORMAL|LOW|HIGH) "NORMAL">

  <!ELEMENT TO (#PCDATA)>
  <!ELEMENT FROM (#PCDATA)>
  <!ELEMENT CC (#PCDATA)>

  <!ELEMENT BCC (#PCDATA)>
  <!ATTLIST BCC
    HIDDEN CDATA #FIXED "TRUE">

  <!ELEMENT SUBJECT (#PCDATA)>
  <!ELEMENT BODY (#PCDATA)>

  <!ENTITY SIGNATURE "Bill">

]>
```

The DTD now includes an entity declaration. But as with other declarations, this is not much good unless it is used, or referenced, in the actual XML document.

ENTITY REFERENCES

You'll recall from Chapter 3 that entity references use a specific syntax within a document: &*EntityName*;. When a processor encounters an entity reference in a document, the reference tells the processor that it should replace that reference with the content declared in the entity. Code Listing 4-3 shows changes to the XML sample document (which you can find in the Chap04\Lst4_3.xml file on the companion CD) and adds an entity reference:

```
<?xml version="1.0"?>

<!DOCTYPE EMAIL [
  <!ELEMENT EMAIL (TO+, FROM, CC*, BCC*, SUBJECT?, BODY?)>
  <!ATTLIST EMAIL
    LANGUAGE (Western|Greek|Latin|Universal) "Western"
    ENCRYPTED CDATA #IMPLIED
    PRIORITY (NORMAL|LOW|HIGH) "NORMAL">

  <!ELEMENT TO (#PCDATA)>
  <!ELEMENT FROM (#PCDATA)>
  <!ELEMENT CC (#PCDATA)>

  <!ELEMENT BCC (#PCDATA)>
  <!ATTLIST BCC
    HIDDEN CDATA #FIXED "TRUE">

  <!ELEMENT SUBJECT (#PCDATA)>
  <!ELEMENT BODY (#PCDATA)>

  <!ENTITY SIGNATURE "Bill">
]>

<EMAIL LANGUAGE="Western" ENCRYPTED="128" PRIORITY="HIGH">
  <TO>Jodie@msn.com</TO>
  <FROM>&SIGNATURE;@msn.com</FROM>
  <CC>Philip@msn.com</CC>
  <BCC>Naomi@msn.com</BCC>
  <SUBJECT>Sample Document with Entity References</SUBJECT>

  <BODY>
    Hello, this is &SIGNATURE;.
    Take care, -&SIGNATURE;
  </BODY>
</EMAIL>
```

Code Listing 4-3.

Notice that in this code, an entity reference to the entity *SIGNATURE* appears wherever the word *Bill* should appear. Figure 4-4 shows how the document looks when it is processed and displayed.

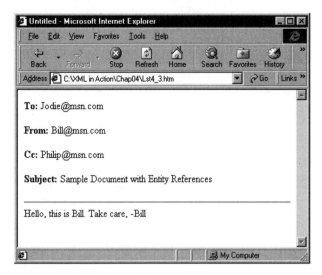

Figure 4-4. *An XML document that uses entities.*

To briefly demonstrate the power of entities, let's change the *SIGNATURE* entity declaration to the following:

```
<!ENTITY SIGNATURE "Colleen">
```

When the document is processed, at each location in which the *SIGNATURE* entity is referenced, the content will appear changed, as shown in Figure 4-5.

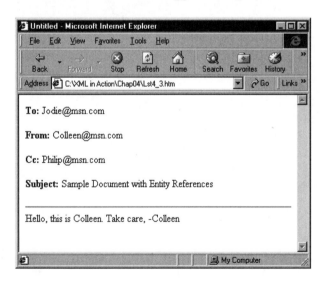

Figure 4-5. *Changing an entity declaration changes content throughout the document.*

PARAMETER ENTITIES

Although parameter entities work in much the same way that general entities work, they have one important syntactical difference. Parameter entities use the percent symbol (%)

in both the declaration and the reference. In the entity declaration, the percent symbol follows the keyword *!ENTITY* but precedes the entity name, as shown here. (Note that a single space is required before and after the % symbol.)

```
<!ENTITY % ENCRYPTION
  "40bit CDATA #IMPLIED
  128bit CDATA #IMPLIED">
```

This entity can now be referenced elsewhere in the DTD. For example:

```
<!ELEMENT EMAIL (TO+, FROM, CC*, BCC*, SUBJECT?, BODY?)>
  <!ATTLIST EMAIL
    LANGUAGE (Western|Greek|Latin|Universal) "Western"
    ENCRYPTED %ENCRYPTION;
    PRIORITY (NORMAL|LOW|HIGH) "NORMAL">
```

Notice that the parameter entity reference (*%ENCRYPTION;*) uses the same basic format used by the general entity reference, except that the % replaces the &. Also notice that a space is not required following the % in the entity reference.

> **NOTE**
>
> Parameter entities are restricted to the DTD. You cannot reference a parameter entity within an XML document element.

As you can see, parameter entities can be a powerful way to create your own shorthand in your DTDs and make them more concise and better organized. These entities should be used with caution, however, since they can create complexity within a document that makes it difficult to manage. For example, you could reference several other parameter entities inside a single parameter entity declaration. As the author, you must be sure that those references actually point to something and that the content is valid.

The *IGNORE* and *INCLUDE* Keywords

The *IGNORE* and *INCLUDE* keywords can be used by authors to turn portions of the DTD "on" or "off." *IGNORE* and *INCLUDE* are used in the DTD to create conditions in the document that are suitable for various purposes. For example, using *IGNORE* and *INCLUDE* allow an author to test various structures while tracking the variations. *IGNORE* and *INCLUDE* are used in much the same way that *CDATA* is used:

```
<![IGNORE [DTD section]]>
<![INCLUDE [DTD section]]>
```

Neither keyword can appear inside a declaration, and each *DTD section* must include an entire declaration or a set of declarations, comments, and white space. Here is an example of how the keywords can be used:

```
<![IGNORE[<!ELEMENT BCC (#PCDATA)>
<!ATTLIST BCC
  HIDDEN CDATA #FIXED "TRUE">]]>
<![INCLUDE[<!ELEMENT SUBJECT (#PCDATA)>]]>
```

This fragment tells the processor to ignore the Bcc element and attribute list and to include the Subject element. As you look over this code, you might think that the *IGNORE* keyword seems useful but that the *INCLUDE* keyword seems unnecessary. You could accomplish the same effect by eliminating the *INCLUDE* keyword. However, *INCLUDE* proves its worth any time you want to quickly change what is being included or ignored in the document. Consider the following code, which changes both keywords into parameter entities and then places content within the appropriate sections:

```
<!ENTITY % SECURE "IGNORE">
<!ENTITY % UNSECURE "INCLUDE">
<![%SECURE; [any number of declarations go here]]>
<![%UNSECURE; [any number of declarations go here]]>
```

In this case, the various declarations can be turned on or off easily by changing their placement or by modifying the entity declarations.

Processing Instructions

Processing instructions (PIs) provide instructions for the application that's processing the document. PIs usually appear in the document prolog, but they can be placed anywhere in the XML document. The most common PI is the XML declaration included at the top of our sample XML documents:

```
<?xml version="1.0"?>
```

PIs are written with the sequence <?, followed by the PI name, followed by a value or instruction, and concluded with ?>. The name, or *PI Target,* identifies which application should be looking at the PI. See section 2.6 in the XML 1.0 specification for more details about PIs.

NOTE

XML has reserved names beginning with the characters *x, m,* and *l* for its own use. Apart from this restriction, PIs can be used to send instructions to any application that is processing the document.

Here are examples of other PIs:

```
<?AVI CODEC="VIDEO1" COLORS="256"?>
<?WAV COMPRESSOR="ADPCM" BITS="8" RESOLUTION="16"?>
```

Comments

Comments are one of a DTD's "miscellaneous" parts. Although comments are not required, they are widely used for making a document more readable to authors. You can add comments as a way to explain the purpose of a certain section of the DTD, to indicate what references mean, and for other purposes. Obviously, comments come in handy as reminders of your coding intentions if you need to go back to the DTD and make changes later or if another author works on the document. Comments are not restricted to the DTD and can be used throughout a document. Since comments benefit only the human reader, any true XML processor will ignore them. Comments appear between comment tags (<!-- -->) and can include any combination of text, markup, and symbols, except the combination of symbols that make up the comment tags. (See section 2.5 in the XML 1.0 specification for more details about comments.) The following boldface code shows how a comment might look in a document:

```
<?xml version="1.0"?>

<!DOCTYPE EMAIL [
<!-- This document could be used as an email template. -->
  <!ELEMENT EMAIL (TO+, FROM, CC*, BCC*, SUBJECT?, BODY?)>
  <!ATTLIST EMAIL
    LANGUAGE (Western|Greek|Latin|Universal) "Western"
    ENCRYPTED CDATA #IMPLIED
    PRIORITY (NORMAL|LOW|HIGH) "NORMAL">

  <!ELEMENT TO (#PCDATA)>
    ⋮
```

NOTE

It is considered good practice to provide well-commented documents and DTDs. Having said that, the sample code in this book will not use many comments because of space considerations.

External DTDs

You've probably noticed that the sample document (shown in Code Listing 4-3 on page 63) has grown quite large. You've also probably noticed that the majority of the document space is taken up by the DTD. You can separate documents and DTDs to make them a bit easier to work with. After creating a separate DTD, you can reference it within any document.

To separate the DTD portion of our sample XML document, you simply cut the DTD portion and paste it into a new text file. The new filename should have the extension *.dtd*.

Code Listing 4-4 shows the stand-alone DTD file named Lst4_4.dtd:

```
<?xml version="1.0"?>

<!ELEMENT EMAIL (TO+, FROM, CC*, BCC*, SUBJECT?, BODY?)>
<!ATTLIST EMAIL
  LANGUAGE (Western|Greek|Latin|Universal) "Western"
  ENCRYPTED CDATA #IMPLIED
  PRIORITY (NORMAL|LOW|HIGH) "NORMAL">
```

Code Listing 4-4.   *(continued)*

```
<!ELEMENT TO (#PCDATA)>
<!ELEMENT FROM (#PCDATA)>
<!ELEMENT CC (#PCDATA)>

<!ELEMENT BCC (#PCDATA)>
<!ATTLIST BCC
  HIDDEN CDATA #FIXED "TRUE">

<!ELEMENT SUBJECT (#PCDATA)>
<!ELEMENT BODY (#PCDATA)>

<!ENTITY SIGNATURE "Bill">
```

If you compare the internal DTD in the previous example with this newly created external DTD, you'll find that they are exactly alike. For this DTD to work, however, you must add a reference to it in the sample XML document. This is shown in Code Listing 4-5 (also in Chap04\Lst4_5.xml on the companion CD). The reference to the new DTD file is shown in boldface type:

```
<?xml version="1.0"?>
<!DOCTYPE EMAIL SYSTEM "Lst4_4.dtd">

<EMAIL LANGUAGE="Western" ENCRYPTED="128" PRIORITY="HIGH">
  <TO>Jodie@msn.com</TO>
  <FROM>&SIGNATURE;@msn.com</FROM>
  <CC>Philip@msn.com</CC>
  <BCC>Naomi@msn.com</BCC>
  <SUBJECT>Sample Document with External DTD</SUBJECT>

  <BODY>
    Hello, this is &SIGNATURE;.
    Take care, -&SIGNATURE;
  </BODY>
</EMAIL>
```

Code Listing 4-5.

Separating the DTD from the document greatly reduces the size of the XML document file and provides some other benefits. Now that the DTD is a separate file, it can be used in other documents by anyone who has access to it. Another author can create a document using the same structure with completely different content. And because the new document would follow the DTD, it could be read by any application that knows how to process that DTD.

This brings us back to the concept that opened this chapter—document objects.

Class DTDs

It should be clear to you now that using a DTD can allow you to create a document with the same basic properties as the original but for a different purpose. This brings us back to the concept of inheritance. By creating a DTD that is used by many documents, you are creating a *base class DTD*. This base class DTD is the rule book upon which all other documents of this class will be based. Every author who uses the DTD must obey the rules outlined in the DTD—almost. By using a combination of internal and external DTDs, an author can *subclass* a document and change some properties. Code Listing 4-6 demonstrates subclassing. (You can find this document in Chap04\Lst4_6.xml on the companion CD.)

```
<?xml version="1.0"?>
<!DOCTYPE EMAIL SYSTEM "Lst4_4.dtd" [
  <!ENTITY SIGNATURE "Joe">
]>

<EMAIL LANGUAGE="Western" ENCRYPTED="128" PRIORITY="HIGH">
  <TO>Jodie@msn.com</TO>
  <FROM>&SIGNATURE;@msn.com</FROM>
  <CC>Philip @msn.com</CC>
  <BCC>Naomi@msn.com</BCC>
  <SUBJECT>Sample Document with External DTD</SUBJECT>

  <BODY>
    Hello, this is &SIGNATURE;.
    Take care, -&SIGNATURE;
  </BODY>
</EMAIL>
```

Code Listing 4-6.

This document overrides the external, or base class, DTD with an internal DTD subset. If an XML processor encounters both an internal DTD and an external DTD, it uses the first declaration that it finds—the one in the internal DTD. In other words, the first one in wins. By declaring an entity with the name *SIGNATURE* and giving it the value *Joe*, the document above overrides the entity in the class DTD of the same name. Now any time the entity reference *SIGNATURE* is used in this document, the value *Joe* will appear instead of *Bill*, which appeared in the original DTD.

Required Markup Declaration

As stated in Chapter 3, a well-formed document does not need to read or process a DTD. While such practice might be fine in many situations, in some cases this can cause problems. For example, every external entity must be declared, even in well-formed documents. In this case, the processor might not need to process an external DTD, but it might need to process an internal DTD so that the necessary entity declarations will be properly read and dealt with.

Still other cases might exist in which all the DTDs must be processed for the document to be properly interpreted. To deal with such situations, XML includes in the XML declaration a *required markup declaration* or RMD. The RMD tells the processor how it should deal with the DTD. The RMD can have one of three values:

- *NONE*, which indicates that the document can be processed without reading any part of the DTD, neither internal nor external.

- *INTERNAL*, which specifies that the processor must process the internal DTD if it's available.

- *ALL*, which specifies that the processor must read and process any available internal and external DTDs.

An example of how the RMD is used is shown below. In this case, the processor knows that it need not consult any DTD:

```
<?xml version="1.0" RMD="NONE"?>
```

If no RMD is declared, *ALL* is assumed by the processor.

Vocabularies

Vocabularies represent a practical use of the topics covered in this chapter. An *XML vocabulary* is a set of the actual elements and the structure for a specific document type. Vocabularies are defined in a DTD that serves as the rule book for that vocabulary. Vocabularies are currently in use both on the Internet and in some organizations and businesses. One of the first and probably most well-known vocabularies is the Channel Definition Format (CDF) used to define Web pages that are designed to be sent automatically, or "pushed," to client users.

Vocabularies are well suited to vertical applications and are likely to be used to develop data interchange systems for specific industries, such as telecommunications, pharmaceuticals, and the legal establishment, to name a few. Vocabularies are also well suited for more horizontal applications, such as the information push application mentioned above. As of this writing, several vocabularies exist or are in development. Following are some of these vocabularies with descriptions of how they might be used.

CHANNEL DEFINITION FORMAT

Channel Definition Format (CDF) is used to describe the behavior of Web pages in a push model of delivery. CDF is currently used by Microsoft Internet Explorer and describes such processes as download schedule, channel bar display, page usage, and frequency of updates.

OPEN FINANCIAL EXCHANGE

Open Financial Exchange (OFX) is currently an SGML application that is used by software packages to communicate to financial institutions. OFX will soon be based on XML.

OPEN SOFTWARE DESCRIPTION

Open Software Description (OSD) is a data format used to allow updating and installation of software via the Internet. This is especially useful for notifying users when new versions of software are available and providing a mechanism for users to obtain the programs over the Internet.

ELECTRONIC DATA INTERCHANGE

Electronic Data Interchange (EDI) is currently used worldwide for data exchange and transaction support. In its current implementation, however, it can be used only by organizations that have been set up to exchange information using compatible systems. XML can greatly expand the reach of EDI and make it more accessible to a larger number of organizations. Efforts are currently under way to move EDI to an XML-based format.

Part 3

Putting XML to Work

Chapter 5
Scripting XML

O ne of the strongest messages coming from the proponents of XML is the idea that "XML is about data." One of the frequent questions posed by those interested in XML is "How do I get that XML data on my Web pages?" This chapter will help answer that question. We'll look at how the XML processor works and the kinds of data it can generate. We'll also begin to examine the *XML object model,* which provides an interface through scripting or some other coding mechanism that allows an author to access XML data; and we will demonstrate how the object model relates to XML data. Most importantly, we will look at the power of scripting and its ability to place and manipulate XML data on an HTML page. A modified version of the sample document from Chapter 4 is used throughout this chapter. For simplicity's sake, document validation using a Document Type Definition (DTD) is not included.

A Scripting Refresher

While this chapter doesn't provide a full introduction to scripting, it does review some aspects of Web-page scripting that you'll need in order to successfully work through the samples throughout the rest of this book. This section is included as a refresher; you should be familiar with a scripting language, such as Microsoft JScript or Microsoft VBScript, and you should have worked at least a bit with Dynamic HTML.

NOTE

All the scripting examples in this book will be written in Microsoft JScript.

HTML and Scripts

Just as HTML elements require the use of tags, getting scripts ir ɔ an HTML file requires that a special set of tags be included, as shown here:

```
<SCRIPT LANGUAGE="JavaScript">
<!--
⋮
-->
</SCRIPT>
```

The opening <SCRIPT> tag can include a *LANGUAGE* attribute that allows the author to specify which scripting language is used: JScript, VBScript, or another language.

JScript vs. JavaScript

JScript is similar to Netscape's JavaScript. So which product should you specify in your scripts? If you are using Microsoft Internet Explorer, the JScript engine will be used, no matter whether you specify *JScript* or *JavaScript* in the *LANGUAGE* attribute of the <SCRIPT> tag. On the other hand, other browsers might not recognize a *LANGUAGE* attribute of *JScript*, and using that value would result in errors. Since *JavaScript* is widely recognized by many browsers, you are less likely to receive errors if you specify it in the *LANGUAGE* attribute of the <SCRIPT> tag.

Although scripts can occur anywhere within an HTML document, their best and widely accepted location is in the document's head section. Since scripts often need to interact with other elements on a page and since HTML documents load and run asynchronously, putting scripts in the head section helps assure that they will get loaded first and will be available when they're needed.

NOTE

If you have used other scripting languages, you might be interested to know that Internet Explorer can act as a *scripting host*. This means that it can host and work with scripting languages other than those that shipped with it. This allows script authors to use those languages that are perhaps more familiar to them, such as REXX and PERL. For more information on script hosting, visit *http://msdn.microsoft.com/scripting/default.htm?/scripting/hosting/hosting.htm*.

The Dynamic HTML Object Model

Internet Explorer (versions 4 and later) provides a powerful and flexible object model for HTML elements. This object model provides access to (exposes) every element on the page as an object, complete with *properties* (information about an object) and *methods* (ways to take action on an object). Examples of properties that are exposed through the object model are colors, text, element position, and element attributes.

NOTE

This section briefly discusses the Dynamic HTML object model. Later in the chapter, you'll learn about the XML object model. As this is being written, the W3C just issued a language-neutral *Document object model* (DOM) Level 1 specification that will help provide a mechanism for interoperability between HTML and XML. The XML object model used by Microsoft maps to DOM Level 1, and Microsoft intends to track future W3C activities on DOM.

Code Listing 5-1 shows the Dynamic HTML object model in action.

```
<!DOCTYPE HTML PUBLIC "-//W3C//DTD HTML 3.2 Final//EN">
<HTML>

  <HEAD>
    <SCRIPT LANGUAGE="JavaScript"
      FOR="window" EVENT="onload">
      alert ("Background color is " +
        document.bgColor + ".")
    </SCRIPT>

    <SCRIPT LANGUAGE="JavaScript">
      function changeColor()
        {
        document.bgColor = "red";
        alert ("Background color is " +
          document.bgColor + ".")
        }
    </SCRIPT>

    <TITLE>Code Listing 5-1</TITLE>
  </HEAD>

  <BODY BGCOLOR="white" ONCLICK="changeColor()">
  </BODY>

</HTML>
```

Code Listing 5-1.

The page in the sample (included on the companion CD in the Chap05\Lst5_1.htm file) uses a script that dynamically changes the background color of the page by changing the *document.bgColor* property when a user clicks on the document page. Similar scripting techniques will be used later in the chapter (and later in this book) when you work with the XML object model.

Event Handlers

Scripts often need to react to some event that occurs on the page. In Code Listing 5-1, the *document* object generates an event when the user clicks on the page. That *onclick* event triggers an action on the page; an *event handler* starts the action by calling a script *function*. An event handler typically waits for a specific event to happen and then springs into action when it does. A common event handler used in Web-page scripts triggers an action when the document is loaded, as shown below (from Code Listing 5-1):

```
<SCRIPT LANGUAGE="JavaScript"
  FOR="window" EVENT="onload">
  alert ("Background color is " +
    document.bgColor + ".")
</SCRIPT>
```

Another type of event handler is the *inline event handler* that is also demonstrated in Code Listing 5-1:

```
<BODY BGCOLOR="white" ONCLICK="changeColor()">
```

This type of handler is incorporated directly into the tag or object that generates the event.

Working with Object Properties

A *property* is a characteristic of an object. For example, HTML's *img* object has the *SRC* attribute, which is a property that identifies the source filename, and the *WIDTH* and *HEIGHT* attributes, which are properties that identify the dimensions of the image. Most object properties can be read and changed while the object (including the *document* object) is being used, as shown in Code Listing 5-1. Working with object properties is essential to writing effective scripts, and object properties are often needed when writing scripts that use the XML object model.

Object Naming

Object naming follows a *dot notation* format—a combination of the name of the object and the name of the child object, property, event, or method separated by periods, or dots. Dot notation is a convenient naming convention to use for working with objects in scripts. Within the dot notation, you can read the hierarchy of an object from left to right: for example, *window.document.image1.height* tells you that *height* is a property of the *image1* object, *image1* is a child object of the *document* object, and the *document* object is a child object of the *window* object. In some cases, the naming convention can be shortened. For example, since the *image1* object exists in the same window and document in which the script is running, the property name could be shortened to *image1.height*. In this case, the window and document are assumed to be the same window and document in which the *image1* object exists.

Code Listing 5-2 (included on the companion CD in the Chap05\Lst5_2.htm file) shows an example of some of the scripting principles discussed above.

```
<!DOCTYPE HTML PUBLIC "-//W3C//DTD HTML 3.2 Final//EN">
<HTML>

  <HEAD>
    <SCRIPT LANGUAGE="JavaScript">
      function showStats()
        {
        widthData.innerText =
          "Image width is " + image1.width + ".";
        heightData.innerText =
          "Image height is " + image1.height + "."
        }
```

Code Listing 5-2.

(continued)

```
      function smaller()
        {
        image1.width = image1.width ? 25;
        image1.height = image1.height ? 25;
        showStats()
        }

      function bigger()
        {
        image1.width = image1.width + 25;
        image1.height = image1.height + 25;
        showStats()
        }
      </SCRIPT>

      <TITLE>Code Listing 5-2</TITLE>
    </HEAD>

  <BODY>
    <INPUT TYPE="Button" NAME="smaller" VALUE="Smaller"
      onclick="smaller()">
    <INPUT TYPE="Button" NAME="bigger" VALUE="Bigger"
      onclick="bigger()">

    <P>
      <IMG ID="image1" SRC="star.gif" WIDTH=172 HEIGHT=152
        onclick="showStats()">

    <P>
      <SPAN ID="widthData"></SPAN>
      <BR>
      <SPAN ID="heightData"></SPAN>

  </BODY>
</HTML>
```

The script on this page accesses the *width* and *height* properties of the *image1* object to change the size of the image on the page when the user clicks the appropriate button. Each button's event handler triggers the appropriate script function. Finally, the *innerText* properties of two Span elements are used to display the image dimensions.

Using Scripts with XML

This ends our whirlwind tour of HTML scripting. Later in this chapter, you'll see that many of the techniques used for HTML scripting are also used in XML scripting. Scripts allow you to create powerful, dynamic, data-aware pages with XML.

The XML Processor

Previous chapters focused on the data that goes into the XML processor. So you should now understand the rules and regulations for getting data into the processor and making sure that the data is in order. Now it's time to see the payoffs for that hard work.

Because XML only describes data and doesn't include instructions for how the processor should display that data, you need a way to manipulate the data into a workable format for eventual display. This is where the XML processor comes in. It should be apparent from previous examples that the primary job of the processor is to parse and validate the XML data. But the processor also manipulates the data into a format that can be used by an application. This is obviously another important processor function, since the data would not be useful if it could not be displayed. The processor, then, acts as a middle layer between the data and the display mechanism.

XML Processors from Microsoft

If you are using Microsoft Internet Explorer, it comes with a built-in XML processor. This processor, Msxml, is designed as a Windows component and can be used as a Microsoft ActiveX control in Web pages or in Visual Basic or C++ applications. Microsoft has also codeveloped a Java-based XML processor with DataChannel, Inc. For more information on the Java processor, visit the DataChannel Web site at *http://www.datachannel.com*.

The Right Processor for the Job

Several commercial, shareware, and freeware XML processors are available—some are validating processors and others are nonvalidating. A nonvalidating processor provides performance benefits because it does not have to read and process a DTD. In many instances, well-formed XML code is good enough, so it's not necessary for the processor to go through the overhead of validating a document.

Many of the available processors are written in the Java programming language. While that might not seem very important, in fact the language in which the processor was written can make a difference in performance and availability. For example, although Java applications (including *applets*) tend to be slower than C++-based applications, Java can often work on multiple platforms. C++-based applications are typically smaller and faster. So generally speaking, if you are after the best performance and validation is not important to you, using a nonvalidating C++ processor is the way to go. But if you need to validate your documents and work on the widest range of platforms, a validating Java processor should be used.

XML: The Parent/Child Relationship

As you'll recall from previous chapters, XML documents are highly structured and must follow strict rules to be well-formed or valid. This structure imposes a specific hierarchical order for XML elements. You will see that all XML documents are organized into a "family tree" of parent/child elements.

Back to Basics

Remember that an XML document can have only one root element. Remember also that every element must nest properly—that is, a child element's closing tag must appear before the parent element's closing tag. The following code demonstrates a proper tree structure and a correct parent/child relationship among tags and elements:

```
<ROOT>
  <C1-ROOT.Child>
    <Ca-C1.Child></Ca-C1.Child>
    <Cb-C1.Child></Cb-C1.Child>
    <Cc-C1.Child></Cc-C1.Child>
  </C1-ROOT.Child>

  <C2-ROOT.Child>
    <Ca-C2.Child></Ca-C2.Child>
    <Cb-C2.Child></Cb-C2.Child>
    <Cc-C2.Child></Cc-C2.Child>
  </C2-ROOT.Child>
</ROOT>
```

This hierarchical tree shows how each subelement is a child of a higher element, with the root element on top. Now if some lines are added to connect the "branches," you can clearly see the tree structure of the document.

```
<ROOT>
 |-<C1-ROOT.Child>
 |  |-<Ca-C1.Child></Ca-C1.Child>
 |  |-<Cb-C1.Child></Cb-C1.Child>
 |  |-<Cc-C1.Child></Cc-C1.Child>
 |-</C1-ROOT.Child>
 |
 |-<C2-ROOT.Child>
 |  |-<Ca-C2.Child></Ca-C2.Child>
 |  |-<Cb-C2.Child></Cb-C2.Child>
 |  |-<Cc-C2.Child></Cc-C2.Child>
 |-</C2-ROOT.Child>
</ROOT>
```

All true XML documents are structured in similar ways, although the actual size and complexity of the documents can vary enormously. To further illustrate this concept, let's look at an example of improperly nested elements:

```
<ROOT>
  <C1-ROOT.Child>
    <Ca-C1.Child>
    <Cb-C1.Child>
    </Ca-C1.Child>
    </Cb-C1.Child>
    <Cc-C1.Child></Cc-C1.Child>
</ROOT>
  </C1-ROOT.Child>
```

In the fifth line, the Ca element is closed *inside* what is now its child element, Cb. Also, the Root element closes before the C1 element closes (as shown in the eighth line). This structure would result in an error from an XML processor.

Although the examples on the previous page are good for illustrative purposes, an actual XML document might help you to see how the hierarchical structure works. Code Listing 5-3, which you can also find in the Chap05\Lst5_3.xml file on the companion CD, shows a simple XML document:

```xml
<?xml version="1.0"?>
<EMAIL>
  <TO>Jodie@msn.com</TO>
  <FROM>Bill@msn.com</FROM>
  <CC>Philip@msn.com</CC>
  <SUBJECT>My document is a tree</SUBJECT>
  <BODY>This is an example of a tree structure</BODY>
</EMAIL>
```

Code Listing 5-3.

Let's send this code through the command-line processor and output the results in "tree mode." The output is shown in Code Listing 5-4, which you can also find in the Chap05\Lst5_4.txt file on the companion CD.

```
DOCUMENT
|---XMLDECL
|   |---ATTRIBUTE version "1.0"
+---ELEMENT EMAIL
    |---ELEMENT TO
    |   +---PCDATA "Jodie@msn.com"
    |---ELEMENT FROM
    |   +---PCDATA "Bill@msn.com"
    |---ELEMENT CC
    |   +---PCDATA "Philip@msn.com"
    |---ELEMENT SUBJECT
    |   +---PCDATA "My document is a tree"
    +---ELEMENT BODY
        +---PCDATA "This is an example of a tree structure"
```

Code Listing 5-4.

NOTE

The use of the command-line processor is covered in the Introduction of this book.

As you can see in this code listing, this well-formed document follows the expected structure, and the result of the processor is a correct tree format. You must understand the parent/child relationships among elements in an XML document to understand how to get data from an XML document.

The XML Object Model

You just saw that when an XML processor parses a document, it creates a treelike structure of all the elements included in the document. Keep in mind that this structure exists only in the computer's memory until something is done with it. While this data can be output for display as is, for the data to be really useful, authors need to be able to access the data in a consistent way. This can be done if the author understands where the data fits in the document structure.

The XML object model meets this need. It provides an interface that allows an author to access the XML data. The object model exposes properties, methods, and the actual content (data) contained in an object. Since the structure of an XML document is in the form of a tree, you might expect that the object model would let you access the branches, called *nodes*, of the tree. And you would be correct. The object model lets authors view all parts of the tree, from the root level through its branches. (This chapter will provide an introduction to some parts of the XML object model; later chapters will present more details.)

From XML to HTML

Let's start at the beginning with a simple HTML document. We'll add the mechanisms necessary to read and process an XML document and finally add some scripts to get the XML data onto the HTML page.

Creating the Basic HTML Page

Code Listing 5-5 (included on the companion CD in the Chap05\Lst5_5.htm file) shows a basic HTML page. We will build into this page everything we need to access and display an XML document.

```
<!DOCTYPE HTML PUBLIC "-//W3C//DTD HTML 3.2 Final//EN">
<HTML>

  <HEAD>
    <TITLE>Code Listing 5-5</TITLE>
  </HEAD>

  <BODY>
  </BODY>

</HTML>
```

Code Listing 5-5.

As mentioned earlier, the XML processor acts as the middle layer between the XML document and the HTML page (or any other application, for that matter). We need to create an *instance* of the XML processor as an object on our Web page so that we can interact with the page through scripting. How you *instantiate* the parser object depends on which processor you use.

> **NOTE**
>
> Creating an instance of, or instantiating, a processor means that you start the processor application (Msxml, for example) and that it is available in memory for you to work with.

Assuming that you are using a Microsoft processor, you can use either the Microsoft ActiveX control in C++ or the Java-based applet. If you decide to use the Java applet, you need to include an Applet element in the body of your document. This element should look similar to the code below:

```
<BODY>
  <APPLET CODE=com.ms.xml.dso.XMLDSO.class
    WIDTH=100% HEIGHT=0 ID=xmldso MAYSCRIPT=true>
  <!-- In next line, replace filename with XML document name. -->
  <PARAM NAME="URL" VALUE="filename">
  </APPLET>
</BODY>
```

Adding the Scripts

Unless you are using Microsoft Internet Explorer 5, XML data is not automatically loaded when the page is loaded. You must include a script to load XML data when the page loads. We'll add a simple script for the *document.onload* event that starts a function called *loadDoc*. This function includes all the code that parses the XML data.

```
<SCRIPT LANGUAGE="JavaScript" FOR=window EVENT=onload>
  loadDoc();
</SCRIPT>
```

Here's the script that creates an instance of the processor and reads the XML document:

```
<SCRIPT LANGUAGE="JavaScript">
  var xmlDoc = new ActiveXObject("microsoft.xmldom");
  xmlDoc.load("Lst5_3.xml");

  function loadDoc()
    {
    if (xmlDoc.readyState == "4")
      start()
    else
      window.setTimeout("loadDoc()", 4000);
    }
```

(continued)

```
function start()
  {
  var rootElem = xmlDoc.documentElement;
  var toVar = rootElem.childNodes.item(0).text;
  }
</SCRIPT>
```

Now the coding starts to get interesting. Let's go through this script a piece at a time. The first section of the script instantiates the XML processor and tells it what document to use:

```
var xmlDoc = new ActiveXObject("microsoft.xmldom");
xmlDoc.load("Lst5_3.xml");
```

This code uses the ActiveX object *microsoft.xmldom* and assigns the instance to the variable *xmlDoc*. Then the name of the XML file (Lst5_3.xml) is passed to the *load* method of the ActiveX control instance.

The next part of the script defines the *loadDoc* function, which checks the *readyState* property of the XML processor. When the processor reaches a *readyState* of 4 (meaning that the document is fully loaded), the *start* function is called.

NOTE

The *readyState* property can have several possible values. For more information, see the *readyState* document property in Appendix A.

The last part of the script defines the *start* function. This function "walks" the XML document tree and pulls out the data. This is really where we get into the XML object model.

Let's look at the code again:

```
function start()
  {
  var rootElem = xmlDoc.documentElement;
  var toVar = rootElem.childNodes.item(0).text;
  }
```

The first line of the function sets the variable *rootElem* to the root node of the XML document. The root node is the single document element discussed earlier and in previous chapters. Here are corresponding lines in the document, the tree, and the code:

```
<?xml version="1.0"?>
<EMAIL>
```

is at the same level as

```
DOCUMENT
|---XMLDECL
|    |---ATTRIBUTE version "1.0"
+---ELEMENT EMAIL
```

which is referenced by the script in the line

```
var rootElem = xmlDoc.documentElement;
```

The second line of the function gets the text content of the first child of the root element (the first child is the To element) by using the *childNodes.item(0)* property, and assigns the value to the variable *toVar*. In this line, the code has walked to another level of the document tree.

Here is where this level maps in the document, tree, and code:

```
<?xml version="1.0"?>
<EMAIL>
<TO>Jodie@msn.com</TO>
```

is at the same level in the tree as

```
DOCUMENT
|---XMLDECL
|    |---ATTRIBUTE version "1.0"
+---ELEMENT EMAIL
     |---ELEMENT TO
     |    +---PCDATA "Jodie@msn.com"
```

which corresponds to the code

```
var toVar = rootElem.childNodes.item(0).text;
```

Code Listing 5-6 puts all the code into our HTML document. The entire page, in a file named Chap05\Lst5_6.htm, is accessible on the companion CD.

```
<!DOCTYPE HTML PUBLIC "-//W3C//DTD HTML 3.2 Final//EN">
<HTML>

  <HEAD>
    <SCRIPT LANGUAGE="JavaScript" FOR=window EVENT=onload>
      loadDoc()
    </SCRIPT>

    <SCRIPT LANGUAGE="JavaScript">
      var xmlDoc = new ActiveXObject("microsoft.xmldom");
      xmlDoc.load("Lst5_3.xml");

      function loadDoc()
        {
        if (xmlDoc.readyState == "4")
          start()
        else
          window.setTimeout("loadDoc()", 4000);
        }
```

Code Listing 5-6.

(continued)

```
      function start()
        {
        var rootElem = xmlDoc.documentElement;
        var toVar = rootElem.childNodes.item(0).text;
        }
    </SCRIPT>

    <TITLE>Code Listing 5-6</TITLE>
  </HEAD>

  <BODY>
  </BODY>

</HTML>
```

If you understand this code, you'll understand how to instantiate an XML processor application, load an XML document, walk the document tree, and get data from the tree. Believe it or not, the difficult part is over! These are the basics upon which all other XML document processing is built.

Now we'll open the page to see how it looks. The results are shown in Figure 5-1.

NOTE

If you are creating your own HTML page to match this sample, you will need to copy the XML document named Chap05\Lst5_3.xml from the companion CD for the page to work. The XML document should be placed in the same folder that contains your HTML page.

Figure 5-1. *A sample HTML page that has processed an XML document.*

Displaying the Data

If your page looks just like the one shown in Figure 5-1, the page is working perfectly! This page is really not much to look at because we haven't done anything with the data we're getting from the XML document. Examine the code closely and you'll see that nothing on the page tells the data how it should look or whether it should even appear on the page.

Making the data appear on the page takes a bit more work, so before doing that, let's make sure the code is working properly. To quickly determine whether we are getting the data we expect from the XML document, we can display an alert box that contains the value returned from an XML variable. First we'll change the *start* method so that it contains the following code:

```
function start()
  {
  var rootElem = xmlDoc.documentElement;
  var toVar = rootElem.childNodes.item(0).text;
  alert(toVar);
  }
```

You should see an alert box like the one shown here:

The alert box shows that the variable contains the correct value. Now we need to get the data on the page. Doing so requires an additional HTML element that contains the content and additional script code to place the content on the HTML page. First let's add the HTML element for the content. In the body of the HTML document, we'll add the following element:

```
<DIV ID="to" STYLE="font-weight:bold;font-size:16">
  To:
  <SPAN ID="todata" STYLE="font-weight:normal"></SPAN>
</DIV>
```

This Div element provides formatting and layout for the data. The element contains a Span element that will actually contain the data obtained from the XML document. You will notice that the Div element also contains some formatting information that makes the data look presentable. Notice as well that the Span element has an ID of *todata* so that we can refer to it in our script code.

We now need to add the script code that will insert the XML data into the Span element. To do that, we'll go back to the *start* function and replace the call to the *alert* method with the following:

```
todata.innerText = toVar;
```

This tells the document to replace the text in the object *todata* (which happens to be empty) with the value of the variable *toVar*. You'll recall that we set the value of *toVar* in the line above this one so that it contains data from our XML document. The code, which you can find in the Chap05\Lst5_7.htm file on the companion CD, should now look like that shown in Code Listing 5-7.

```
<!DOCTYPE HTML PUBLIC "-//W3C//DTD HTML 3.2 Final//EN">
<HTML>

  <HEAD>
    <SCRIPT LANGUAGE="JavaScript" FOR=window EVENT=onload>
      loadDoc()
    </SCRIPT>

    <SCRIPT LANGUAGE="JavaScript">
      var xmlDoc = new ActiveXObject("microsoft.xmldom");
      xmlDoc.load("Lst5_3.xml");

      function loadDoc()
        {
        if (xmlDoc.readyState == "4")
          start()
        else
          window.setTimeout("loadDoc()", 4000);
        }

      function start()
        {
        var rootElem = xmlDoc.documentElement;
        var toVar = rootElem.childNodes.item(0).text;
        todata.innerText = toVar;
        }
    </SCRIPT>

    <TITLE>Code Listing 5-7</TITLE>
  </HEAD>

  <BODY>
    <DIV ID="to" STYLE="font-weight:bold;font-size:16">
      To:
      <SPAN ID="todata" STYLE="font-weight:normal"></SPAN>
    </DIV>
  </BODY>

</HTML>
```

Code Listing 5-7.

Now when the page is opened, the data is displayed as HTML data, as shown in Figure 5-2.

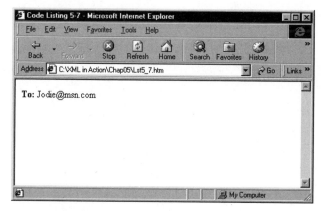

Figure 5-2. *XML data displayed as HTML data.*

This document is almost done; but before we complete it, we should make one small optimization that will reduce the complexity of the code and reduce the size of the script. In the current script, we are assigning the XML value to a variable and then replacing the text in the Span element with the value of the variable. Instead, we can take a shortcut and put the XML data into the Span element in one step. So the code

```
var toVar = rootElem.childNodes.item(0).text;
todata.innerText = toVar;
```

becomes

```
todata.innerText = rootElem.childNodes.item(0).text;
```

This is a small change, but optimizations like this one can really make a difference in a large document.

Now let's add the HTML code and scripting needed to display the rest of the elements in the XML document. To do that, we can simply reproduce the steps discussed above for every element that we want to display.

NOTE

Before looking at the code below or on the companion CD, see if you can do this on your own. Remember, you need an HTML element that will contain the data and some script code to retrieve the data and make it appear on the HTML page.

Code Listing 5-8 (on the companion CD in Chap05\Lst5_8.htm) contains the finished page with all the necessary HTML and script code.

```
<!DOCTYPE HTML PUBLIC "-//W3C//DTD HTML 3.2 Final//EN">
<HTML>

  <HEAD>
    <SCRIPT LANGUAGE="JavaScript" FOR=window EVENT=onload>
      loadDoc()
    </SCRIPT>

    <SCRIPT LANGUAGE="JavaScript">
      var xmlDoc = new ActiveXObject("microsoft.xmldom");
      xmlDoc.load("Lst5_3.xml");

      function loadDoc()
        {
        if (xmlDoc.readyState == "4")
          start()
        else
          window.setTimeout("loadDoc()", 4000);
        }

      function start()
        {
        var rootElem = xmlDoc.documentElement;
        todata.innerText = rootElem.childNodes.item(0).text;
        fromdata.innerText = rootElem.childNodes.item(1).text;
        ccdata.innerText = rootElem.childNodes.item(2).text;
        subjectdata.innerText = rootElem.childNodes.item(3).text;
        bodydata.innerText = rootElem.childNodes.item(4).text;
        }
    </SCRIPT>

    <TITLE>Code Listing 5-8</TITLE>
  </HEAD>

  <BODY>
    <DIV ID="to" STYLE="font-weight:bold;font-size:16">
      To:
      <SPAN ID="todata" STYLE="font-weight:normal"></SPAN>
    </DIV>
    <BR>

    <DIV ID="from" STYLE="font-weight:bold;font-size:16">
      From:
      <SPAN ID="fromdata" STYLE="font-weight:normal"></SPAN>
    </DIV>
    <BR>
```

Code Listing 5-8.

```
   <DIV ID="cc" STYLE="font-weight:bold;font-size:16">
     Cc:
     <SPAN ID="ccdata" STYLE="font-weight:normal"></SPAN>
   </DIV>
   <BR>

   <DIV ID="subject" STYLE="font-weight:bold;font-size:16">
     Subject:
     <SPAN ID="subjectdata" STYLE="font-weight:normal"></SPAN>
   </DIV>
   <BR>

   <HR>
   <SPAN ID="bodydata" STYLE="font-weight:normal"></SPAN>
 </BODY>

</HTML>
```

The finished document is displayed as shown in Figure 5-3.

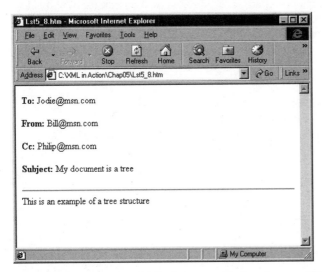

Figure 5-3. *A complete XML document displayed as an HTML page.*

Measuring the Costs and Benefits

Before we go any further, let's address the potential hesitation some of you might experience about XML after seeing the amount of work involved in getting XML data on an HTML page. You might think that it would have been much easier to create the document by hand in HTML. You wouldn't have needed all that script code or the separate XML document, and creating a single HTML document would have been much simpler.

While it is obvious that a lot of work is involved for you to create the simple document used in the example, some enormous benefits can be realized by using XML, including the following:

◆ **Data-independent Web pages** The HTML document created in this chapter can be used as a template for any XML content that fits that predefined model. Although creating the HTML page took some work, the document can be used over and over with different content. If we wanted to create many different versions of the same document, we could simply create new XML files and plug them in to the HTML template instead of creating many separate HTML files from scratch.

◆ **Easy data creation** The other side of the first point is that modifying or replacing the content in any way does not imply that you work with HTML. For example, to translate the content into a different language, only the XML file would need to be changed. While that might not seem useful with small documents, it would be beneficial with large or complex documents. The next point expands on this idea.

◆ **Increased returns on increased complexity** It's a toss-up whether using XML makes sense for developing simple documents. But when a document needs to be complex, using XML makes the most sense. Imagine a highly complex Web page or Web site that requires that data be changed or updated on a regular basis. Instead of having to constantly edit or update your HTML files, you can use XML to provide the data after creating an HTML document only once. In addition, the Web-site administrator would never need to go in and edit the HTML code. The same benefits apply to other complex systems that use XML as a data source, even if they do not include HTML documents.

◆ **Data in a standardized format** Because the data is separate from the display formatting, the XML format can be used as an interchange mechanism between incompatible data sources. In this scenario, XML does not care how the data is being used. If each system can read and write XML, the data can be interchanged between them.

These are just a few of the ways XML can make data more powerful and flexible. While it's true that additional time is needed up front to get XML working, the benefits can far outweigh the costs in most applications. It should also be noted that the purpose of many of the examples in this chapter is to demonstrate how XML documents are structured and how the processor works to extract data from a document. As you will see in later chapters, there are other ways to get XML data into a Web page or application, such as the XML Data Source Object (covered in Chapter 6), XSL (Extensible Stylesheet Language, Chapter 8), and XSL Patterns (Chapter 9). In addition, Microsoft Internet Explorer 5 adds support for XML Data Islands (Chapter 11), which allows you to include XML code directly in an HTML page without needing a separate XML document. These methods can add more benefits to the use of XML for structuring and storing data.

Beyond the Basics—
More Scripting Techniques

The simple email sample file in this chapter demonstrates how you can access the XML object model and work with XML data. A closer look at the document and its scripts reveals that simplicity comes with a cost. In an effort to keep the scripts on the easy side, some techniques have been incorporated that would prove to be less than ideal in many situations. Consider the following:

◆ The script code that accesses the XML document tree and extracts the data assumes that we know not only how many elements exist but what each element's type is, since we address each one by index. While this type of code might work in some applications, it would be totally inadequate in others.

◆ The script code addresses each element separately. While this might work fine for small documents, it would become tedious and potentially error-prone in large or complex documents.

◆ The HTML document is not totally data independent. The HTML tags used for layout and formatting contain text (such as To: and From:). If this document needed to be translated into other languages, it would require that both the XML document and the HTML document be edited.

We will now look at some scripting techniques that will help us avoid some of the pitfalls just described.

Walking the XML Document Tree

While in the previous example the author was required to know the number and type of elements in the XML document, this situation can be easily avoided by using some other properties and methods in the XML object model. First let's take Code Listing 5-8 and replace the *start* function with the following code:

```
function start()
  {
  var newHTML = "";
  rootElem = xmlDoc.documentElement;
  for (el=0; el<rootElem.childNodes.length; el++)
    {
    alert(rootElem.childNodes.item(el).text);
    }
  }
```

Loading the HTML file now should produce a series of five dialog boxes that contain the contents of the elements in the XML document, such as the dialog box shown on the next page.

One of the changes made in the preceding code uses the object model (the property *rootElem.childNodes.length*) to ask the XML document how many child elements the root element contains. The script then enters a loop and walks through all the children of the root element, requesting the text contained in each element until the last one is reached. Now we don't need to know how many elements or child elements exist or their types. Since our document structure is simple, we need to use only one loop to access all the content; you could do this looping as often as necessary to access all the elements and child elements in a more complex document. You can even find out if an element has children by using the *childNodes* property of an element. This property returns a value if children exist and returns *null* if they do not. (This and the many other parts of the XML object model are fully described in Appendix A.)

In this example, the value for each element is displayed in an alert box since we have no way of knowing which HTML tag should receive what data. Remember, we no longer know that a one-to-one relationship exists between XML document elements and HTML elements. We can work around this by having the script create the HTML elements on the fly. We'll change the body of the HTML document to the following:

```
<BODY>
  <DIV ID="content">
  </DIV>
</BODY>
```

Quite a reduction! This works because we no longer require hard-coded elements to contain the content. We now need to add the script code that will create the HTML elements on the fly as the data is read from the XML document, by changing the *start* function to the following:

```
function start()
  {
  var newHTML = "";
  rootElem = xmlDoc.documentElement;

  for (el=0; el<rootElem.childNodes.length; el++)
    {
    if (el != rootElem.childNodes.length-1)
      {
      newHTML = newHTML +
        "<SPAN STYLE='font-weight:bold;font-size:16'>" +
        rootElem.childNodes.item(el).nodeName +
        ": </SPAN><SPAN STYLE='font-weight:normal'>" +
        rootElem.childNodes.item(el).text + "</SPAN><P>";
      }
```

```
    else
      {
      newHTML = newHTML +
        "<HR><SPAN STYLE='font-weight:normal'>" +
        rootElem.childNodes.item(el).text + "</SPAN><P>";
      }
    }

  content.innerHTML = newHTML;
  }
```

This script code accomplishes several things. Each time the script encounters a new XML element, it creates a new HTML element that includes all the formatting information for that element. It then adds that element to the variable *newHTML*. The script also uses an *if* statement to test for the last element in the document. When the last element is reached, different formatting is applied. Finally, the script assigns the contents of the *newHTML* variable to the Div element named *content*. Since the variable *newHTML* contains valid HTML code, the page is displayed as we intended. Code Listing 5-9 (also in Chap05\Lst5_9.htm on the companion CD) shows the completed page with all of our changes.

```
<!DOCTYPE HTML PUBLIC "-//W3C//DTD HTML 3.2 Final//EN">
<HTML>

  <HEAD>
    <SCRIPT LANGUAGE="JavaScript" FOR=window EVENT=onload>
      loadDoc()
    </SCRIPT>

    <SCRIPT LANGUAGE="JavaScript">
      var xmlDoc = new ActiveXObject("microsoft.xmldom");
      xmlDoc.load("Lst5_3.xml");

      function loadDoc()
        {
        if (xmlDoc.readyState == "4")
          start()
        else
          window.setTimeout("loadDoc()", 4000);
        }

      function start()
        {
        var newHTML = "";
        rootElem = xmlDoc.documentElement;
```

Code Listing 5-9.   *(continued)*

```
        for (el=0; el<rootElem.childNodes.length; el++)
          {
          if (el != rootElem.childNodes.length-1)
            {
            newHTML = newHTML +
              "<SPAN STYLE='font-weight:bold;font-size:16'>" +
              rootElem.childNodes.item(el).nodeName +
              ": </SPAN><SPAN STYLE='font-weight:normal'>" +
              rootElem.childNodes.item(el).text + "</SPAN><P>";
            }

          else
            {
            newHTML = newHTML +
              "<HR><SPAN STYLE='font-weight:normal'>" +
              rootElem.childNodes.item(el).text + "</SPAN><P>";
            }
          }
        content.innerHTML = newHTML;
        }
    </SCRIPT>

    <TITLE>Code Listing 5-9</TITLE>
  </HEAD>

<BODY>
  <DIV ID="content">
  </DIV>
</BODY>

</HTML>
```

When you open this page, it should look like the one shown in Figure 5-4.

In Figure 5-4, you will notice that the document looks much like the document in Figure 5-3. The difference between the two is that here the HTML page is completely data independent. All the data is retrieved from the XML document, so that we can accomplish the same results with more flexible and compact code.

To further demonstrate this, let's add a Bcc element to the XML document Lst5_3.xml, as shown here.

```
<?xml version="1.0"?>
<EMAIL>
  <TO>Jodie@msn.com</TO>
  <FROM>Bill@msn.com</FROM>
  <CC>Philip@msn.com</CC>
```

```
<BCC>Naomi@microsoft.com</BCC>
<SUBJECT>My document is a tree</SUBJECT>
<BODY>This is an example of a tree structure</BODY>
</EMAIL>
```

Now when our sample HTML page is opened, the Bcc element is included in the document, even though no changes were made to the HTML code. The result is shown in Figure 5-5.

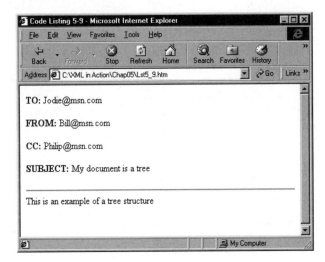

Figure 5-4. *Displaying the XML document content.*

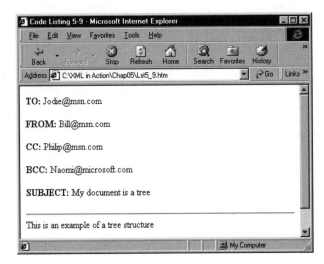

Figure 5-5. *Adding an element to the XML document does not require a change in the HTML code.*

This page is now completely data driven. Even so, the point of putting the data into HTML is to get the exact layout and formatting that we want for the data. As you might suspect, we still need to know quite a bit about what kind of data the XML document contains or we would not know how to apply the formatting. For example, the code tests for the last element in the XML document because we know that the last element is the body and should be formatted differently than other elements.

Note that while using these techniques can make an HTML document much more flexible and powerful, the document is still only a template for a specific class of XML document or documents. This makes HTML and XML perfect complements to one another.

Error Handling

Scripting is terrific when everything works, but it can be annoying, especially to the user, when problems occur. The XML object model provides several ways for authors to handle errors when they occur as a result of the XML document. One of these is the document object's *parseError* property, which provides information about problems that occur in an XML document so that authors can deal with them and users might not have to.

The *parseError* property provides a code for every error that occurs. An author can use these codes to:

◆ Help debug XML documents or scripts

◆ Inform the user of problems and provide suggestions for resolution

◆ Trap for certain kinds of errors and fix them behind the scenes

The sample code below shows how the *parseError* property might be used to inform a user of a problem.

```
var xmlDoc = new ActiveXObject("microsoft.xmldom");
xmlDoc.load("Lst5_3.xml");

if (xmlDoc.parseError.reason == "")
  alert("Document loaded successfully");

else
  alert("The following error occurred: " +
    xmlDoc.parseError.errorCode)
```

This technique can be used both for debugging and for shielding users from errors. The document object and its many properties are covered in more detail in Appendix A.

Chapter 6
XML As Data

T he past few chapters focused on the building blocks of XML—how XML files are built, the rules that govern their structure, and how properties and methods of the XML object model are accessed and manipulated through script. This chapter shifts our attention toward content, or data. After all, *data* is what XML is all about. Here our focus will be on using XML as a data source in much the same way that a Microsoft Access or Microsoft SQL database might be used. This chapter covers XML data typing and building data structures in XML. It also gives us the chance to work with the XML Data Source Object (DSO) and to examine how to use the DSO to read and write data.

Data Typing in XML

If you are familiar with databases or programming, you know that generally a piece of data possesses certain characteristics or conforms to a specific format that brands it a *string*, a *number*, a *date*, a *currency*, or another *data type*. So far, the XML data we've worked with in previous chapters has been of the single type *string*, or text data. However, XML data types allow authors to specify element data as objects that can be interpreted as different types.

It is important to distinguish the element type from its data type. Chapter 4 looked at how to define element types in a Document Type Definition (DTD). You will remember that an element can contain data that is either parsed character data (*#PCDATA*) or character data (*CDATA*). The DTD can further define the element by its context or position in the structure. This method of element typing indicates the semantics of the element (such as Age representing how old a person is) but does not describe the type of data the element contains (such as Age containing a number). Parsed character data and character data are both string data types. You'll recall from Chapter 4 that additional types can be specified for XML attributes. These types are restated in the table below:

Attribute Type	Usage
CDATA	Only character data can be used in the attribute.
ENTITY	Attribute value must refer to an external binary entity declared in the DTD.
ENTITIES	Same as ENTITY, but allows multiple values separated by white space.
ID	Attribute value must be a unique identifier. If a document contains ID attributes with the same value, the processor should generate an error.
IDREF	Value must be a reference to an ID declared elsewhere in the document. If the attribute does not match the referenced ID value, the processor should generate an error.

Attribute Type	Usage
IDREFS	Same as *IDREF*, but allows multiple values separated by white space.
NMTOKEN	Attribute value is any mixture of name token characters, which must be letters, numbers, periods, dashes, colons, or underscores.
NMTOKENS	Same as *NMTOKEN*, but allows multiple values separated by white space.
NOTATION	Attribute value must refer to a notation declared elsewhere in the DTD. Declaration can also be a list of notations. The value must be one of the notations in the list. Each notation must have its own declaration in the DTD.
Enumerated	Attribute value must match one of the included values. For example: *<!ATTLIST MyAttribute (content1|content2)>*.

The attribute types in the above table are known as *primitive data types*. The Microsoft XML processor (Msxml) also supports *rich data types,* which represent the kinds of data types found in traditional programming languages and database systems. Data typing, as discussed in this chapter, focuses on rich data types and indicates the parser class that is used to interpret the data as something other than just a string.

NOTE

The attribute types in the above table are identified in section 3.3.1 of the XML 1.0 specification (included on the companion CD).

Strong Typing vs. Weak Typing

Data typing falls into two basic contexts: *strong typing* and *weak typing*. In strong typing, an element must always contain a single type of data. The content in the element must conform to a strict set of rules regarding its type. For example, you might have an element named *Part* that must always contain an *integer*. It could not contain a *string*, a *date*, or even a *decimal*. Data is usually strongly typed in database APIs such as ODBC (Open Database Connectivity) or JDBC (Java Database Connectivity).

Weak typing, as you might guess, allows multiple types of data to exist in a single element. So if our Part element was specified to have a weak type, it might contain an *integer*, a *string*, a *name*, a *date*, or some combination of types.

Specifying Data Types

You specify data types in an XML document using the *dt:dt* attribute in an element. The syntax is *dt:dt="datatype"*, where *datatype* represents one of the supported data types. In the following example, the Id element is of type *number*.

```
<?xml version="1.0"?>
<PRODUCT xmlns:dt="urn:schemas-microsoft-com:datatypes">
  <PART>
    <ID dt:dt="number">4535645.234</ID>
    <NAME>widget</NAME>
  </PART>
</PRODUCT>
```

NOTE

The unusual syntax of the *dt:dt* attribute is because of the fact that data types are defined by a particular *namespace*. You might also have noticed the *namespace declaration* in the second line of the above code, which declares the *datatypes* namespace. Namespaces use special prefixes to uniquely identify elements and attributes. See the section "XML Namespaces" later in this chapter.

The table below identifies some of the more common data types. For a complete list of supported data types, see the section "Supported Data Types" in Appendix B of this book.

Data Type	Description	Example
boolean	1 or 0	*1; 0*
char	String (one character only)	*a*
float	A signed or unsigned whole number or fraction. No effective limit on number of digits. Can contain an exponent.	*34234.376; 477*
int	An unsigned whole number, no exponent.	*345*
number	A signed or unsigned whole number or fraction. No effective limit on number of digits. Can contain an exponent.	*−23; 567556; 443.34; 67E12*
string	*#PCDATA*	*This is a string.*
uri	Universal Resource Identifier	*http://mspress.microsoft.com*

Whenever a node is assigned a type, the data in that node will conform to the specified type, despite the data's original format. Consider this Number element, for example:

```
<NUMBER dt:dt="int">-255</NUMBER>
```

This element will be processed as its typed value: the integer 255. It will not be processed as −255. This type conversion is important to understand when working with data types, because unexpected results can occur if you are not careful.

Working with Data Types in Script

The XML object model allows scripts access to data types. As is true of other objects in the object model, the *data type* object is exposed and available to the script code. The element node properties *dataType* and *nodeTypedValue* allow the content author to access the data types of any node in the content tree. Let's look at how these properties work in script code, using the XML document shown in Code Listing 6-1.

> **NOTE**
>
> Throughout the rest of this chapter we will work with an XML document containing information for a wildflower plant catalog. A copy of the catalog document is included on the companion CD in the Chap06\Lst6_1.xml file. A portion of the file is shown in Code Listing 6-1.

```
<CATALOG xmlns:dt="urn:schemas-microsoft-com:datatypes">
  <PLANT>
    <COMMON>Bloodroot</COMMON>
    <BOTANICAL>Sanguinaria canadensis</BOTANICAL>
    <ZONE>4</ZONE>
    <LIGHT>Mostly Shady</LIGHT>
    <PRICE dt:dt="fixed.14.4">2.44</PRICE>
    <AVAILABILITY dt:dt="dateTime">1999-03-15</AVAILABILITY>
  </PLANT>

  <PLANT>
    <COMMON>Columbine</COMMON>
    <BOTANICAL>Aquilegia canadensis</BOTANICAL>
    <ZONE>3</ZONE>
    <LIGHT>Mostly Shady</LIGHT>
    <PRICE dt:dt="fixed.14.4">9.37</PRICE>
    <AVAILABILITY dt:dt="dateTime">1999-03-06</AVAILABILITY>
  </PLANT>

  <PLANT>
    <COMMON>Marsh Marigold</COMMON>
    <BOTANICAL>Caltha palustris</BOTANICAL>
    <ZONE>4</ZONE>
    <LIGHT>Mostly Sunny</LIGHT>
    <PRICE dt:dt="fixed.14.4">6.81</PRICE>
    <AVAILABILITY dt:dt="dateTime">1999-05-17</AVAILABILITY>
  </PLANT>
</CATALOG>
```

Code Listing 6-1.

Next we'll create an HTML page to work with the data in our XML document. Code Listing 6-2 (Chap06\Lst6_2.htm on the companion CD) uses the XML object model to walk through elements in the document tree and pull out the data we want.

NOTE

For more detail on the XML object model, see Appendix A, "The XML Object Model."

THE *dataType* PROPERTY

In Code Listing 6-2, the *dataType* property is used to get the data type of the price node.

```
<!DOCTYPE HTML PUBLIC "-//W3C//DTD HTML 3.2 Final//EN">
<HTML>

  <HEAD>
    <SCRIPT LANGUAGE="JavaScript" FOR=window EVENT=onload>
      loadDoc();
    </SCRIPT>

    <SCRIPT LANGUAGE="JavaScript">
      var xmlDoc = new ActiveXObject("microsoft.xmldom");
      xmlDoc.load("Lst6_1.xml");

      function loadDoc()
        {
        if (xmlDoc.readyState == "4")
          start();
        else
          window.setTimeout("loadDoc()", 4000);
        }

      function start()
        {
        var rootElem = xmlDoc.documentElement;
        var plantNode = rootElem.childNodes.item(0);
        var plantLength = plantNode.childNodes.length;
        for (cl=0; cl<plantLength; cl++)
          {
          currNode = plantNode.childNodes.item(cl);
          switch (currNode.nodeName)
            {
            case "PRICE":
              alert("The data type of this node is " +
```

Code Listing 6-2.

```
                currNode.dataType + ".");
            break;
        }
      }
    }
  }
  </SCRIPT>

  <TITLE>Code Listing 6-2</TITLE>
</HEAD>

<BODY>
</BODY>

</HTML>
```

When you run the code in Code Listing 6-2, the *start* function displays the value *fixed.14.4* because *fixed.14.4* is the data type specified in the XML document.

THE *nodeTypedValue* PROPERTY

This property is the typed value of a node, which may differ from the value as it is formatted in the document. Code Listing 6-3 (Chap06\Lst6_3.htm on the companion CD) uses the *nodeTypedValue* property to display the typed value.

```
<!DOCTYPE HTML PUBLIC "-//W3C//DTD HTML 3.2 Final//EN">
<HTML>

<HEAD>
  <SCRIPT LANGUAGE="JavaScript" FOR=window EVENT=onload>
    loadDoc();
  </SCRIPT>

  <SCRIPT LANGUAGE="JavaScript">
    var xmlDoc = new ActiveXObject("microsoft.xmldom");
    xmlDoc.load("Lst6_1.xml");

    function loadDoc()
      {
      if (xmlDoc.readyState == "4")
        start();
      else window.setTimeout("loadDoc()", 4000);
      }
```

Code Listing 6-3.

(continued)

```
    function start()
      {
      var rootElem = xmlDoc.documentElement;
      var plantNode = rootElem.childNodes.item(0);
      var plantLength = plantNode.childNodes.length;
      for (cl=0;cl<plantLength;cl++)
        {
        currNode = plantNode.childNodes.item(cl);
        switch (currNode.nodeName)
          {
          case "AVAILABILITY":
            alert("The typed value of this node is " +
              currNode.nodeTypedValue + ".");
            break;
          }
        }
      }
    </SCRIPT>

    <TITLE>Code Listing 6-3</TITLE>
  </HEAD>

  <BODY>
  </BODY>

</HTML>
```

This code displays the value *Mon Mar 15 00:00:00 PST 1999* rather than *1999-03-15* because the type specified is *dateTime*. Even though the data can appear as a date (without a time) when the XML document is displayed, the *nodeTypedValue* property for the node is its typed value, not just a date.

CHANGING THE DATA TYPE

You can change the data type of an element or attribute through a process called data type *coercion,* or *casting.* However, you can convert only from a primitive data type to a rich data type. XML does not support conversions between different rich data types. To change the data type of an element or attribute, you set its *dataType* property to a different rich data type. You can also use the *dataType* property to retrieve the current rich data type of an element or attribute. Note that the *dataType* property can be used to retrieve a rich data type only. If an element or attribute is a primitive data type, its *dataType* property will be the null value. Code Listing 6-4 (Chap06\Lst6_4.htm on the companion CD) shows an example of how this works.

```
<!DOCTYPE HTML PUBLIC "-//W3C//DTD HTML 3.2 Final//EN">
<HTML>

  <HEAD>
    <SCRIPT LANGUAGE="JavaScript" FOR=window EVENT=onload>
      loadDoc();
    </SCRIPT>

    <SCRIPT LANGUAGE="JavaScript">
      var xmlDoc = new ActiveXObject("microsoft.xmldom");
      xmlDoc.load("Lst6_1.xml");

      function loadDoc()
        {
        if (xmlDoc.readyState == "4")
          start();
        else
          window.setTimeout("loadDoc()", 4000);
        }

      function start()
        {
        var rootElem = xmlDoc.documentElement;
        var plantNode = rootElem.childNodes.item(0);
        var plantLength = plantNode.childNodes.length;
        for (cl=0; cl<plantLength; cl++)
          {
          currNode = plantNode.childNodes.item(cl);
          switch (currNode.nodeName)
            {
            case "ZONE":
              alert("The data type of this node is " +
                currNode.dataType + ".");
              currNode.dataType = "number";
              alert("The new data type of this node is " +
                currNode.dataType + ".");
              break;
            }
          }
        }
    </SCRIPT>

    <TITLE>Code Listing 6-4</TITLE>
  </HEAD>

  <BODY>
  </BODY>

</HTML>
```

Code Listing 6-4.

This example changes the data type of the Zone element from its default primitive data type (*#PCDATA*) to a number. The processor will now treat the value of this element as a numeric value instead of just text.

The table below lists the rich data type coercions supported by Msxml. Note that these coercions might not work with other XML processors.

Rich Data Type	Description
bbin.base64	MIME-style Base64 encoded binary block.
bin.hex	Hexadecimal digits representing octets.
boolean	0 (false) or 1 (true).
char	One-character string.
date	Date, in a subset of the ISO 8601 format, without the time data. Example: 1998-11-02.
dateTime	Date, in a subset of the ISO 8601 format, with optional time but no zone. Fractional seconds can be as precise as nanoseconds. Example: 1988-07-09T18:39:09.
dateTime.tz	Date, in a subset of the ISO 8601 format, with optional time and optional zone. Fractional seconds can be as precise as nanoseconds. Example: 1988-07-09T18:39:09-08:00.
fixed.14.4	Same as *number*, but supports no more than 14 digits to the left of the decimal point and no more than 4 to the right.
float	Real number with essentially no limit on the number of digits. Optionally contains a leading sign, fractional digits, and/or an exponent. Values from 1.7976931348623157E+308 to 2.2250738585072014E-308.
int	Number with optional sign, no fractions, and no exponent.
number	Number with essentially no limit on the number of digits. Optionally contains a leading sign, fractional digits, and/or an exponent.
time	Time, in a subset of the ISO 8601 format, with no date and no time zone. Example: 06:18:35.
time.tz	Time, in a subset of the ISO 8601 format, with no date but optional time zone. Example: 03:1525-04:00.
i1	Integer represented in 1 byte. A number with optional sign, no fractions, and no exponent. Examples: 1, 34, -165.
i2	Integer represented in 2 bytes. A number with optional sign, no fractions, and no exponent. Examples: 1, 244, -56433.
i4	Integer represented in 4 bytes. A number with optional sign, no fractions, and no exponent. Examples: 1, 556, -34234, 156645, -2005000700.

Rich Data Type	Description
i8	Integer represented in 8 bytes. A number with optional sign, no fractions, and no exponent. Examples: 1, 646, −65333, 2666345433454, −2007000800090090.
r4	Real number with essentially no limit on the number of digits. Optionally contains a leading sign, fractional digits, and/or an exponent. Values from 3.40282347E+38F to 1.17549435E−38F.
r8	Same as *float.*
ui1	Unsigned 1-byte integer. An unsigned number with no fractions and no exponent. Examples: 1, 255.
ui2	Unsigned 2-byte integer. An unsigned number with no fractions and no exponent. Examples: 1, 255, 65535.
ui4	Unsigned 4-byte integer. An unsigned number with no fractions and no exponent. Examples: 1, 660, 2005000000.
ui8	Unsigned 8-byte integer. An unsigned number with no fractions and no exponent. Example: 1582437474934.
uri	Uniform Resource Identifier (URI). Example: urn:schemas-flowers-com:wildflowers.
uuid	Hexadecimal digits that represent octets. Optionally contains embedded hyphens that are ignored. Example: 333C7BC4-460F-11D0-BC04-0080C7055A83.

XML Namespaces

Namespaces represent a critical concept in terms of understanding XML and working with it as a data source. As you have already seen, the data (content) of an XML document is retrieved by examining individual nodes within the document. This works because the hierarchical structure of XML documents and the rules of validity and well-formedness that govern XML document creation ensure that each node in a document is unique. This, in turn, guarantees that only one reference exists for any one node. The potential for problems arises, however, when you use XML documents in a collaborative environment. For example, two (or more) documents might contain elements with the same names but different semantics. (And the documents might even be structured in the same way.) If it were necessary to use both documents in a single environment, there would be confusion about the overlapping elements. Consider the following XML code:

```
<AUTOMOBILE>
  <ID>232-HDF</ID>
</AUTOMOBILE>

<DOG>
  <ID>Rover</ID>
</DOG>
```

Here the Automobile element and the Dog element each contain an Id element, but the Id element has a different meaning in each case. If these elements came from different sources but were combined into a single document, as shown in the following code, the Id elements would lose their meaning.

```
<FAMILY>
  <MOM>
  ⋮
  </MOM>

  <DAD>
  ⋮
  </DAD>

  <KIDS>
  ⋮
  </KIDS>

  <AUTOMOBILE>
    <ID>232-HDF</ID>
  </AUTOMOBILE>

  <DOG>
    <ID>Rover</ID>
  </DOG>
</FAMILY>
```

This is a very real problem and will become pervasive as XML is used more widely on the Web and in organizations. The solution is XML namespaces, which offer a way to create names that remain unique no matter where the elements are used.

Creating Unique Names via XML Namespaces

The term *namespace* in traditional programming parlance means a set of names in which no duplicates exist. Because the nature of XML allows authors to define their own tag sets, which could likely result in duplicate names among XML documents, the term namespaces in XML has some additional connotations. *Namespaces* in XML is a methodology for creating universally unique names in an XML document by identifying element names with a unique external resource. A *namespace* in XML is therefore a collection of names that is identified by a Uniform Resource Identifier (URI). A namespace can be qualified or unqualified.

QUALIFIED NAMES

A qualified name in XML is composed of two parts: the *namespace name* and the *local part*. The namespace name, which is a URI, selects the namespace. The local part is the local document element or attribute name. Because a URI is always unique, the namespace name combined with the local part creates a universally unique element name. To be able to use a namespace in an XML document, you include a *namespace declaration* in the prolog of the document. A *namespace prefix* can also be included in the declaration. You can then attach the prefix with a colon to the local part to associate the local part with the namespace name.

Let's look at how this works. In the following document, we'll declare two namespaces with prefixes and then use those namespaces in the document.

```
<?xml version="1.0"?>
<?xml:namespace ns="http://inventory/schema/ns" prefix="inv"?>
<?xml:namespace ns="http://wildflowers/schema/ns" prefix="wf"?>
<PRODUCT>
  <PNAME>Test1</PNAME>
  <inv:quantity>1</inv:quantity>
  <wf:price>323</wf:price>
  <DATE>6/1</DATE>
</PRODUCT>
```

In the above code, the prefixes are used to identify elements that are part of the selected namespace. The result is not only unique names, but the preservation of the semantic value of the names as well. The inv:quantity and wf:price elements now contain fully qualified names that will be unique no matter where they are used. The prefix is part of the element name and must always be included to indicate that the element belongs to the namespace.

> **NOTE**
>
> All namespaces in this chapter, with the exception of the *datatypes* namespace covered earlier, are examples only. The *datatypes* namespace really exists and can be used as described in the section "Specifying Data Types."

UNQUALIFIED NAMES

An unqualified name does not have an associated namespace name. Typical XML element names are unqualified since they do not specify a namespace. For example, all element names in the following XML code are unqualified and would not be universally unique.

```
<PRODUCT>
  <NAME>Bloodroot</TITLE>
  <QUANTITY>10</QUANTITY>
</PRODUCT>
```

NAMESPACE SCOPE

The prolog is not the only option for the location of the namespace declaration. Instead, you can include the namespace declaration directly within an element that is part of the namespace. Simply include the declaration the first time the element is used, as shown here.

```
<PRODUCT>
  <PNAME>Test1</PNAME>
  <inv:quantity>1</inv:quantity>
  <wf:price
    xmlns:wf="urn:schemas-wildflowers-com:xml-prices">
    323
  </wf:price>
  <DATE>6/1</DATE>
</PRODUCT>
```

The namespace is then available within the context of that element. In other words, that element and all its children can use the namespace. If the namespace is declared in the document element, that namespace can be used throughout the entire document.

DEFAULT NAMESPACES

You can make a namespace the default by declaring it without assigning a prefix. In this case, the namespace is assumed within the context of the element in which it was declared, as shown in the following code:

```
<CATALOG>
  <INDEX>
    <ITEM>Trees</ITEM>
    <ITEM>Wildflowers</ITEM>
    ⋮
  </INDEX>

  <PRODUCT xmlns:wf="urn:schemas-wildflowers-com">
    <NAME>Bloodroot</NAME>
    <QUANTITY>10</QUANTITY>
    <PRICE>$2.44</PRICE>
  </PRODUCT>
</CATALOG>
```

The Product element in the above code contains a namespace declaration without an associated prefix. As such, the namespace is assumed for the Product element and all of its child elements but not for any elements outside the Product element. The only exception occurs when a child element contains another namespace declaration, which overrides the default namespace declaration. The following code shows an example:

```
<CATALOG>
  <INDEX>
    <ITEM>Trees</ITEM>
    <ITEM>Wildflowers</ITEM>
    ⋮
  </INDEX>

  <PRODUCT xmlns:wf="urn:schemas-wildflowers-com">
    <NAME>Bloodroot</NAME>
    <inv:quantity
      xmlns:wf="urn:schemas-wildflowers-com:xml-inventory">
      10
    </inv:quantity>
    <PRICE>$2.44</PRICE>
  </PRODUCT>
</CATALOG>
```

Here the default namespace is overridden for the inv:quantity element only.

DECLARING THE NAMESPACE AS A URL OR URN

Because all URLs are unique, they can be used to provide uniqueness to namespace names. If a namespace is mapped to a URL, that namespace is unique in the entire context of where the namespace is used.

Another scenario might be where a namespace schema exists that identifies all the names in the namespace and how they should be structured. While it is not the goal of the XML namespace name to provide a mechanism for retrieving that schema, such a method could exist using Uniform Resource Names (URNs).

> **NOTE**
>
> A *schema* is a document definition, similar to a DTD but using a special XML vocabulary named XML-Data. Schemas and XML-Data are covered in Chapter 10. With regard to namespaces, a schema can be used to define all the names contained in the namespace. For example, a schema might define *dt* as the prefix that is mapped to the namespace name and *string* as a name within the namespace. In this case, the element name dt:string could be used in the XML document.

A URN can provide a mechanism for locating and retrieving a schema file that defines a particular namespace. While similar functionality could be provided by an ordinary URL, a URN is more robust and easier to manage for this purpose because a URN can refer to more than one URL.

> **NOTE**
>
> For more information about URNs, visit *http://www.ncsa.uiuc.edu/InformationServers/ Horizon/URN/urn.html.*

The following code shows how a URN might be used in the context of an XML namespace:

```
<CATALOG>
  <INDEX>
    <ITEM>Trees</ITEM>
    <ITEM>Wildflowers</ITEM>
    ⋮
  </INDEX>

  <wf:product xmlns:wf="urn:schemas-wildflowers-com">
    <wf:name>Bloodroot</wf:name>
    <QUANTITY>10</QUANTITY>
    <PRICE>$2.44</PRICE>
  </wf:product>
</CATALOG>
```

Here a schema for the namespace might be found at the location identified by the URN, and the processing application would know how to retrieve that schema. The schema would detail the elements of the namespace that could be used in the document.

ATTRIBUTE NAMESPACES

Namespaces can apply to attributes as well as elements, and to make it easy, the naming mechanism is the same for both, as shown in the following example.

```
<wf:product TYPE="plant" class:kingdom="plantae"
  xmlns:wf="urn:wildflowers:schemas:product"
  xmlns:class="urn:bio:botany:classification">
  <PNAME>Test1</PNAME>
  <QUANTITY>1</QUANTITY>
  <PRICE>323</PRICE>
  <DATE>6/1</DATE>
</wf:product>
```

In this example, both the wf:product element and the *class:kingdom* attribute have associated namespace declarations. The attribute namespace is used in a similar fashion to the element namespace.

Namespaces will become increasingly important as new vocabularies and XML-based technologies develop. There are already technologies that rely on namespaces, such as XML-Data, XML data types, and SMIL (Synchronized Multimedia Integration Language). Chapter 10 includes practical examples of how XML namespaces are used by XML-Data.

Using the XML Data Source Object

So far in this chapter, we have used the XML document as a source of data, but we did it by loading the document into the processor, walking the document tree, and working with the data one node at a time. This technique has demonstrated how you can work with XML in much the same way as you would work with records in a database. However, there is another way to work with XML data. Using the XML DSO, you can *bind* data to controls on an HTML page. This lets you work with the data one node at a time, if you want, but you can also work with the data in "chunks," or multiple nodes at a time, without having to walk the document tree.

NOTE

The XML DSO is supported by Microsoft Internet Explorer versions 4 and later.

Working with One Record at a Time

Using the XML DSO and the object model, you can continue to walk an XML document tree in much the same way as you have been doing. The significant difference, though, is that the data is bound to specific controls on the page and the controls are automatically populated with data from the DSO. Let's look at how this works in Code Listing 6-5 (Chap06\Lst6_5.htm on the companion CD).

Code Listing 6-5 uses a modified version of Lst6_1.xml, named Lst6_1a.xml, that does not include any data types from the *datatypes* namespace. As of this writing (using the beta version of Msxml), the DSO does not support namespaces. It is expected that namespaces will be supported in the released version.

```
<!DOCTYPE HTML PUBLIC "-//W3C//DTD HTML 3.2 Final//EN">
<HTML>

  <HEAD>
    <SCRIPT FOR="window" EVENT="onload">
      var xmlDso = xmldso.XMLDocument;
      xmlDso.load("Lst6_1a.xml");
    </SCRIPT>

    <TITLE>Code Listing 6_5</TITLE>
  </HEAD>

  <BODY>
    <OBJECT WIDTH="0" HEIGHT="0"
      CLASSID="clsid:550dda30-0541-11d2-9ca9-0060b0ec3d39"
      ID="xmldso">
    </OBJECT>

    <DIV ID="catalog">
      <SPAN STYLE="font-weight:bold">Common Name: </SPAN>
      <SPAN ID="common" DATASRC=#xmldso
        DATAFLD="COMMON" STYLE="color:blue">
      </SPAN>
      <BR>

      <SPAN STYLE="font-weight:bold">Botanical Name: </SPAN>
      <SPAN ID="botan" DATASRC=#xmldso
        DATAFLD="BOTANICAL" STYLE="color:blue">
      </SPAN>
      <BR>

      <SPAN STYLE="font-weight:bold">Zone: </SPAN>
      <SPAN ID="zone" DATASRC=#xmldso
        DATAFLD="ZONE" STYLE="color:blue">
      </SPAN>
      <BR>
```

Code Listing 6-5.   *(continued)*

```
      <SPAN STYLE="font-weight:bold">Light Needs: </SPAN>
      <SPAN ID="light" DATASRC=#xmldso
        DATAFLD="LIGHT" STYLE="color:blue">
      </SPAN>
      <BR>

      <SPAN STYLE="font-weight:bold">Price: </SPAN>
      <SPAN ID="price" DATASRC=#xmldso
        DATAFLD="PRICE" STYLE="color:blue">
      </SPAN>
      <BR>
    </DIV>

    <P>
      <INPUT TYPE=button VALUE="Previous Plant"
        ONCLICK="xmldso.recordset.moveprevious()">
      <INPUT TYPE=button VALUE="Next Plant"
        ONCLICK="xmldso.recordset.movenext()">

  </BODY>
</HTML>
```

Code Listing 6-5 loads the document Lst6_1a.xml into the XML DSO and binds various data elements to Span elements in the HTML page. Notice that a Span element appears for every element we want to display that corresponds to an element in the XML document. For example, the code below binds the Price element from the DSO to the Span element named *price* in the HTML page:

```
<SPAN ID="price" DATASRC=#xmldso
  DATAFLD="PRICE" STYLE="color:blue">
</SPAN>
```

The *DATASRC* attribute specifies the DSO to use (a pound sign followed by the name of the data source object), and the *DATAFLD* attribute specifies the element that is supplying the data. By this method, data is bound to some control or HTML element. The resulting display is as shown in Figure 6-1.

SINGLE-VALUE ELEMENTS

In our example, only one *recordset,* or set of element data, is in use at any given time. This is due to the characteristics of the HTML element to which the data is bound. Most elements, like Span elements, are *single-value* elements; that is, only one piece of data can be bound to the element at any given time. Because only one piece of data can be used at a time, the data that is in use is considered the *current* recordset. You might also notice from Code Listing 6-5 that a separate Span element is needed for each value in the recordset.

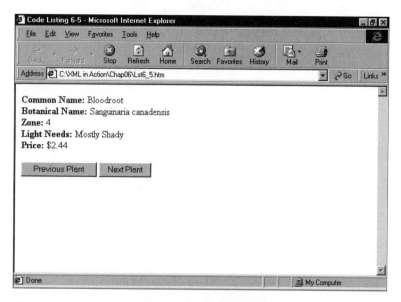

Figure 6-1. *Using the XML DSO to display XML data on an HTML page.*

MOVING THROUGH THE RECORDSETS

As you can see in Figure 6-1, the HTML page contains two buttons that the user can click to essentially walk the document. The buttons are tied to methods in the DSO that move forward or backward through the data: the *recordset.moveprevious* method moves to the recordset immediately preceding the current recordset in the data source, and the *recordset.movenext* method moves to the recordset immediately following the current recordset. You might notice that using the DSO lets us get a lot of functionality with only a little script code.

Viewing All the Data in a Data Source Document

You can use the XML DSO to view all the data in a source document without walking the document tree and pulling the data out. You use the same data-binding technique just discussed, but this time the data is bound to a multiple-value element rather than several single-value elements. Currently, the only multiple-value element in HTML is the Table element. Code Listing 6-6 (Chap06\Lst6_6.htm on the companion CD) shows how data can be bound to a table to view the entire contents of our XML document.

```
<!DOCTYPE HTML PUBLIC "-//W3C//DTD HTML 3.2 Final//EN">
<HTML>

  <HEAD>
    <SCRIPT FOR="window" EVENT="onload">
      var xmlDso = xmldso.XMLDocument;
```

Code Listing 6-6.

(continued)

```
        xmlDso.load("Lst6_1a.xml");
    </SCRIPT>

    <TITLE>Code Listing 6_6</TITLE>
</HEAD>

<BODY>
    <OBJECT WIDTH="0" HEIGHT="0"
        CLASSID="clsid:550dda30-0541-11d2-9ca9-0060b0ec3d39"
        ID="xmldso">
    </OBJECT>

    <TABLE DATASRC=#xmldso BORDER="1"
        CELLSPACING="5" CELLPADDING="2">

        <THEAD>
            <TH>Common Name</TH>
            <TH>Botanical Name</TH>
            <TH>Zone</TH>
            <TH>Light</TH>
            <TH>Price</TH>
            <TH>Availability</TH>
        </THEAD>

        <TR ALIGN="center">
            <TD><DIV DATAFLD="COMMON"></TD>
            <TD><DIV DATAFLD="BOTANICAL"></TD>
            <TD><DIV DATAFLD="ZONE"></TD>
            <TD><DIV DATAFLD="LIGHT"></TD>
            <TD><DIV DATAFLD="PRICE"></TD>
            <TD><DIV DATAFLD="AVAILABILITY"></TD>
        </TR>

    </TABLE>
</BODY>

</HTML>
```

In this example, data is bound to cells of the table. Because the Table element is a multiple-value element, the table is built on the fly, based on the amount of data available. The result is a fully populated table that contains all the data in the document, as shown in Figure 6-2.

NOTE

The table is built asynchronously for performance reasons. Rendering an entire table in memory before displaying it could cause a long delay if the dataset is large.

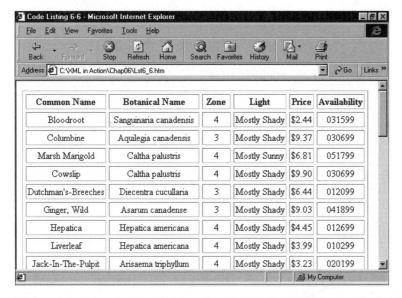

Figure 6-2. *Using the XML DSO and an HTML Table element to display XML data.*

USING HIERARCHICAL DATA IN XML

One of the big advantages to using XML as a data source is that, unlike many standard Web-based data sources, XML allows you to use hierarchical data. So, instead of being able to work with only columns and rows, you can work with the complete XML document tree. To demonstrate this, we'll reorganize our wildflower document, as shown in Code Listing 6-7 (Chap06\Lst6_7.xml on the companion CD).

```
<CATALOG>
  <REGION>
    <ZONE>3</ZONE>

    <PLANT>
      <COMMON>Columbine</COMMON>
      <BOTANICAL>Aquilegia canadensis</BOTANICAL>
      <LIGHT>Mostly Shady</LIGHT>
    </PLANT>

    <PLANT>
      <COMMON>Dutchman's-Breeches</COMMON>
      <BOTANICAL>Diecentra cucullaria</BOTANICAL>
      <LIGHT>Mostly Shady</LIGHT>
    </PLANT>
```

Code Listing 6-7.   *(continued)*

```
    <PLANT>
      <COMMON>Ginger, Wild</COMMON>
      <BOTANICAL>Asarum canadense</BOTANICAL>
      <LIGHT>Mostly Shady</LIGHT>
    </PLANT>
  </REGION>

  <REGION>
    <ZONE>4</ZONE>

    <PLANT>
      <COMMON>Bloodroot</COMMON>
      <BOTANICAL>Sanguinaria canadensis</BOTANICAL>
      <LIGHT>Mostly Shady</LIGHT>
    </PLANT>

    <PLANT>
      <COMMON>Marsh Marigold</COMMON>
      <BOTANICAL>Caltha palustris</BOTANICAL>
      <LIGHT>Mostly Sunny</LIGHT>
    </PLANT>

    <PLANT>
      <COMMON>Cowslip</COMMON>
      <BOTANICAL>Caltha palustris</BOTANICAL>
      <LIGHT>Mostly Shady</LIGHT>
    </PLANT>
  </REGION>
</CATALOG>
```

Notice in this code listing that the plants are organized by region, thus adding another "level" to the document tree. The XML DSO allows us to bind data from any level of the tree, resulting in highly complex views of the data. To display the data in Code Listing 6-7, we will create an HTML page that contains three nested tables, each one bound to a different level of the document tree. The HTML code is shown in Code Listing 6-8 (Chap06\Lst6_8.htm on the companion CD).

```
<!DOCTYPE HTML PUBLIC "-//W3C//DTD HTML 3.2 Final//EN">
<HTML>

  <HEAD>
    <SCRIPT FOR="window" EVENT="onload">
      var xmlDso = xmldso.XMLDocument;
```

Code Listing 6-8.

```
        xmlDso.load("Lst6_7.xml");
    </SCRIPT>

    <TITLE>Code Listing 6-8</TITLE>
  </HEAD>

  <BODY>
    <OBJECT WIDTH="0" HEIGHT="0"
      CLASSID="clsid:550dda30-0541-11d2-9ca9-0060b0ec3d39"
      ID="xmldso">
    </OBJECT>

    <TABLE CELLSPACING="6" ID="catalog">
      <TR>
        <TD>
          <TABLE BORDER="2" DATASRC=#xmldso>
            <TR>
              <TD STYLE="font-size:18; font-weight:bold">
                <SPAN>Zone: </SPAN><SPAN DATAFLD="ZONE"></SPAN>
              </TD>
            </TR>

            <TR>
              <TD>
                <TABLE DATASRC=#xmldso DATAFLD="PLANT">
                  <THEAD ALIGN="left">
                    <TH>Common Name</TH>
                    <TH>Botanical Name</TH>
                    <TH>Light Requirement</TH>
                  </THEAD>

                  <TR>
                    <TD><DIV DATAFLD="COMMON"></TD>
                    <TD><DIV DATAFLD="BOTANICAL"></TD>
                    <TD><DIV DATAFLD="LIGHT"></TD>
                  </TR>

                </TABLE>
              </TD>
            </TR>
          </TABLE>
        </TD>
      </TR>
    </TABLE>

  </BODY>
</HTML>
```

Notice that for each level of the hierarchy that we want to traverse, we insert a *DATASRC* attribute. When we want to pull out data, we use a *DATAFLD* attribute. The result is a set of nested tables that automatically display the hierarchical data, as shown in Figure 6-3.

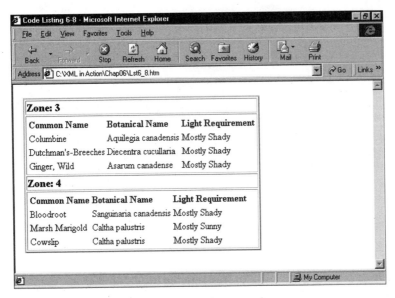

Figure 6-3. *A set of nested tables bound to XML data.*

Putting It All Together

In this section we will put together many of the data source concepts we discussed to create an XML-based application for the Web, commonly known as a *weblication*. Our weblication will incorporate the data from our wildflower document into an online store. Our store will allow the users to add their names to the data store, select plants, add plants to their shopping lists, and view their current lists. All the plant data will come from the Lst6_1a.xml file. All the user data will be stored in a separate XML file that contains only user information. Our online store will operate through an HTML document that makes use of the XML object model to read and write the data. In this example, we will use both the XML DSO and the standard XML parser.

First let's look at all the documents that we will need for this example. Then we will walk through the code so that you will understand how it functions. You have already seen the first document we will need that contains all the wildflower plant information. Remember that Lst6_1a.xml was used in Code Listing 6-5, beginning on page 117.

The next piece we need is the XML document that will form the structure for our user, or customer, information. This document is shown in Code Listing 6-9 and is located in Chap06\Lst6_9.xml on the companion CD.

```
<CUSTOMERS>
  <CUSTOMER>
    <CNAME></CNAME>
    <PNAME></PNAME>
    <QUANTITY></QUANTITY>
    <PRICE></PRICE>
    <DATE></DATE>
  </CUSTOMER>
</CUSTOMERS>
```

Code Listing 6-9.

Notice that this document does not yet contain any data. We will add data to this structure when we open the store! Each customer's data is organized in a Customer element that contains a customer name (Cname element). Each Customer element also provides information on one product, which includes the product's name (Pname element), quantity (Quantity element), price (Price element), and date purchased (Date element). The last piece of our store is the HTML document that contains all the logic needed to run the store and display the data. Code Listing 6-10 shows all the HTML code, which you can also find in the Chap06\Lst6_10.htm file on the companion CD.

```
<!DOCTYPE HTML PUBLIC "-//W3C//DTD HTML 3.2 Final//EN">
<HTML>

  <HEAD>
    <STYLE>
      .category {font-weight:bold; font-size:14}
      .fdata {font-size:16; color:#000099}
      .pdata {font-size:14; font-weight:bold}
      .cdata {font-size:16; color:#993300}
    </STYLE>

    <SCRIPT LANGUAGE="JavaScript" FOR="window" EVENT="onload">
      var xmlDso = xmldso.XMLDocument;
      xmlDso.load("Lst6_1a.xml");
      var xmlDso2 = xmldso2.XMLDocument;
      xmlDso2.load("Lst6_9.xml");
    </SCRIPT>

    <SCRIPT SRC=ShowXML.js>
    </SCRIPT>

    <SCRIPT LANGUAGE="JavaScript">
      function doMenu()
        {
        if (fmenu.style.display == "none")
          fmenu.style.display = "";
```

Code Listing 6-10. *(continued)*

```
      else
        fmenu.style.display = "none";
      }

  function goRecord(indexNum)
    {
    var row = window.event.srcElement;
    var c = row.recordNumber - 1;
    xmldso.recordset.MoveFirst();
    while (c > 0)
      {
      xmldso.recordset.MoveNext();
      c = c - 1;
      }
    doMenu();
    }

  function mouseHover(state)
    {
    var row = window.event.srcElement;
    var colorChange = ((state == "over") ? "#ffff00" : "");
    row.style.backgroundColor = colorChange;
    }

  function updateList()
    {
    var custVal = custName.value;
    if (custVal == "")
      alert ("You must enter a customer name.")
    else
      addToList();
    }

  function addToList()
    {
    var pmatch = 0;
    var cmatch = 0;
    var rootElem = xmldso2.XMLDocument.documentElement;
    var rootChild = rootElem.childNodes;
    var childNum = rootChild.length;
    var currDate = new Date();
    fullDate = (currDate.getMonth() + 1) + "/";
    fullDate += currDate.getDate() + "/";
    fullDate += currDate.getYear();

    for (i = 0; i < childNum; i++)
      {
```

```javascript
        var currNode = rootChild.item(i);
        if (currNode.nodeName == "CUSTOMER")
          {
          var custChild = currNode.childNodes;
          var cnameNode = custChild.item(0);
          var pnameNode = custChild.item(1);
          if (cnameNode.text == custName.value)
            {
            cmatch = 1;
            }
          else
            {
            cmatch = 0;
            }
          if (pnameNode.text == common.innerText)
            {
            pmatch = 1;
            }
          else
            {
            pmatch = 0;
            }
          }
        if (cmatch == 1 && pmatch == 1)
          {
          xmldso2.recordset.moveFirst();
          for (ds = 0; ds <= i; ds++)
            {
            if (ds != i)
              {
              xmldso2.recordset.moveNext();
              }
            }
          break;
          }
        }

if (cmatch != 1 && pmatch != 1)
  {
  xmldso2.recordset.AddNew();
  xmldso2.recordset("CNAME") = custName.value;
  xmldso2.recordset("PNAME") = common.innerText;
  xmldso2.recordset("QUANTITY") = "1";
  xmldso2.recordset("PRICE") = price.innerText;
  xmldso2.recordset("DATE") = fullDate;
  }
else
  {
```

(continued)

```
    if (cmatch == 1 && pmatch == 1)
      {
      xmldso2.recordset("QUANTITY") =
        parseInt(xmldso2.recordset("QUANTITY")) + 1;
      }
    else
      {
      if (cmatch != 1)
        {
        xmldso2.recordset.AddNew();
        xmldso2.recordset("CNAME") = custName.value;
        xmldso2.recordset("PNAME") = common.innerText;
        xmldso2.recordset("QUANTITY") = "1";
        xmldso2.recordset("PRICE") = price.innerText;
        xmldso2.recordset("DATE") = fullDate;
        }
      else
        {
        if (cmatch == 1)
          {
          xmldso2.recordset.AddNew();
          xmldso2.recordset("CNAME") = custName.value;
          xmldso2.recordset("PNAME") = common.innerText;
          xmldso2.recordset("QUANTITY") = "1";
          xmldso2.recordset("PRICE") = price.innerText;
          xmldso2.recordset("DATE") = fullDate;
          }
        }
      }
    }

  showList();
  }

function showList()
  {
  var hold = 0;
  var rootElem = xmldso2.XMLDocument.documentElement;
  var rootChild = rootElem.childNodes;
  var childNum = rootChild.length;
  var purTable = "<TABLE CELLSPACING='5'><THEAD ALIGN='center'>" +
    "<TH>Name</TH><TH>Quantity</TH><TH>Date</TH></THEAD>"
  for (i = 0; i < childNum; i++)
    {
    var currNode = rootChild.item(i);
    if (currNode.nodeName == "CUSTOMER")
      {
      var custChild = currNode.childNodes;
```

```
            var custNum = custChild.length;
            for (ci = 0; ci < custNum; ci++)
              {
              var currCustNode = custChild.item(ci);
              if (currCustNode.nodeName == "CNAME")
                {
                var currCustName = custName.value;
                if (currCustNode.text == currCustName)
                  {
                  hold = 1;
                  }
                else
                  {
                  hold = 0;
                  }
                }
              if (currCustNode.nodeName == "PNAME")
                {
                if (hold == 1)
                  {
                  purTable = purTable + "<TR ALIGN='center'><TD>" +
                    currCustNode.text + "</TD>";
                  }
                }
              if (currCustNode.nodeName == "QUANTITY")
                {
                if (hold == 1)
                  {
                  purTable = purTable +"<TD>"+ currCustNode.text +"</TR>";
                  }
                }
              }
            if (currCustNode.nodeName == "DATE")
              {
              if (hold == 1)
                {
                purTable = purTable +"<TD>"+ currCustNode.text +"</TR>";
                }
              }
            }
          }
      purTable = purTable + "</TABLE>"
      PTData.innerHTML = purTable
      }
  </SCRIPT>

  <TITLE>Code Listing 6-10</TITLE>
</HEAD>
```

```
<BODY>
  <OBJECT WIDTH="0" HEIGHT="0"
    CLASSID="clsid:550dda30-0541-11d2-9ca9-0060b0ec3d39"
    ID="xmldso">
  </OBJECT>

  <OBJECT WIDTH="0" HEIGHT="0"
    CLASSID="clsid:550dda30-0541-11d2-9ca9-0060b0ec3d39"
    ID="xmldso2">
  </OBJECT>

  <TABLE STYLE="position:absolute; left:10; top:10"
    CELLSPACING="6" ID="catalog">
    <TR>
      <TD ALIGN="right" CLASS="category">Common Name:</TD>
      <TD><DIV CLASS="fdata" ID="common"
        DATASRC=#xmldso DATAFLD="COMMON">
      </TD>
    </TR>

    <TR>
      <TD ALIGN="right" CLASS="category">Botanical Name:</TD>
      <TD><DIV CLASS="fdata" ID="botan"
        DATASRC=#xmldso DATAFLD="BOTANICAL">
      </TD>
    </TR>

    <TR>
      <TD ALIGN="right" CLASS="category">Zone:</TD>
      <TD><DIV CLASS="fdata" ID="zone"
        DATASRC=#xmldso DATAFLD="ZONE">
      </TD>
    </TR>

    <TR>
      <TD ALIGN="right" CLASS="category">Light Needs:</TD>
      <TD><DIV CLASS="fdata" ID="light"
        DATASRC=#xmldso DATAFLD="LIGHT">
      </TD>
    </TR>

    <TR>
      <TD ALIGN="right" CLASS="category">Price:</TD>
      <TD><DIV CLASS="fdata" ID="price"
        DATASRC=#xmldso DATAFLD="PRICE">
      </TD>
    </TR>
  </TABLE>
```

```
<DIV STYLE="position:absolute; left:300; top:20">
  <SPAN>Customer Name:</SPAN>
  <INPUT TYPE="Text" NAME="custName">
  <BR>
  <INPUT TYPE="Button" NAME="SL" VALUE="Buy It!"
    onClick="updateList()">
  <INPUT TYPE="Button" NAME="Show" VALUE="Show XML Data"
    onClick="ShowXML(xmldso2.XMLDocument);">
  <DIV ID=PTData></DIV>
</DIV>

<INPUT TYPE="Button" NAME="Flowers" VALUE="Wildflowers"
  STYLE="position:absolute; left:10; top:170"
  onClick="doMenu()">

<TABLE ID="fmenu"
  STYLE="position:absolute; left:10; top:192;
    display:none; cursor:hand"
  DATASRC=#xmldso
  CELLSPACING="0" CELLPADDING="0" BORDER="1"
  onMouseOver = "mouseHover('over')"
  onMouseOut = "mouseHover('out')"
  onClick = "goRecord()">

  <TR>
    <TD><DIV DATAFLD=COMMON></TD>
  </TR>
</TABLE>

</BODY>
</HTML>
```

When this HTML page is run, it displays the online storefront and waits for the user to interact, as shown in Figure 6-4. Information about the first plant in the document, the Bloodroot, is displayed by default. After entering a name in the Customer Name field, the customer can select a plant from the list by clicking the Wildflowers button. Clicking the "Buy It!" button adds the selected plant to the customer's shopping list, as shown in Figure 6-5 on the following page.

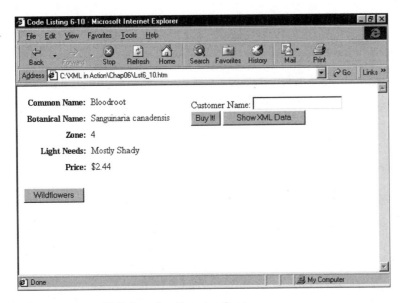

Figure 6-4. *An XML-based online storefront.*

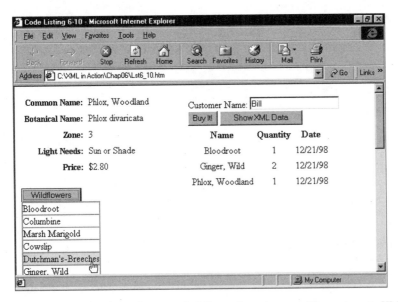

Figure 6-5. *"Purchases" are tracked for each customer with a separate XML structure.*

The code above might look a bit complex, so let's walk through it a piece at a time so that you will understand how it works.

The Style Sheet

The first section near the top of Code Listing 6-10, beginning on page 125, is a style sheet:

```
<STYLE>
  .category {font-weight:bold; font-size:14}
  .fdata {font-size:16; color:#000099}
  .pdata {font-size:14; font-weight:bold}
  .cdata {font-size:16; color:#993300}
</STYLE>
```

This sets up some text styles that we will use later.

The *onload* Script

This script loads the appropriate XML documents into the XML DSO objects. This happens as soon as the page is loaded so that the documents are ready to be worked with when they are needed.

The Linked Script

You'll notice that there is a *linked script* called *ShowXML.js* in a separate Script element. This is used to open a new window and build an XML tree for the *xmldso2* object. I won't go into the details of this script, but you can see how it works by clicking the Show XML Data button. I have included this button so that you can see how the XML data changes as you interact with the elements on the page.

The Remaining Script

The next Script element contains all the remaining functions that are used on the page.

THE *doMenu* FUNCTION

The *doMenu* function alternately shows and hides the list of plants when the Wildflowers button is clicked. Because we want the data for this list to come from our XML data source, we must create our own list instead of using an HTML form. Most "built-in" HTML forms require you to predefine your list items and don't have the fancy rollover functionality that we want.

THE *goRecord* FUNCTION

The *goRecord* function changes the record in the XML DSO based on the item that was selected in the Wildflowers list. The list maintains a one-to-one correspondence with the data in the XML document because the list is bound to that data. So if and when the data changes, the list is updated to reflect those changes.

THE *mouseHover* FUNCTION

The *mouseHover* function changes the color of a menu item when the user moves the mouse over the item. This highlighting allows the user to easily see what item is selected.

THE *updateList* FUNCTION

The *updateList* function does several things. When the user clicks Buy It!, *updateList* checks to determine whether a user exists in the Customer Name field. If not, it displays a message warning the user to add a customer name. If a name is found in the Customer Name field, *updateList* calls the *addToList* function.

THE *addToList* FUNCTION

This is the most complex function in the script. One of the reasons for this is that this function is designed to be relatively smart. For example, if a user has already added a plant to his or her shopping list, we don't want to add it again, but rather, we just want to increment the quantity. Also, the function needs to check for new customer names and add them to the data source. To accomplish these and other tasks, this function walks the entire XML document (Lst6_9.xml) to determine whether the specified customer name already exists in the data source. If it finds a match, it checks to see if the customer has already added the current plant to his or her shopping list. If no match is found, the function adds a new customer to the XML document and then adds the plant information for that customer. If the plant is found but does not belong to the current customer, it creates a new customer and adds the plant to his or her shopping list. If it finds both the plant and the customer, it simply increments the quantity for that plant. When all this work is done, the function calls the *showList* function for display.

THE *showList* FUNCTION

The *showList* function creates a table that contains the plant names and quantities for the current customer. The table is built on the fly based on the data contained in the XML source.

The Control Section

The next section in the code is the control section, where the two XML DSO controls are added to the page. Since we need to work with two XML documents at the same time, we need one control for each document.

```
<OBJECT WIDTH="0" HEIGHT="0"
  CLASSID="clsid:550dda30-0541-11d2-9ca9-0060b0ec3d39"
  ID="xmldso">
</OBJECT>

<OBJECT WIDTH="0" HEIGHT="0"
  CLASSID="clsid:550dda30-0541-11d2-9ca9-0060b0ec3d39"
  ID="xmldso2">
</OBJECT>
```

Notice that both controls are set with dimensions of zero. Since we want only the data from the controls, there is no reason to take up space on the page displaying them.

The Wildflower Information Table

This section establishes the table that will display the plant information for each "record" in the data source. Note that each cell contains a Div element that is bound to an element in the XML data source.

```
<TABLE STYLE="position:absolute; left:10; top:10"
  CELLSPACING="6" ID="catalog">
  <TR>
    <TD ALIGN="right" CLASS="category">Common Name:</TD>
    <TD><DIV CLASS="fdata" ID="common"
      DATASRC=#xmldso DATAFLD="COMMON">
    </TD>
  </TR>

  <TR>
    <TD ALIGN="right" CLASS="category">Botanical Name:</TD>
    <TD><DIV CLASS="fdata" ID="botan"
      DATASRC=#xmldso DATAFLD="BOTANICAL">
    </TD>
  </TR>

  <TR>
    <TD ALIGN="right" CLASS="category">Zone:</TD>
    <TD><DIV CLASS="fdata" ID="zone"
      DATASRC=#xmldso DATAFLD="ZONE">
    </TD>
  </TR>

  <TR>
    <TD ALIGN="right" CLASS="category">Light Needs:</TD>
    <TD><DIV CLASS="fdata" ID="light"
      DATASRC=#xmldso DATAFLD="LIGHT">
    </TD>
  </TR>

  <TR>
    <TD ALIGN="right" CLASS="category">Price:</TD>
    <TD><DIV CLASS="fdata" ID="price"
      DATASRC=#xmldso DATAFLD="PRICE">
    </TD>
  </TR>
</TABLE>
```

Whenever the DSO is updated by a user selecting an item from the Wildflowers list, the data in the bound table is automatically updated as well. Remember that tables are multiple value elements. Normally we would set the *DATASRC* attribute in the Table element. But if we did that here, it would display all the data at once! Since we just want it a node, or record, at a time, we bind the data source to each individual cell in the table.

The Customer Area and Function Buttons

This next section displays the input box for the customer name, and it displays the Buy It! and Show XML Data buttons. (The Buy It! button is used to display the customer's shopping list, and the Show XML Data button is used to display the customer data source.) This section also contains an empty Div element, which gets filled with data from the *showList* function when the Buy It! button is clicked. The last button is the Wildflowers button, which displays the list of wildflowers when clicked. It is outside the main Div element since it is positioned differently on the page.

```
<DIV STYLE="position:absolute; left:300; top:20">
  <SPAN>Customer Name:</SPAN>
  <INPUT TYPE="Text" NAME="custName">
  <BR>
  <INPUT TYPE="Button" NAME="SL" VALUE="Buy It!"
    onClick="updateList()">
  <INPUT TYPE="Button" NAME="Show" VALUE="Show XML Data"
    onClick="ShowXML(xmldso2.XMLDocument);">
  <DIV ID=PTData></DIV>
</DIV>

<INPUT TYPE="Button" NAME="Flowers" VALUE="Wildflowers"
  STYLE="position:absolute; left:10; top:170"
  onClick="doMenu()">
```

The List Table

This section contains the table that serves as the wildflower list.

```
<TABLE ID="fmenu"
  STYLE="position:absolute; left:10; top:192;
    display:none; cursor:hand"
  DATASRC=#xmldso
  CELLSPACING="0" CELLPADDING="0" BORDER="1"
  onMouseOver = "mouseHover('over')"
  onMouseOut = "mouseHover('out')"
  onClick = "goRecord()">

  <TR>
    <TD><DIV DATAFLD=COMMON></TD>
  </TR>
</TABLE>
```

Notice that instead of binding individual cells to DSO data fields as we did above, the entire table is bound to the DSO. This allows the table to be populated by the entire list of wildflower names instead of by just one record. The list is hidden until it is activated by the *doMenu* function.

Using XML as Application Data

This simple example shows how XML can be used for real-world applications. It uses XML in a somewhat different way than might be expected because it not only serves as a data source but also acts as a data storage mechanism. This brings the discussion of XML as data full circle. In addition to being a document semantics and structure language, XML can also serve as a powerful data storage and retrieval mechanism. As you will see in later chapters, there are even more powerful ways to manipulate, search, and display XML data, using technologies such as XSL and XSL Patterns.

Chapter 7
Linking with XML

The growth of the World Wide Web during the past several years has been nothing short of phenomenal. If one were to look at some of the factors contributing to that growth, surely the ability for information to be linked to other sources of information around the globe has had much to do with the Web's popularity. Indeed, the term "Web" was inspired by the medium's ability to link documents to other documents, and to link those documents to still other documents, and so on. The engine that drives the linking capability of the Web is an HTML mechanism. Millions of documents on the Web are connected via this simple but powerful system of linking one piece of information to another using the Anchor (<A>) tag.

In this chapter, we will look at how linking is accomplished with HTML. We will compare the similarities between HTML linking and XML linking and examine how XML provides a more powerful way to connect information on the Web through an XML application called XLink. Finally, we will take a brief look at XPointer, the mechanism that allows linking to the internal structures of an XML document.

> **NOTE**
>
> At the time of this writing, the XLink specification is at the working draft stage with the W3C. As such, all the information in this chapter is based on the current version of the specification, which you can find at *http://www.w3.org/TR/WD-xlink*. Also, at this time, there is no available processing software that supports XLink. So while this chapter provides code samples, they are based solely on the draft specification. Because of possible future changes to the specification, these samples might not work properly when software support becomes available for the XLink specification.

Simple Links the HTML Way

If you use the World Wide Web or work with HTML, you are probably familiar with the way HTML accomplishes linking. A text link is usually identified by a change in the format—such as a color change or an underline—of the text serving as the *origin* of the link. Also, most Web browsers change the mouse cursor to a hand or another type of pointer when it passes over a link. When you click a link, either a new document opens—the *target* of the link—to replace the current one or a new browser window opens containing the new document. Even though the target is displayed slightly differently in these two scenarios, the same basic event is happening—the origin document is "jumping," one way, to a new location, usually another document. This sort of linking is known as *simple linking* because the links work in only one direction. HTML provides two basic methods for linking to other documents: the Anchor element and the Link element.

You might assume that you use links in a two-way manner when you click the Back button on your Web browser. But this is not really two-way linking. The Back button does not use HTML code to move back to the previous document. Instead, the browser saves, or caches, the document location and simply goes back to the previous document when the Back button is clicked. This feature is specific to the individual browser, not to HTML.

HTML Links with the Anchor Element

The Anchor element is by far the most often used method of working with links in HTML. The Anchor element supports many attributes, but the most widely used attribute is the ubiquitous *HREF*. The *HREF* attribute uses a URL (the location of the target of the link) or a *fragment identifier* as its value. A fragment identifier provides a link to a predetermined portion of the same or another document. A fragment identifier can stand alone, which specifies that the link is to a location in the same document, or it can be attached to a URL, which indicates that the target is a location in a separate document. Code Listing 7-1 (Chap07\Lst7_1.htm on the companion CD) demonstrates a simple link with a fragment identifier.

```
<!DOCTYPE HTML PUBLIC "-//W3C//DTD HTML 3.2 Final//EN">
<HTML>

  <HEAD>
    <TITLE>Code Listing 7-1</TITLE>
  </HEAD>

  <BODY>
    This is a
    <A HREF="Lst7_2.htm#jumplocation">simple link</A>
    in HTML that uses the Anchor element.
  </BODY>

</HTML>
```

Code Listing 7-1.

The page, including the link, is shown in Figure 7-1.

In Code Listing 7-1, a fragment identifier is appended to the URL so that when the target document (Lst7_2.htm) is opened, the jump should land at the place identified by the name *jumplocation*. Code Listing 7-2 (Chap07\Lst7_2.htm on the companion CD) shows the code for the target document containing an internal link.

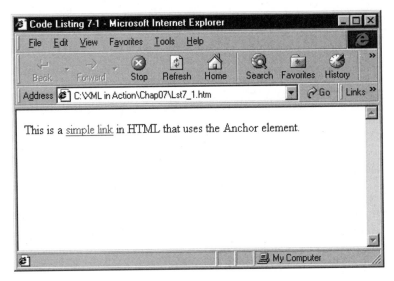

Figure 7-1. *An HTML page containing a link origin.*

```
<!DOCTYPE HTML PUBLIC "-//W3C//DTD HTML 3.2 Final//EN">
<HTML>

  <HEAD>
    <TITLE>Code Listing 7-2</TITLE>
  </HEAD>

  <BODY>
    Here is the new document!

    <BR><BR><BR><BR><BR><BR><BR><BR><BR><BR><BR><BR>
    <BR><BR><BR><BR><BR><BR><BR><BR><BR><BR><BR>
    <BR><BR><BR><BR><BR><BR><BR><BR><BR><BR><BR>
    <BR><BR><BR><BR><BR><BR><BR><BR><BR><BR><BR>
    <BR><BR><BR><BR><BR><BR><BR><BR><BR><BR><BR>

    <A NAME="jumplocation">
      This is the location for the
      jump from the previous document.
    </A>
```

Code Listing 7-2.

```
Clicking
<A HREF="#samedocjump">here</A>
will take you to another part of this document
by using a fragment identifier.

<BR><BR><BR><BR><BR><BR><BR><BR><BR><BR><BR><BR><BR><BR>
<BR><BR><BR><BR><BR><BR><BR><BR><BR><BR><BR><BR><BR><BR>
<BR><BR><BR><BR><BR><BR><BR><BR><BR><BR><BR><BR><BR><BR>
<BR><BR><BR><BR><BR><BR><BR><BR><BR><BR><BR><BR><BR><BR>

<A NAME=samedocjump>
   Here is the location for the jump in this document.
   Click <A HREF="#top">here</A>
   to go to the top of this document.
</A>

</BODY>
</HTML>
```

NOTE

Code Listing 7-2 contains a lot of line break (<BR>) tags. These were included to simulate a large document; they create a lot of space between the lines so that the links can be demonstrated. Line break tags are not required for links to work in normal circumstances.

When the link shown in Code Listing 7-1 is activated (the user clicks the link), the document shown in Code Listing 7-2 (Lst7_2.htm) opens and jumps to the location specified in the link by the fragment identifier, in this case *jumplocation*. Notice that Code Listing 7-2 includes an Anchor element containing just a *NAME* attribute. The value of the attribute is *jumplocation*, and it tells the HTML code shown in Code Listing 7-1 where to jump. If an element by this name was missing from the target document, the document shown in Code Listing 7-2 would open but would not jump to a specific location.

Following the Anchor element named *jumplocation* in Code Listing 7-2 is another link, this time to a location in the same document. Even though this internal link looks the same as an external link, as shown in Figure 7-2, you know that the link points to a location within the current document because the target for the link is a fragment identifier with no URL. As always, an Anchor element including the name of the target must exist for the link to work.

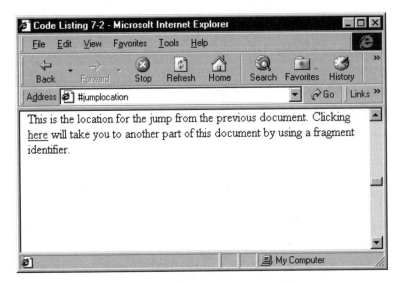

Figure 7-2. *An internal link using a fragment identifier.*

Linking to External Documents with the Link Element

The Link element can be used only in the head section of the document and is not used to jump to a target location; instead, this element is used to establish a relationship between the current document and some other document or object. In Code Listing 7-3 (Chap07\Lst7_3.htm on the companion CD), the Link element is used to link a style sheet to the document. The style sheet can then be used as though it were part of the original document. In this way, the Link element acts much like an Image element with its *SRC* attribute in that the element links to an external object and makes it part of the current document.

```
<!DOCTYPE HTML PUBLIC "-//W3C//DTD HTML 3.2 Final//EN">
<HTML>

  <HEAD>
    <LINK REL="stylesheet" HREF="Styles.css">
    <TITLE>Code Listing 7-3</TITLE>
  </HEAD>

  <BODY>
    <SPAN CLASS=style1>This text uses style1</SPAN>
    <BR>
    <SPAN CLASS=style2>This text uses style2</SPAN>
  </BODY>

</HTML>
```

Code Listing 7-3.

Even though the Link element in Code Listing 7-3 contains an *HREF* attribute, the link does not jump to the document specified in the URL but, rather, links the target document back to the source document.

The linking mechanisms shown previously, especially the Anchor element, have been used for years, by millions of people, on hundreds of millions of Web pages. So why does XML change all that by including its own linking specification? Well, the good news is that XML does not change the simple linking mechanisms used by HTML, such as the Anchor element and the Link element. Instead, the XML linking specification starts with these simple mechanisms and extends the concept of linking into powerful new ways to work with linked information.

XLink: The XML Linking Mechanism

The XML specification does not contain a "built-in" method for linking. Instead, a proposal for linking in XML is accomplished through an XML vocabulary called XLink. XLink uses XML to define all the pieces necessary to build links into XML documents. XLink defines two basic kinds of links: simple links and extended links. XLink is designed to maintain the simplicity of linking in HTML, but it provides more power and extensibility when needed. To accomplish this, the creators of XLink developed the specification around several design goals, as shown below.

GOAL 1: XLINK SHALL BE STRAIGHTFORWARDLY USABLE OVER THE INTERNET.   This goal relates directly to the idea that the simple linking mechanisms currently in use should still work in XML. In addition, this goal supports the idea that XLink should work well on the Internet without being too complicated, despite any new features that are introduced.

GOAL 2: XLINK SHALL BE USABLE BY A WIDE VARIETY OF LINK USAGE DOMAINS AND OF CLASSES OF LINKING APPLICATION SOFTWARE.   This goal identifies the desire for XLink to be extensible beyond just Web applications. XLink should be flexible enough to map to various uses and work with a variety of software applications.

GOAL 3: THE XLINK EXPRESSION LANGUAGE SHALL BE XML. XLink is an application of XML. The goal was not to create a completely new language, but just to create a vocabulary of XML. By using XML as the expression language, XLink uses an established structure and format and does not require authors and software application designers to learn a new language.

GOAL 4: THE XLINK DESIGN SHALL BE PREPARED QUICKLY. As is true with XML itself, the creators of XLink knew that if a mechanism for linking in XML was not prepared relatively quickly by the XML community, other organizations and vendors would probably work to create their own proprietary method for linking in XML. This would work against the open, standardized roots of the XML language.

GOAL 5: THE XLINK DESIGN SHALL BE FORMAL AND CONCISE. This goal is another carryover from the goals of the XML language. The designers of XLink know that if the specification is to be adopted by the industry, it has to be easy to understand and use. This goal helped the designers focus on keeping the verbiage of the specification formal and on keeping the specification as small as possible.

GOAL 6: XLINKS SHALL BE HUMAN-READABLE. Because XLink is created using XML, XLink should be as easy to understand as XML. XLink should be easy for humans to read; reading XLink should not require that a computer decipher what is going on in the code.

GOAL 7: XLINKS MAY RESIDE OUTSIDE THE DOCUMENTS IN WHICH THE PARTICIPATING RESOURCES RESIDE. This goal relates directly to the extensibility of the XLink language. As you will see, XLink goes beyond the simple one-way links of HTML and can provide links that point to more than one resource. This is exactly what the XLink designers had in mind.

GOAL 8: XLINK SHALL REPRESENT THE ABSTRACT STRUCTURE AND SIGNIFICANCE OF LINKS. This goal is based on some of the philosophy behind the XLink language. The designers decided that not only should XLink provide the mechanics of linking in XML, but that links created using XLink should be able to describe the semantics of links and identify their relationship to the objects or resources to which they are connecting. This kind of data will provide the user with information, such as the role of the link, in addition to the resources the link is using.

GOAL 9: XLINK MUST BE FEASIBLE TO IMPLEMENT. Just as XLink must be easy to understand by human readers and easy to author, links must be easy to implement by application developers. Again, the designers of the language knew that if the language was going to be widely adopted, it would have to be easy to implement. At the time of this writing, few, if any, applications use XLink, so whether this goal is met remains to be seen.

Simple Links in XML

Although XML can do the same type of document linking that can be done with HTML, you should start thinking of linking in XML as connecting *resources*. That is, XLink can connect to any resource that can be reached via a locator in the linking element. This concept is not particular to XLink, as the notion of resources is inherent to the workings of the World Wide Web. The difference here is that XLink provides a much more sophisticated syntax for defining link elements and behavior, such as allowing links to occur in more than one direction. XLink is also more flexible, allowing a document to link to any type of resource that is reachable on the Web.

A simple link in XLink can have the same functionality as that of the Anchor element in HTML. Simple links are *inline* links, just as they are in HTML. That is, the link is part of the element and links can connect in only one direction. A simple link has only one resource identifier, or *locator*. The locator, such as the *HREF* attribute in the Anchor element, contains data about the link. In XLink, *all* of the locator information is contained within the linking element. This means that the processing application does not need to search for any other information about the locator. So in Code Listings 7-1 and 7-2, if the origin and target documents were both XML documents, the target document would not need to include elements containing the names of the fragment identifiers, since all of the necessary locator information would have been contained within the linking element. Since HTML does not provide this level of functionality, let's look at how to create a link in XML.

We create an XML simple link in our first link example. Creating even a simple link element in XML is more complicated than merely creating an Anchor element and assigning an *HREF* value. Remember that XML is a metalanguage, so creating a new element that can be used in a document requires that you declare the element and all of its attributes. The good news is that XML and the XLink specification provide you with a lot of powerful options for creating links.

We will create a simple link element named SLINK. Below is the element declaration and attribute list as they might appear in a Document Type Definition (DTD).

> **NOTE**
>
> Nothing is inherently special about the name SLINK for this element. In fact, you don't even need to create an element that is used only for links (as is the Anchor element in HTML); you could make any element a link element. So you have a lot of options for linking information in XML documents!

```
<!ELEMENT SLINK ANY>
<!ATTLIST SLINK
  XML:LINK CDATA #FIXED "simple"
  HREF CDATA #REQUIRED
  INLINE (true|false) "true"
  ROLE CDATA #IMPLIED
  TITLE CDATA #IMPLIED
  SHOW (replace|new|embed) #IMPLIED
  ACTUATE (auto|user) #IMPLIED
  BEHAVIOR CDATA #IMPLIED
  CONTENT-ROLE CDATA #IMPLIED
  CONTENT-TITLE CDATA #IMPLIED
>
```

You'll notice that the familiar *HREF* attribute appears in this element, but all the other attributes used are new. Let's go through them and discuss their purposes.

XML:LINK

The designers of XLink knew they needed to come up with a reliable way for processing software to recognize an element as a linking element. They could have done this by reserving a tag name (such as <A> in HTML), by reserving an attribute name, or by leaving it completely up to the application software. They chose to reserve an attribute name, believing that this provided a balance between allowing authors to define their own elements and maintaining the linking element as a *link* part of the structure of the element. The result is the designated attribute *XML:LINK*, which can have the value *simple* or *extended*. The preceding example assigns the value of *simple* since we are creating a simple link. (We will look at extended links later in this chapter.) In use, the Slink element would appear in a document as shown below:

```
<SLINK XML:LINK="simple" HREF="http://mspress.microsoft.com">
  Microsoft Press Home Page
</SLINK>
```

The *XML:LINK* attribute is included in the Slink element above, but since the attribute is declared with a fixed value in the element declaration, the element itself does not need to include the *XML:LINK* attribute for it to work.

HREF

Every linking element in XML must have a resource *locator*. The locator identifies the resource to which the link will connect. The locator attribute in XLink is *HREF*, and it works in XLink just as it does in HTML. Locators also contain some functionality not provided by HTML, as discussed in the following sidebar.

Locators and Fragment Identifiers

Let's take a look at some of the extended functionality of locators in XLink. In HTML, a locator, identified by the *HREF* attribute, could contain a fragment identifier as shown here:

```
This is a <A HREF="Lst7_2.htm#jumplocation">simple link</A>
```

A fragment identifier provides a link to a predetermined portion of the same or another document. In XML, the locator can provide information that allows the application to follow a link based on a document's structure, an element ID, or even an element's content. This is done through the XML XPointer addressing mechanism, which uses the syntax shown in either of the following two lines:

```
HREF="uri#Xpointer"
HREF="uri|Xpointer"
```

XPointers, which will be covered in detail in the latter part of this chapter, allow authors to follow links into any part of an XML document, using a wide variety of ways to specify what is needed. And since the locator mechanism provides a flexible traversal method, the pointer might return only a small portion of the target document, saving bandwidth and client-side processing.

INLINE

An XLink linking element is either inline or out-of-line. (For more information on these types of links, see "Inline Extended Links" and "Out-of-Line Extended Links" later in this chapter.) An inline link serves as one of its own resources—that is, the linking element contains content as well as the target of the link. Again, the HTML Anchor element is a great example of this type of link. The Anchor element also contains content as well as the target of the link. In our example, the default value of *true* is part of the *INLINE* attribute declaration, so it is not necessary to specify the attribute in the element.

ROLE

ROLE is a great feature of XLink linking elements. The *ROLE* attribute identifies to the application software the link's meaning or significance. Note that this attribute is meant to provide information about the link as a whole, not just the link's remote resource. This information is meant for the application to understand, not for a human reader. By using *ROLE*, you can provide the application with much more detailed information about links than simply where they go. For example, some links might lead to glossary terms, others might lead to background information on a certain topic, and some might lead to property information for a resource (such as version information). Applications can now get this kind of information directly from the link and act appropriately.

> **NOTE**
>
> Many of the attributes described in this section are used for resource semantics—that is, they are included to provide information about the meaning or context of a resource. Some attributes are used for remote resource semantics and some for local resource semantics. These uses will be noted where appropriate.

TITLE

The *TITLE* attribute is akin to the <ALT> tag in HTML. The *TITLE* attribute contains a displayable label or text phrase that can be used to provide supplemental information to the user. It is a remote resource attribute: the *TITLE* information is not intended to pertain to the link as a whole, but rather to provide information to the user as to how the resource relates to the link. While the *ROLE* attribute is intended for the machine, the *TITLE* attribute is intended for the user.

SHOW

The *SHOW* attribute is part of XML's remote resource semantics and is probably one of the most noted improvements over HTML linking. The *SHOW* attribute accepts *replace*, *new*, and *embed* as values; these values describe how the link should be traversed. The *replace* value indicates that the local resource is replaced with the remote resource, which is the most common technique used by HTML links. In the real world, this is what happens when a browser jumps to a new page when a user clicks a link. The *new* value specifies that the target resource should be opened in a new context. Similar functionality is provided in HTML with the *TARGET* attribute of the Anchor element: the target of the link opens in the new context, usually another browser window. If no context is found with that name, a new context is created (usually by opening a new browser window). The *embed* value indicates the cool new technique for traversing a link. If the *embed* value is specified, the content of the link target is embedded in the content of the link source. For example, imagine a document that contains a link to background information on a particular subject. When the user clicks that link with the *embed* value specified, the information is displayed in context, right inside the source document.

ACTUATE

The *ACTUATE* attribute, part of the remote resource semantics, specifies how the link should be traversed. *ACTUATE* can accept the values *auto* or *user*. The *auto* value indicates that the link should be traversed automatically when the link is processed by the application. The *user* value specifies that the link should be traversed by some external mechanism, such as a mouse click.

NOTE

You might begin to see that combining certain attributes can add a whole new dimension to linking information. For example, by combining the *SHOW=embed* attribute with the *ACTUATE=auto* attribute, an author could create a document that contains many embedded links. When the document is opened by a user, all the links are traversed automatically and embedded directly into the document. The result is a compound document containing information gathered from various sources that are invisible to the user.

BEHAVIOR

Until now, most attributes we have seen work to describe the link: they define what it is, the parts that make it up, and so on. The *BEHAVIOR* attribute, which is part of the remote resource semantics, provides a space for the link author to fully describe what should happen when the link is activated. For example, you can think of a link as having before and after states. The before state is how the link looks before it is activated. This could include font, color, and other formatting. (Note that XLink itself does not provide ways to control link formatting, since that should be handled by the application.) The after state occurs after the link is activated, where link behavior comes into play. While the *SHOW* and *ACTUATE* attributes indicate basic behaviors, the *BEHAVIOR* attribute is unconstrained, which means that it can contain any type of instruction that can be communicated to the application processing the link. *BEHAVIOR* is meant to provide additional behavioral information beyond *SHOW* and *ACTUATE*, but XLink does not specify what particular values the *BEHAVIOR* attribute can contain.

CONTENT-ROLE

This attribute works in much the same way as the *ROLE* attribute, but it is specific to local resources. It identifies to the application the purpose of the local resource as part of the link. As with the *ROLE* attribute, this information is meant to be used by the application, not by the human reader.

CONTENT-TITLE

CONTENT-TITLE is another local resource semantic attribute that provides information to the user about the local part of the link. Similar in function to the *TITLE* attribute, *CONTENT-TITLE* is meant for human readers.

IMITATING HTML LINKS WITH XML

Now that you understand the process of creating simple links, let's look at how you can re-create all the functionality (and then some) of the HTML Anchor element using XLink constructs. This example will help demonstrate how XML linking can imitate the functions of HTML linking, and it will also show some of the differences XML can make. Let's start with a basic element declaration.

```
<!ELEMENT ANCHOR ANY>
<!ATTLIST ANCHOR
  XML:LINK CDATA #FIXED "simple"
  HREF CDATA #REQUIRED
  TITLE CDATA #IMPLIED
  INLINE (true|false) "true"
  SHOW (replace|new|embed) "replace"
  ACTUATE (auto|user) "user"
>
```

This is a good start. The most commonly used attributes of the HTML Anchor element are included, which alone would allow us to write a simple Anchor element in XML that would match an HTML link, as shown here:

```
<A HREF="http://www.microsoft.com">Microsoft Home Page</A>
```

To completely finish our Anchor element reproduction, however, we'll have to add more attributes supported by the HTML Anchor element, including *REV*, *REL*, *NAME*, and *TARGET*. Two of these, *REV* and *REL*, will require that we remap them to XML attributes to make them work (more on this later).

ATTRIBUTE MAPPING

Sometimes it's necessary to map existing XLink attribute names to other attribute names. This can occur, for example, if an existing XML document contains elements whose attribute names conflict with XLink attribute names. This is a problem particularly if you want to use those elements as linking elements. You also might want to map existing XLink attribute names to HTML attribute names so that you can more closely approximate the syntax of HTML, and possibly even use existing HTML links.

To accomplish these kinds of tasks, XLink provides an attribute mapping mechanism: the *XML:ATTRIBUTES* attribute. The basic syntax is the keywords *XML:ATTRIBUTES* followed by name pairs separated by white space. The first name in each name pair is the XLink attribute name, and the second name in each pair is the attribute name that will "play the role" of the first name.

Let's look at this in an example. Since the HTML attributes *REV* and *REL* are equaled in XLink by *ROLE* and *CONTENT-ROLE*, we will remap the XML attributes in our XML version of the Anchor element. Here is how this is done:

```
XML:ATTRIBUTES CDATA #FIXED "ROLE REV CONTENT-ROLE REL"
```

This tells the processing application, "When you encounter the *REV* attribute in this element, map it to the XLink *ROLE* attribute, and when you encounter the *REL* attribute in this element, map that to the XLink *CONTENT-ROLE* attribute."

Now let's add this attribute map to our element declaration, along with the *REV* and *REL* attribute declarations.

```
<!ELEMENT ANCHOR ANY>
<!ATTLIST ANCHOR
  XML:LINK CDATA #FIXED "simple"
  XML:ATTRIBUTES CDATA #FIXED "ROLE REV CONTENT-ROLE REL"
  HREF CDATA #REQUIRED
  TITLE CDATA #IMPLIED
  INLINE (true|false) "true"
  SHOW (replace|new|embed) "replace"
  ACTUATE (auto|user) "user"
  REV CDATA #IMPLIED
  REL CDATA #IMPLIED
>
```

Finally, we can add our declarations for the *NAME* and *TARGET* attributes.

```
<!ELEMENT ANCHOR ANY>
<!ATTLIST ANCHOR
  XML:LINK CDATA #FIXED "simple"
  XML:ATTRIBUTES CDATA #FIXED "ROLE REV CONTENT-ROLE REL"
  HREF CDATA #REQUIRED
  TITLE CDATA #IMPLIED
  INLINE (true|false) "true"
  SHOW (replace|new|embed) "replace"
  ACTUATE (auto|user) "user"
  REV CDATA #IMPLIED
  REL CDATA #IMPLIED
  TARGET CDATA #IMPLIED
  NAMEID #IMPLIED
>
```

We now have an XML Anchor element that behaves just like an HTML Anchor element and supports the same attributes. While it is beneficial to know and understand that XLink can reproduce the simple links found in HTML, XLink is capable of much more than that. XLink's extended links take the concept of linking information to a new level.

Extended Links in XML

As stated earlier, the main difference between simple links and extended links is that extended links can connect any number of resources, not just one local and one remote resource, as HTML does. Using extended links, authors can define groups of possible destinations from a single origin. For example, suppose you want to provide links to multiple news stories from a single category, such as sports. Instead of needing a special control or a lot of code, extended links would supply all the information needed to provide the multiple links.

Extended links also provide other capabilities, mentioned briefly here and discussed more thoroughly in the following sections.

- Enabling links in read-only resources. A document can contain outgoing links even if it cannot be modified to contain inline links.

- Enabling filtering of relevant links. Filtering can be done on the fly, and mechanisms can exist for the user to perform real-time filtering of link resources.

INLINE EXTENDED LINKS

With power comes complexity, and extended links do add a bit more complexity to the equation. Below is a basic inline extended-link element declaration:

> **NOTE**
>
> As with a simple link, an extended link can be declared with any element name. The name *ELINK* is used here only as an example.

```
<!ELEMENT ELINK ANY>
<!ATTLIST ELINK
  XML:LINK CDATA #FIXED "extended"
  INLINE (true|false) "true"
  ROLE CDATA #IMPLIED
  TITLE CDATA #IMPLIED
  SHOW (replace|new|embed) #IMPLIED
  ACTUATE (auto|user) #IMPLIED
  BEHAVIOR CDATA #IMPLIED
  CONTENT-ROLE CDATA #IMPLIED
  CONTENT-TITLE CDATA #IMPLIED
>
```

You will notice that this code looks similar to the simple link declaration we created earlier, but with two changes. First, the *XML:LINK* attribute contains the value *extended* instead of *simple*, since this is an extended link. Second, no *HREF* attribute is declared. This is because with extended links, the locators must be contained in a separate set of elements. These elements are identified as locator elements. As you will see, using this method for defining locators allows the author to specify many locators for one linking element. As with other elements, the locator element must be declared. Next let's look at a locator element declaration.

```
<!ELEMENT ELOCATOR ANY>
<!ATTLIST ELOCATOR
  XML:LINK CDATA #FIXED "locator"
  HREF CDATA #REQUIRED
```

(continued)

```
ROLE CDATA #IMPLIED
TITLE CDATA #IMPLIED
SHOW (replace|new|embed) #IMPLIED
ACTUATE (auto|user) #IMPLIED
BEHAVIOR CDATA #IMPLIED
>
```

Notice that the *XML:LINK* attribute contains the value *locator* to identify that this element is an XLink locator. You can also see that the *HREF* attribute is used.

Let's look at how this structure might work in an XML document. Based on the previous declarations, the linking element might look like the code shown here:

```
<ELINK XML:LINK="extended">minivan review
  <ELOCATOR TITLE="Chrysler Town and Country" HREF="Chrysler.htm"/>
  <ELOCATOR TITLE="Ford Windstar" HREF="Ford.htm"/>
  <ELOCATOR TITLE="Chevrolet Venture" HREF="Chevy.htm"/>
  <ELOCATOR TITLE="Honda Odyssey" HREF="Honda.htm"/>
  <ELOCATOR TITLE="Nissan Quest" HREF="Nissan.htm"/>
  <ELOCATOR TITLE="Toyota Sienna" HREF="Toyota.htm"/>
</ELINK>
```

This format provides the processor with all the information it needs for the extended link. It is up to the application, however, to decide what to do with this information. For example, the application could present the link in the same way it presents any other Web link, as shown in Figure 7-3.

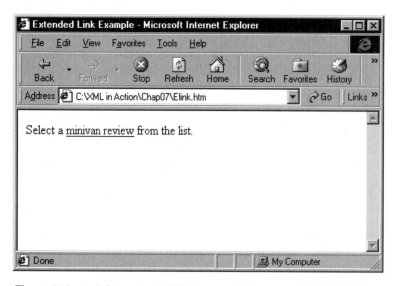

Figure 7-3. *An inline extended link, presented as any other Web link.*

But when the link is clicked, the application can do whatever the author has programmed it to do. For example, the application can present the user with a list of possible locations, depending on the contents of the locator list, as shown in Figure 7-4.

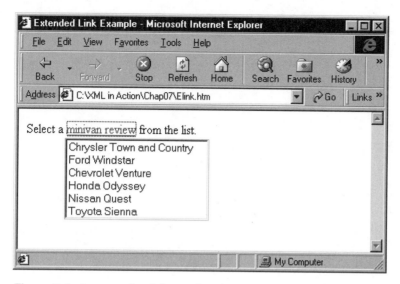

Figure 7-4. *An example of the results of clicking an inline extended link.*

One big advantage to this technique that might not be readily apparent is that all the documents in the list can be available to all the other documents, thus creating interrelated connections among all the documents. This can be done if the element declarations and the locator elements are put into a separate XML document that can be accessed by all the documents in the locator list. Let's look at an example of this using another kind of extended link, the out-of-line extended link.

OUT-OF-LINE EXTENDED LINKS

The previous example took the concept of an inline link and added another dimension to it. But the local resource, the link text itself, was part of the whole link. In other words, an inline link requires the link text in order to complete the link. Extended links allow authors to create links in which the local resource is not part of the link. This means that an element or portion of content can be a link, even if it was not originally authored to serve in that way. These links are called *out-of-line links,* and using them can be a powerful and flexible way to link information. To create an out-of-line link, we use the same extended-link element declaration and locator element declaration that we created for the inline extended link. When the element is inserted into a document, however, a change needs to be made. In the element tag, we need to set the *INLINE* attribute to *false* to indicate that the element is an out-of-line link.

```
<ELINK XML:LINK="extended" INLINE="false">
  <ELOCATOR TITLE="Chrysler Town and Country" HREF="#Chrysler"/>
  <ELOCATOR TITLE="Ford Windstar" HREF="#Ford"/>
  <ELOCATOR TITLE="Chevrolet Venture" HREF="#Chevy"/>
  <ELOCATOR TITLE="Honda Odyssey" HREF="#Honda"/>
  <ELOCATOR TITLE="Nissan Quest" HREF="#Nissan"/>
  <ELOCATOR TITLE="Toyota Sienna" HREF="#Toyota"/>
</ELINK>
```

(continued)

```
<REVIEW ID="Chrysler">
  <TITLE="Chrysler Town and Country"</TITLE>
  <!-- This is the Chrysler section -->
</REVIEW>

<REVIEW ID="Ford">
  <TITLE="Ford Windstar"</TITLE>
  <!-- This is the Ford section -->
</REVIEW>

<REVIEW ID="Chevy">
  <TITLE="Chevrolet Venture"</TITLE>
  <!-- This is the Chevrolet section -->
</REVIEW>

<REVIEW ID="Honda">
  <TITLE="Honda Odyssey"</TITLE>
  <!-- This is the Honda section -->
</REVIEW>

<REVIEW ID="Nissan">
  <TITLE="Nissan Quest"</TITLE>
  <!-- This is the Nissan section -->
</REVIEW>

<REVIEW ID="Toyota">
  <TITLE="Toyota Sienna"</TITLE>
  <!-- This is the Toyota section -->
</REVIEW>
```

In this example, the locators are kept in their own section and are not tied to any local link resources. The locators contain all the information necessary to provide connections to the appropriate sections in the document, but it is up to the application to display the links to the user in some way. The application could, for example, provide a list that is separate from the content that would allow the user to connect to any of the links at any time. This sets up truly multidirectional links and does away with the "forward-and-back" sort of linking that most Web users are accustomed to using.

Let's take this one step further. Suppose an XML document contained in its DTD the Elink and Elocator element declarations we used earlier. Suppose it also included in its document element the following locator elements:

```
<ELINK XML:LINK="extended" INLINE="false">
  <ELOCATOR TITLE="Chrysler Town and Country" HREF="Chrysler.htm"/>
  <ELOCATOR TITLE="Ford Windstar" HREF="Ford.htm"/>
  <ELOCATOR TITLE="Chevrolet Venture" HREF="Chevy.htm"/>
  <ELOCATOR TITLE="Honda Odyssey" HREF="Honda.htm"/>
  <ELOCATOR TITLE="Nissan Quest" HREF="Nissan.htm"/>
  <ELOCATOR TITLE="Toyota Sienna" HREF="Toyota.htm"/>
</ELINK>
```

Now any application that uses this document can make these links available, because the locators are contained in their own document. Again, this creates a multidirectional link structure because a link to any document is accessible from any other document. Another advantage is that because the locator list resides in its own document, the list of links can be managed separately from the documents in which they are used. In addition, this kind of structure could be used to add links to documents that could not ordinarily be edited to contain their own inline links. Finally, the application could check to ensure that the documents identified in the locators are available even before displaying the links—that means no more broken links!

You might begin to see that XLink provides some pretty powerful mechanisms for creating links among XML-based information resources. But you might also see that with the ability to set up multiple targets for links, extended out-of-line links, and multidirectional links, you could end up trying to manage a dizzying number of links. Fortunately, XLink provides a way to help with some of these issues: *extended link groups*.

EXTENDED LINK GROUPS

Extended link groups provide a way to help you manage related link information by setting up elements that contain lists of related documents. To see how this works, let's extend our example from the previous section. Suppose you worked for a consumer magazine, and every month you published reports on new automobiles. Instead of having a single document that contained lists of every vehicle in every vehicle category for every month, you could group the lists to make them easier to manage. To use extended link groups, two elements are required—one to define the group and the other to specify the documents in the group. Here is how the declarations might look:

```
<!ELEMENT GROUP (DOCUMENT*)>
<!ATTLIST GROUP
  XML:LINK CDATA #FIXED "group"
  STEPS CDATA #IMPLIED
>

<!ELEMENT DOCUMENT EMPTY>
<!ATTLIST DOCUMENT
  XML:LINK CDATA #FIXED "document"
  HREF CDATA #REQUIRED
>
```

Notice that these declarations are substantially shorter than some of the previous ones. The only new attribute used is the *STEPS* attribute, which tells the application how many layers of documents to traverse before ending its search. This attribute can be useful when the group contains documents that contain other groups, which contain other documents that contain other groups, and so on. After the element declarations are in place, we need to add the Group and Document elements. This creates our link group.

```
<GROUP STEP=2>
  <DOCUMENT HREF="minivans.htm"/>
  <DOCUMENT HREF="passengercars.htm"/>
```

(continued)

```
    <DOCUMENT HREF="pickups.htm"/>
    <DOCUMENT HREF="sportscars.htm"/>
</GROUP>
```

If a document called Reviews.xml contains this group of elements, the application processes all of the documents and checks for links back to the Review.xml document. If links are found, the application builds a list of links available for Reviews.xml and makes them available to the user. Again, an extended link group provides a way to centralize link management by creating a central "hub" document that contains all the other links. This is illustrated in Figure 7-5. As shown, if a link to a specified resource is not available, the resource itself is not available as a link.

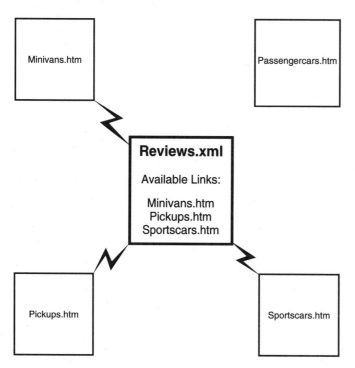

Figure 7-5. *Managing links by using link groups.*

So far, all the links we have looked at connect to external content or fragments within a document. But there is a way to get even more precision when linking inside an XML document. This can be done with another XML-based language called XPointer.

XPointer—Looking Inward

The primary goal of XPointer is to provide a way to address the internal structure of an XML document. In our previous examples, if we wanted to address a specific part of a document we used a fragment identifier that required that the element use an *ID* attribute. XPointer is designed to address the internal structures of a document whether or not they include *ID* attributes. XPointer is a separate language and could easily occupy its own chapter; this section will simply provide an introduction to XPointer and identify a bit of what it can do. Note that XSL (Extensible Stylesheet Language), covered in Chapter 8, provides similar functionality and is currently implemented in Microsoft's Msxml processor.

NOTE

At the time of this writing, XPointer is still in the working draft stage and is not a formal recommendation by the W3C. The information in this section is based on the working specification located at *http://www.w3.org/TR/1998/WD-xptr-19980303*.

XPointer Basics

XPointers work from within the elements and constructs that make up the XML document tree structure. An XPointer contains a series of location terms that specifies a location in the document tree. XPointers, although much more sophisticated than HTML fragment identifiers, can be used in much the same way that fragment identifiers are used. A location term can use the syntax on either of the following two lines:

```
HREF="uri#Xpointer"
HREF="uri|Xpointer"
```

If the pound sign (#) is used as the separator, it serves as an indication that the client should process the connection. If the pipe symbol (|) is used as the separator, the connection mechanism is left open. This provides an opportunity for the link connection to be handled on the server side, potentially saving bandwidth.

A *location term* requires a location source—this is just a way of telling the XPointer where to start in the document structure. Each location term uses a keyword and can contain arguments. The keyword specifies the location source, such as *Root*, *Id*, and so on, which tells the XPointer where to start. The arguments provide further information about where the XPointer should go within the source. For example, a location term could be this,

```
Child(2, PRODUCT)
```

which means "the second Product element among the children of the current element."

Location terms can map to absolute locations, relative locations, spanning locations, attribute locations, or string locations. Let's look at some of the different types of location terms so that we can understand how they work.

ABSOLUTE LOCATION TERMS

An *absolute location term* points to a specific place in the document structure. It does not require a location source. An absolute location term can be used to establish a location source, or it can serve as its own self-contained XPointer. Absolute location terms support the following keywords:

◆ *ROOT*—The *Root* keyword specifies that the location source is the root element of the containing resource. This is the default keyword if no other keyword is specified. Because the purpose of a location term is to point into a document, this keyword would be used rarely, if ever.

- *Origin*—This keyword generates a useful location source if the XPointer is being processed because of a traversal request (such as a link). If the XPointer begins with *Origin*, the location source is the resource from which the traversal took place.

- *Id*—The *Id* keyword uses the more common technique of document traversal, the *ID* and *NAME* pair. The traversal starts at the element with an *ID* that matches the specified *NAME*.

- *Html*—This keyword mimics the action performed by the fragment identifier in an HTML document. The *Html* keyword contains a *NAMEVALUE* attribute. The location source is the first Anchor element that contains a *NAME* attribute whose value matches that of the *NAMEVALUE* attribute in the location term.

An example of an absolute location term is shown below:

```
Id(PRODUCT)
```

RELATIVE LOCATION TERMS

The keywords for relative location terms are dependent on the existence of a location source. If a location source does not exist, the XPointer assumes the root element of the resource that contains the term. The following keywords are supported by relative location terms.

- *Child*—If the *Child* keyword is specified, it identifies the child nodes of the location source. The *Child* keyword selects all the children of the location source.

- *Descendant*—Specifies document nodes that are anywhere within the content of the location source, no matter how many levels deep.

- *Ancestor*—Specifies nodes that contain the location source, or its parent elements.

- *Preceding*—Specifies nodes that appear in the document tree before the location source.

- *Psibling*—Specifies sibling elements that appear before the location source. (Sibling elements share the same parent.)

- *Following*—Specifies nodes that appear in the document tree after the location source.

- *Fsibling*—Specifies sibling elements that appear after the location source.

An example of a relative location term is shown below:

```
Child(2, SECTION)
```

SPANNING LOCATION TERMS

A *spanning location term* points to a subresource by locating the data found between its two arguments. The arguments are relative to the location source for the spanning location term, as shown below:

```
Id(PRODUCT).Span(Child(1), Child(3))
```

ATTRIBUTE LOCATION TERMS

The attribute location term takes an attribute name, finds the attribute, and returns its value. Its usage is shown below:

```
Attr(COLOR)
```

STRING LOCATION TERMS

The string location term selects one or more strings or positions between strings in the location source. String location terms support the following keywords:

- ◆ *InstanceOrAll*—Identifies the ordinal occurrence of the specified string. If the number is positive, the XPointer counts forward from the beginning of the location source. If the number is negative, the XPointer counts backward from the end of the location source. If the value *All* is used, all occurrences of the string are used.

- ◆ *SkipLit*—Specifies the string to be found in the location source.

- ◆ *Position*—Specifies a character offset from the start of the string or strings to the beginning of the final string match.

- ◆ *Length*—Specifies the number of characters to be selected in the string.

   An example of a string location term is shown below:

```
Id(PRODUCT).String(3, "widget")
```

   This brief introduction to XPointer is not meant to provide you with detail on how to implement XPointers in your applications. Rather, it is intended to show you the kinds of detail XPointers can add to your links. Perhaps this will inspire you to look at XPointers in more detail as you begin to work with linking elements in your XML documents.

Chapter 8
XSL: XML with Style

Until now, the XML message has been all about data. XML semantically marks up a document, providing structure and context for the data it contains. However, we've seen nothing in the XML document that indicates how the data should look when it is displayed. So far in this book, HTML has been used to provide the display information; we've walked through the XML document tree and inserted the data from each XML element into an HTML element. While using HTML directly is certainly an effective way to format XML documents, there is another way. XSL (Extensible Stylesheet Language) is a formatting language built especially for use by XML documents. In fact, XSL is an application of XML, so XSL's structure and syntax are the same as those of XML.

In this chapter, we'll examine how XSL works. We'll also work with XSL to create extensible style sheets based on formatting rules. Finally, we'll delve into some advanced features of XSL, such as using scripts with XSL and reordering the XML output.

Style Sheet Basics

XSL is built around the *style sheet mechanism*. Style sheets are generally used to apply styles, or formatting information, consistently throughout a document. The most commonly used form of style sheet on the Web is based on the Cascading Style Sheets (CSS) specification. CSS allows authors to define *classes* of styles that can be applied throughout an HTML document. Let's look at an example of CSS in action to provide a better foundation for our work with XSL later on.

A Look at Cascading Style Sheets

CSS requires two basic components to function properly: the style sheet that contains all the style definitions, or rules, and a document to which these styles will be applied. First let's create a style sheet that contains several style rules. Code Listing 8-1 (Chap08\Lst8_1.css on the companion CD) shows two style rules:

```
H1 {font-style:italic; font-size:24}
.bold16 {font-weight:bold; font-size:16}
```

Code Listing 8-1.

Next we need to create an HTML document that will use this style sheet. This document is shown in Code Listing 8-2 (Chap08\Lst8_2.htm on the companion CD). Notice that the HTML document is linked to the style sheet. The <LINK> tag tells the application to use the style sheet in the document where appropriate.

```
<!DOCTYPE HTML PUBLIC "-//W3C//DTD HTML 3.2 Final//EN">
<HTML>

  <HEAD>
    <TITLE>Code Listing 8-2</TITLE>
    <LINK HREF="Lst8_1.css" REL=STYLESHEET TYPE="text/css">
  </HEAD>

  <BODY>
    <H1>An H1 paragraph</H1>
    <BR>
    <SPAN CLASS=bold16>
      A Span element with the bold16 style rule applied
    </SPAN>
  </BODY>

</HTML>
```

Code Listing 8-2.

The style sheet in Code Listing 8-1 defines two style rules in two different ways. The first rule, *H1*, corresponds directly to the HTML H1 element. In other words, every H1 element in the HTML document will use the style defined in the style sheet rather than the default style for the element. The second style rule, *bold16*, is a class style rule (indicated by the initial dot character) that does not correspond to any particular HTML element. Both style rules contain custom formatting (in other words, I decided what I wanted the style rules to do), but the *bold16* style rule also contains the custom name, *bold16*. In other words, because *bold16* is a class style rule, I could have named it anything I wanted. To use the class style rule in the HTML document, I have to explicitly assign the rule to the Span element using the *CLASS* attribute. Doing so assigns the style rule defined with the matching name to the current element.

When the page is displayed, it looks like the one shown in Figure 8-1.

Now let's get a little tricky with the style sheet so that you can fully understand how CSS works. You know that because the *H1* style rule corresponds to an HTML element, that style will apply to every H1 element included in the document. But you can override the style from the style sheet by including a *class style* for a particular H1 element. For example, you could create an H1 element with a class style of *bold16*, as shown in Code Listing 8-3 (Chap08\Lst8_3.htm on the companion CD).

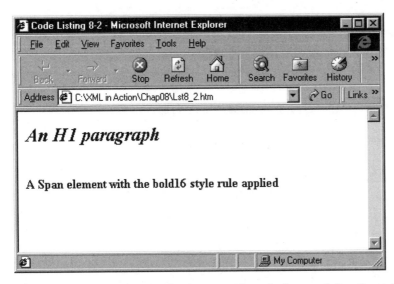

Figure 8-1. *This HTML document uses a CSS style sheet to define the styles for both elements.*

```
<!DOCTYPE HTML PUBLIC "-//W3C//DTD HTML 3.2 Final//EN">
<HTML>

  <HEAD>
    <TITLE>Code Listing 8-3</TITLE>
    <LINK HREF="Lst8_1.css" REL=STYLESHEET TYPE="text/css">
  </HEAD>

  <BODY>
    <H1>An H1 paragraph</H1>
    <BR>
    <SPAN CLASS=bold16>
      A Span element with the bold16 style rule applied
    </SPAN>
    <P>

    <H1 CLASS=bold16>
      An H1 paragraph with an overriding class style
    </H1>
    <BR>
    <SPAN>A Span element with no style rule applied</SPAN>
  </BODY>

</HTML>
```

Code Listing 8-3.

When this page is displayed, the second H1 element is displayed with the *bold16* style, as shown below, instead of just with the *H1* style defined in the style sheet. Note that the overriding style adds new attributes (*font-weight* in our example) and overrides the matching attributes only (in this case, *font-size*). The *font-style* attribute of *italic* is left intact from the *H1* style.

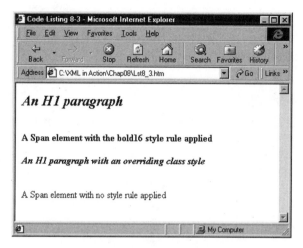

Notice that the second Span element does not contain any style information, so it is displayed with the default settings—essentially, no style at all.

XSL Basics

XSL also uses style sheets. It can accomplish the same level of formatting and flexibility as CSS (and a lot more), but it uses a different approach. XSL is built on the notion of templates, which are in some ways similar to CSS style rules. XSL templates provide the mechanism for applying formatting information to data that matches a specific pattern.

The Parts of XSL

Before going any further, we need to discuss the component parts of XSL. These are important to understand if you are to work effectively with XSL. The XSL language consists of two parts: an XSL transformation language and a formatting object specification. These two parts are kept separate for the reasons described below, but they can work together to provide sophisticated formatting capabilities for document display. The XSL transformation language and the formatting object specification are implemented as XML namespaces. (See Chapter 6 for a discussion of namespaces.)

NOTE

The W3C often uses the term "formatting vocabulary" to describe what I am calling a formatting object specification. Don't let this confuse you. As with other vocabularies, a formatting vocabulary is described as a specification. So for our purposes, a specification and a vocabulary are the same. (See Chapter 4 for details on vocabularies.)

XSL TRANSFORMATION LANGUAGE

The XSL transformation language (*xsl* namespace) is a description of how a processor can transform an XML document from one structure to another. The transformation process in a general sense takes one document tree and transforms it into another document tree. Its most likely and perhaps obvious use (at least initially) would be to convert an XML document from a semantic structure to a display structure, such as converting an XML document to an HTML document. But, in fact, this does not have to be the case since the transformation process is entirely independent of the final output. This allows for tremendous extensibility in the future, since XSL could transform documents into other structures that have not even been thought of yet!

FORMATTING OBJECT SPECIFICATION

The formatting object specification (*fo* namespace) provides for new formatting semantics developed as an XML vocabulary. So a display engine could directly process the formatting information that's in the *fo* namespace (unlike the information in the *xsl* namespace) or a processor could further transform the formatting information into other formatting structures, such as HTML code. The difference between this method and the *xsl* namespace method is that the *fo* namespace method is specifically related to formatting semantics, allowing vocabularies to be developed for specific applications, such as multimedia. The *xsl* namespace capability is focused on Document object model transformation and is independent of formatting semantics.

> **NOTE**
>
> The XSL implementation in Msxml, which ships with Microsoft Internet Explorer 5, focuses almost entirely on outputting HTML code. As such, Msxml is developed around the *xsl* namespace. Accordingly, the rest of this chapter will focus on using the *xsl* namespace.

XSL Style Sheets

As described above, XSL has the ability to transform an XML source document into some arbitrary output structure. This is accomplished through the use of style sheets. XSL style sheets describe the process by which the output structure should be created.

Using Templates

A style sheet consists of one or more *templates* that contain *patterns*. As their name implies, templates provide a structure for the output document. The output elements can be almost anything. XSL templates do not even need to contain any references to XML data. For example, examine the template below:

```
<xsl:template xmlns:xsl="uri:xsl">
  <HTML>
    <HEAD>
      <TITLE>XSL Test</TITLE>
    </HEAD>
```

```
      <BODY>
        <B>This is a test of an XSL template.</B>
      </BODY>
    </HTML>
  </xsl:template>
```

This template produces HTML elements as its output elements. If you look closely, you'll see that this style sheet is not very useful since it outputs static HTML code and does not reference any XML data. However, it does demonstrate how templates describe the output structure. The real power of style sheets is their ability to output XML data to new documents. XSL templates reference XML data via patterns.

PATTERNS

XSL uses patterns to specify the XML elements to which the XSL template applies. This method of pattern matching makes XSL a declarative language as opposed to a procedural language. That is, the patterns describe the specific "branch" in the document tree to match by identifying its hierarchical structure within that tree. For example, *ROOT/NODE1* identifies the pattern as "the Node1 elements that are inside the Root element." Let's look at a simple style sheet to give you a feel for the structure of a template. First we'll need to create an XML document to which the style sheet will be applied.

```
<CATALOG>
  <PLANT>
    <COMMON>Bloodroot</COMMON>
    <BOTANICAL>Sanguinaria canadensis</BOTANICAL>
    <ZONE>4</ZONE>
    <LIGHT>Mostly Shady</LIGHT>
    <PRICE>$7.05</PRICE>
    <AVAILABILITY  USONLY="true">02/01/99</AVAILABILITY>
  </PLANT>
</CATALOG>
```

Next we'll create an XSL style sheet with a single template for the Common element:

```
<?xml version="1.0"?>
<xsl:template xmlns:xsl="uri:xsl">
  <HTML>
    <BODY>
      <xsl:repeat for="CATALOG/PLANT">
        <DIV>
          <SPAN STYLE="font-weight:bold; font-size:20">
            <xsl:get-value for="COMMON"/>
          </SPAN>
        </DIV>
      </xsl:repeat>
    </BODY>
  </HTML>
</xsl:template>
```

When the XML document is processed with the XSL style sheet, the processor outputs the following HTML code:

```
<HTML>
<BODY>
<DIV>
<SPAN STYLE="font-weight:bold; font-size:20">
Bloodroot
</SPAN>
</DIV>
</BODY>
</HTML>
```

NOTE

The examples in this chapter all output HTML code, but keep in mind that the XSL specification supports the output of other structures that are independent of the XSL language.

Now let's look at the template defined in the above style sheet and examine what is taking place when the document is processed.

ANATOMY OF A TEMPLATE

Each template comprises one or more patterns. Our example above contains two patterns. Here is the part that contains the patterns:

```
<xsl:repeat for="CATALOG/PLANT">
  <DIV>
    <SPAN STYLE="font-weight:bold; font-size:20">
      <xsl:get-value for="COMMON"/>
    </SPAN>
  </DIV>
</xsl:repeat>
```

The first pattern specifies any Plant element that is a child of the Catalog element. (You can ignore the *repeat for* statement for now; we'll get to that later.) The second pattern for this rule specifies the Common element. The rule puts whatever data is found in the pattern element into a Span element and applies the style *"font-weight:bold; font-size:20"* to that Span element. So if we were to write this template in English, it might sound something like this: "Repeat the following for every Plant element that is a child of the Catalog element: get the value of its Common element and put that value into a Span element with a font weight of bold and a font size of 20."

A template applies to every element in the document that matches the pattern or patterns defined in the template. To further demonstrate this notion, let's add a few more Plant elements to our example:

```
<CATALOG>
  <PLANT>
    <COMMON>Bloodroot</COMMON>
    <BOTANICAL>Sanguinaria canadensis</BOTANICAL>
```

```
   <ZONE>4</ZONE>
   <LIGHT>Mostly Shady</LIGHT>
   <PRICE>$7.05</PRICE>
   <AVAILABILITY  USONLY="true">02/01/99</AVAILABILITY>
</PLANT>

<PLANT>
   <COMMON>Columbine</COMMON>
   <BOTANICAL>Aquilegia canadensis</BOTANICAL>
   <LIGHT>Mostly Shady</LIGHT>
   <PRICE>$3.20</PRICE>
   <AVAILABILITY>04/08/99</AVAILABILITY>
</PLANT>

<PLANT>
   <COMMON>Marsh Marigold</COMMON>
   <BOTANICAL>Caltha palustris</BOTANICAL>
   <ZONE>4</ZONE>
   <LIGHT>Mostly Sunny</LIGHT>
   <PRICE>$2.90</PRICE>
   <AVAILABILITY>01/09/99</AVAILABILITY>
</PLANT>

<PLANT>
   <COMMON>Cowslip</COMMON>
   <LIGHT>Mostly Shady</LIGHT>
   <PRICE>$3.83</PRICE>
   <AVAILABILITY  USONLY="true">05/19/99</AVAILABILITY>
</PLANT>
</CATALOG>
```

If we process this document with the same XSL style sheet we used in the previous example, the output is as follows:

```
<HTML>
<BODY>
<DIV>
<SPAN STYLE="font-weight:bold; font-size:20">
Bloodroot
</SPAN>
</DIV>
<DIV>
<SPAN STYLE="font-weight:bold; font-size:20">
Columbine
</SPAN>
</DIV>
<DIV>
<SPAN STYLE="font-weight:bold; font-size:20">
Marsh Marigold
</SPAN>
</DIV>
```

(continued)

```
<DIV>
<SPAN STYLE="font-weight:bold; font-size:20">
Cowslip
</SPAN>
</DIV>
</BODY>
</HTML>
```

Notice that the template was applied only to those elements that matched the pattern. All other elements were ignored. This represents some of the power of XSL. By using XSL's pattern matching capabilities, you can completely rearrange the XML data to suit a specific purpose. If you don't want to include an element or elements in the output, you simply do not include a pattern for the element(s). If you want to include only a single element in a very specific part of the XML document, you can create a detailed pattern to translate it for display.

SINGLE TEMPLATE STRUCTURE

Notice that our template started with the <xsl:template xmlns:xsl="uri:xsl"> tag and ended with the </xsl:template> tag. Using this pair of tags, or *container,* makes it easy to apply different portions of a style sheet when more than one template is used, as we'll see shortly. However, since this style sheet contains only one template, the container <xsl:document> </xsl:document> could be used as well. For example, the style sheet below is equivalent to the one above:

```
<?xml version="1.0"?>
<xsl:document xmlns:xsl="uri:xsl">
  <HTML>
    <BODY>
      <xsl:repeat for="CATALOG/PLANT">
        <DIV>
          <SPAN STYLE="font-weight:bold; font-size:20">
            <xsl:get-value for="COMMON"/>
          </SPAN>
        </DIV>
      </xsl:repeat>
    </BODY>
  </HTML>
</xsl:document>
```

Both style sheets are examples of a *single template structure.* That is, each style sheet consists of only one template. A style sheet can also be of a *multiple templates structure,* in which the style sheet contains multiple templates that can be applied independently.

MULTIPLE TEMPLATES STRUCTURE

A multiple templates style sheet uses the container tags <xsl:stylesheet></xsl:stylesheet>. This pair of tags can contain a number of pairs of <xsl:template></xsl:template> tags; each of these pairs can be applied independently. Let's look at an example to see how this works. Code Listing 8-4 shows the XML file we will use for this example.

```
<CATALOG>
  <PLANT BESTSELLER="no">
    <NAME>
      <COMMON>Bloodroot</COMMON>
      <BOTAN>Sanguinaria canadensis</BOTAN>
    </NAME>
    <GROWTH>
      <ZONE>4</ZONE>
      <LIGHT>Mostly Shady</LIGHT>
    </GROWTH>
    <SALESINFO>
      <PRICE>$3.00</PRICE>
      <AVAILABILITY>4/21/99</AVAILABILITY>
    </SALESINFO>
  </PLANT>

  <PLANT BESTSELLER="yes">
    <NAME>
      <COMMON>Columbine</COMMON>
      <BOTAN>Aquilegia canadensis</BOTAN>
    </NAME>
    <GROWTH>
      <ZONE>3</ZONE>
      <LIGHT>Mostly Shady</LIGHT>
    </GROWTH>
    <SALESINFO>
      <PRICE>$9.00</PRICE>
      <AVAILABILITY>4/10/99</AVAILABILITY>
    </SALESINFO>
  </PLANT>
  <PLANT BESTSELLER="no">
    <NAME>
      <COMMON>Marsh Marigold</COMMON>
      <BOTAN>Caltha palustris</BOTAN>
    </NAME>
    <GROWTH>
      <ZONE>4</ZONE>
      <LIGHT>Mostly Sunny</LIGHT>
    </GROWTH>
    <SALESINFO>
      <PRICE>$9.00</PRICE>
      <AVAILABILITY>4/19/99</AVAILABILITY>
    </SALESINFO>
  </PLANT>
</CATALOG>
```

Code Listing 8-4.

The file Chap08\Lst8_4.xml on the companion CD is an expanded version of the document shown in Code Listing 8-4. Since the document contains many repetitive nodes, it was reduced in the book to conserve space.

Code Listing 8-5 shows the style sheet we will use in our example. This style sheet contains several templates. You will see how these templates are independently applied to different parts of the XML document. (You can also find the style sheet on the companion CD in the Chap08\Lst8_5.xsl file.)

```xml
<?xml version="1.0"?>
<xsl:stylesheet xmlns:xsl="uri:xsl">
  <xsl:template match="/">
    <HTML>
      <BODY>
        <TABLE BORDER="1">
          <TR STYLE="font-weight:bold">
            <TD>Common Name</TD>
            <TD>Botanical Name</TD>
            <TD>Zone</TD>
            <TD>Light</TD>
            <TD>Price</TD>
            <TD>Availability</TD>
          </TR>
          <xsl:for-each select="CATALOG/PLANT">
            <TR>
              <xsl:apply-templates/>
            </TR>
          </xsl:for-each>
        </TABLE>
      </BODY>
    </HTML>
  </xsl:template>

  <xsl:template match="NAME">
    <TD><xsl:value-of select="COMMON"/></TD>
    <TD><xsl:value-of select="BOTAN"/></TD>
  </xsl:template>

  <xsl:template match="GROWTH">
    <TD><xsl:value-of select="ZONE"/></TD>
    <TD><xsl:value-of select="LIGHT"/></TD>
  </xsl:template>
```

Code Listing 8-5.

```
    <xsl:template match="SALESINFO">
      <TD><xsl:value-of select="PRICE"/></TD>
      <TD><xsl:value-of select="AVAILABILITY"/></TD>
    </xsl:template>
  </xsl:stylesheet>
```

Notice that the style sheet begins with the <xsl:stylesheet> tag and ends with the </xsl:stylesheet> tag. Since an XML document can have only one root element, and since XSL is an application of XML, the single xsl:stylesheet element allows for the inclusion of multiple xsl:template elements within the style sheet.

Notice that the pattern for the first template is simply "/." This identifies the root of the XML document. Notice also the xsl:for-each element within this template. This element identifies another pattern, *CATALOG/PLANT,* and states that the output structure that follows should apply everywhere that the pattern is matched. Within that output structure is the xsl:apply-templates element. This tells the processor to look for other templates in the style sheet and apply them when a match is found. This is where the multiple templates are brought in. You'll notice three other templates in the style sheet, each having its own pattern. Because the xsl:apply templates element is inside the *CATALOG/PLANT* pattern, the other templates will be applied only when a match is found inside that element. For example, the *NAME* template will apply only to elements that exist in the hierarchy of *CATALOG/PLANT/NAME.*

Before moving on, let's summarize what we have learned thus far. XSL transforms XML into output elements. These output elements are typically used to prepare the data for display by applying some sort of formatting to the XML data, but that is not necessarily the only purpose. This transformation occurs in the following sequence:

1. A style sheet specifies patterns that match data found in an XML document. These patterns are part of individual templates containing output structures.

2. The processor finds the data that matches each pattern and translates that data into the output structure.

3. When the entire style sheet is processed, a new data structure based on the output from the style sheet exists in the computer's memory.

We're now ready to do something with that data.

Displaying the Output Elements

This is where we introduce another piece of the XSL puzzle—the display piece. In our examples, the output from the XSL processor has been HTML code. So we need to get the HTML code into something that can display it. One method would be for the application to write the HTML to a separate file, thus creating a new HTML document. Another method, the method we will use throughout the rest of this book, is simply to insert the HTML code produced by the XSL style sheet into an HTML document. This allows the processing and display to occur within the same document, so there is nothing else the user needs to do to see the results. Code Listing 8-6 (Chap08\Lst8_6.htm on the companion CD) shows the HTML page we will use to display our example.

```
<!DOCTYPE HTML PUBLIC "-//W3C//DTD HTML 3.2 Final//EN">
<HTML>

  <HEAD>
    <SCRIPT LANGUAGE="JavaScript" FOR="window" EVENT="onload">
      var source = new ActiveXObject("Microsoft.xmldom");
      source.load("Lst8_4.xml");

      var style = new ActiveXObject("Microsoft.xmldom");
      style.load("Lst8_5.xsl");
      document.all.item("xslContainer").innerHTML =
        source.transformNode(style.documentElement);
    </SCRIPT>

    <TITLE>Code Listing 8-6</TITLE>
  </HEAD>

  <BODY>
    <DIV ID="xslContainer"></DIV>
  </BODY>
</HTML>
```

Code Listing 8-6.

This HTML page uses a Div element as the container for the HTML output elements produced by the XSL processor. Two XML objects are created—one containing the XML document and the other containing the XSL style sheet. The style sheet object is then applied to the XML object using the *transformNode* method. Figure 8-2 shows the results.

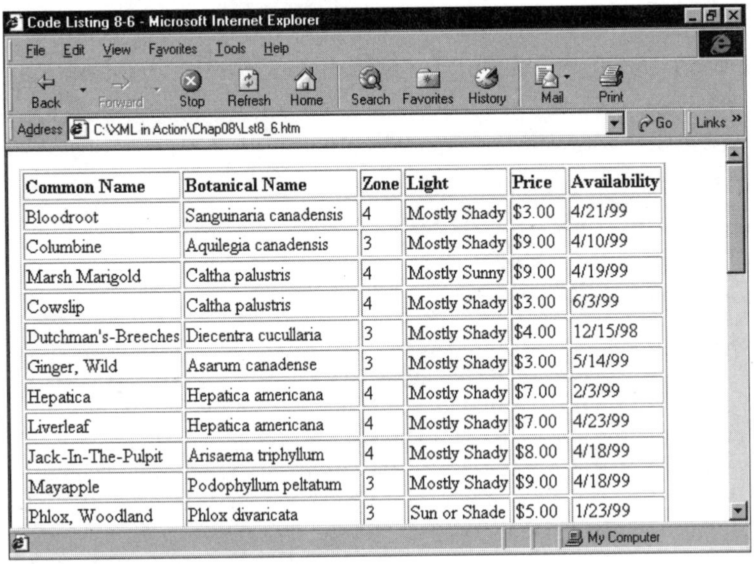

Common Name	Botanical Name	Zone	Light	Price	Availability
Bloodroot	Sanguinaria canadensis	4	Mostly Shady	$3.00	4/21/99
Columbine	Aquilegia canadensis	3	Mostly Shady	$9.00	4/10/99
Marsh Marigold	Caltha palustris	4	Mostly Sunny	$9.00	4/19/99
Cowslip	Caltha palustris	4	Mostly Shady	$3.00	6/3/99
Dutchman's-Breeches	Diecentra cucullaria	3	Mostly Shady	$4.00	12/15/98
Ginger, Wild	Asarum canadense	3	Mostly Shady	$3.00	5/14/99
Hepatica	Hepatica americana	4	Mostly Shady	$7.00	2/3/99
Liverleaf	Hepatica americana	4	Mostly Shady	$7.00	4/23/99
Jack-In-The-Pulpit	Arisaema triphyllum	4	Mostly Shady	$8.00	4/18/99
Mayapple	Podophyllum peltatum	3	Mostly Shady	$9.00	4/18/99
Phlox, Woodland	Phlox divaricata	3	Sun or Shade	$5.00	1/23/99

Figure 8-2. *Using an HTML page to display XSL output.*

Getting Data from XML

As demonstrated in the preceding examples, various XSL elements can be used to extract data from the XML document. XSL elements combined with XSL attributes provide a powerful mechanism for getting precisely the data that is needed from an XML document.

BEING DIRECT

The most straightforward way for you to get data into a template is to use the xsl:value-of element combined with the *select* attribute. The xsl:value-of element retrieves the value of the element indicated by the *select* attribute. This value is then inserted into the template as text. Code Listing 8-7 (Chap08\Lst8_7.xsl on the companion CD) demonstrates this.

```
<?xml version="1.0"?>
<xsl:template xmlns:xsl="uri:xsl">
  <H1><xsl:value-of select="CATALOG/PLANT/NAME/COMMON"/></H1>
  <H2><xsl:value-of select="CATALOG/PLANT/NAME/BOTAN"/></H2>
</xsl:template>
```

Code Listing 8-7.

To use the style sheet in Code Listing 8-7, modify the Lst8_6.htm file to use Lst8_7.xsl as the XSL file, as shown here:

```
var style = new ActiveXObject("Microsoft.xmldom");
style.load("Lst8_7.xsl");
```

When this style sheet is processed, the result is as shown here:

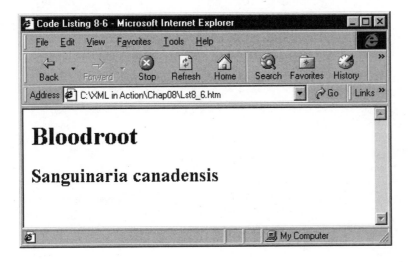

Unless otherwise noted, the rest of the examples in this chapter will use the XML file Lst8_4.xml and the HTML page Lst8_6.htm. You can simply change the name of the XSL file in the HTML page to see the result.

The xsl:value-of element has an attribute equivalent. In other words, you can use curly braces ({}) to cause the value of an XML element to be inserted into an *attribute* of a specified HTML element. For example, in the Div element that follows (which you would include in your XSL document), the value of the CATALOG/PLANT/NAME/COMMON element is inserted into the *ID* attribute of the Div element:

```
<DIV ID={CATALOG/PLANT/NAME/COMMON}></DIV>
```

XSL Patterns will be covered in more depth in Chapter 9. XSL Patterns is a general purpose query and addressing language that can be used to perform queries within or across documents. We will survey parts of XSL Patterns in this chapter when it is necessary to work with XSL.

USING MULTIPLE ELEMENTS

You might have noticed in the previous example that only one element was returned for each xsl:value-of element even though the XML document contained many elements that matched each element's criteria. That is because the xsl:value-of element returns only the first element that matches. To return each element in the document that matches, you can use the xsl:for-each element. Code Listing 8-8 (Chap08\Lst8_8.xsl on the companion CD) shows this strategy in action.

```
<?xml version="1.0"?>
<xsl:template xmlns:xsl="uri:xsl">
  <xsl:for-each select="CATALOG/PLANT/NAME">
    <SPAN STYLE="font-weight:bold; font-size:20">
      <xsl:value-of select="COMMON"/>
    </SPAN>
    <SPAN STYLE="font-weight:bold">
      (<xsl:value-of select="BOTAN"/>)
    </SPAN>
    <P></P>
  </xsl:for-each>
</xsl:template>
```

Code Listing 8-8.

The xsl:for-each element finds every element that matches the value of the *select* attribute and then inserts the output object into the template output. The result is the set of the values of all the elements that match, as shown below:

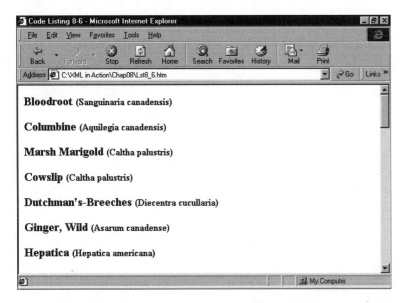

Notice that the patterns in the preceding template specify both the element that is to be repeated (CATALOG/PLANT/NAME) and the target element from which the value is to be obtained. While this works well for data or XML documents that use a consistent or predictable structure, it would not work well for documents that do not have consistent structures. The multiple template style sheet we looked at earlier provides the best mechanism for getting at the appropriate data based on the structure of that data. Let's look at this a bit more closely.

WORKING WITH MULTIPLE TEMPLATES

The multiple templates mechanism allows the XSL processor to direct which template should be applied to a specific pattern of data. The xsl:apply-templates element tells the processor to find an xsl:template element based on the results of a query. The xsl:template element uses the *match* attribute to determine whether the element is a match. In our XML document, each Plant element contains several child elements. The xsl:template elements in Code Listing 8-9 (Chap08\Lst8_9.xsl on the companion CD) filter for just the information needed to make up a price list.

```
<?xml version="1.0"?>
<xsl:stylesheet xmlns:xsl="uri:xsl">
  <xsl:template match="/">
```

Code Listing 8-9.

(continued)

```
    <HTML>
      <BODY>
        <H1>Price List</H1>
        <TABLE CELLSPACING="4" CELLPADDING="2">
          <TR STYLE="font-weight:bold; font-size:18">
            <TD>Name</TD>
            <TD>Price</TD>
            <TD>Available</TD>
          </TR>
          <xsl:for-each select="CATALOG/PLANT">
            <TR>
              <xsl:apply-templates/>
            </TR>
          </xsl:for-each>
        </TABLE>
      </BODY>
    </HTML>
  </xsl:template>

  <xsl:template match="NAME">
    <TD STYLE="font-style:italic; font-size:20">
      <xsl:value-of select="COMMON"/>
    </TD>
  </xsl:template>

  <xsl:template match="SALESINFO">
    <TD><xsl:value-of select="PRICE"/></TD>
    <TD><xsl:value-of select="AVAILABILITY"/></TD>
  </xsl:template>
</xsl:stylesheet>
```

The result is a list of all the plants according to each plant's common name, price, and availability, as shown in Figure 8-3.

All other data in the file is ignored because the style sheet is able, through pattern matching, to select only that data which is relevant. Notice that the xsl:apply-templates element looks for all xsl:template elements that match child elements of the Plant element. Within each template, the *select* attribute selects a specific child element and inserts the value into the template. To further demonstrate this, let's use the same set of XML data but output completely different results. Code Listing 8-10 (Chap08\Lst8_10.xsl) retrieves data relevant to growing information only.

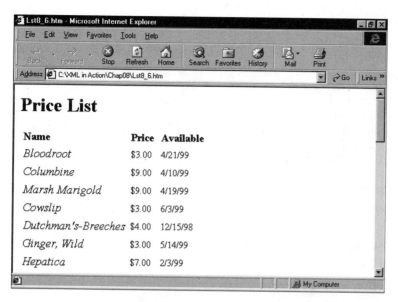

Figure 8-3. *The XSL style sheet retrieves data relevant to the price list only.*

```
<?xml version="1.0"?>
<xsl:stylesheet xmlns:xsl="uri:xsl">
  <xsl:template match="/">
    <HTML>
      <BODY>
        <H1>Growing Information</H1>
        <TABLE CELLSPACING="4" CELLPADDING="2">
          <TR STYLE="font-weight:bold; font-size:18">
            <TD>Botanical Name</TD>
            <TD>Zone</TD>
            <TD>Light Requirement</TD>
          </TR>
          <xsl:for-each select="CATALOG/PLANT">
            <TR>
              <xsl:apply-templates/>
            </TR>
          </xsl:for-each>
        </TABLE>
      </BODY>
    </HTML>
  </xsl:template>
```

Code Listing 8-10.

(continued)

```
<xsl:template match="NAME">
  <TD STYLE="font-style:italic; font-size:20">
    <xsl:value-of select="BOTAN"/>
  </TD>
</xsl:template>

<xsl:template match="GROWTH">
  <TD><xsl:value-of select="ZONE"/></TD>
  <TD><xsl:value-of select="LIGHT"/></TD>
</xsl:template>
</xsl:stylesheet>
```

Here the XML document has not been modified at all; only the style sheet has changed. The result is shown in Figure 8-4.

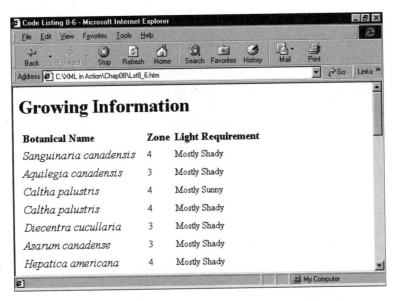

Figure 8-4. *The XSL style sheet now retrieves growing information.*

You can see from these examples that XSL not only allows authors to display precise data from an XML data source, but it can also allow them to completely restructure the XML data based on how the style sheet is authored. So far, our examples have shown basic queries that were used to provide a pattern for the template. As noted earlier, XSL Patterns is covered in depth in Chapter 9. But since XSL uses queries, let's briefly examine how to create queries that can be used in XSL style sheets as a primer for your work in XSL Patterns. We will focus on the capabilities that are especially important to XSL.

Creating Queries in XSL

Queries are the muscle behind XSL. While the term *query* might sound like a highly technical programming term, it should not scare anyone who is new to XSL. As we have already seen, queries, while powerful, provide a simple way for the template to pick out the correct data. Queries provide a way to *address* data by specifying a pattern and then matching that pattern. Queries also provide a sorting mechanism in XSL.

SORTING IN XSL

To sort in XSL, you include the *order-by* attribute with an xsl:apply-templates or xsl:for-each element. The *order-by* attribute specifies the criteria by which the data should be sorted. Code Listing 8-11 (Chap08\Lst8_11.xsl) shows how to display a list of plant names sorted alphabetically.

```xml
<?xml version="1.0"?>

<xsl:stylesheet xmlns:xsl="uri:xsl">
  <xsl:template match="/">
    <HTML>
      <BODY>
        <H1>Growing Information</H1>
        <TABLE CELLSPACING="4" CELLPADDING="2">
          <TR STYLE="font-weight:bold; font-size:18">
            <TD>Name (Sorted Alphabetically)</TD>
          </TR>
          <xsl:for-each select="CATALOG/PLANT" order-by="+ NAME/COMMON">
            <TR>
              <xsl:apply-templates/>
            </TR>
          </xsl:for-each>
        </TABLE>
      </BODY>
    </HTML>
  </xsl:template>

  <xsl:template match="NAME">
    <TD STYLE="font-style:italic; font-size:20">
      <xsl:value-of select="COMMON"/>
    </TD>
  </xsl:template>
</xsl:stylesheet>
```

Code Listing 8-11.

Notice that the syntax of the *order-by* criteria includes a plus sign (+) in front of the actual element name. This indicates how the sort should occur. Use a plus sign (+) to sort in ascending order, and use a minus sign (−) to sort in descending order. The result is shown in Figure 8-5.

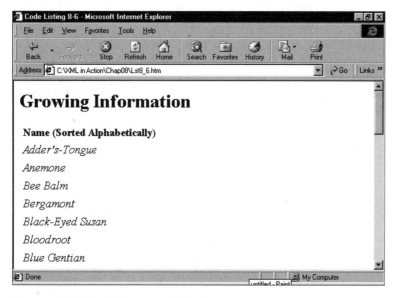

Figure 8-5. *Using XSL to sort XML data.*

USING ELEMENT VALUES IN A QUERY

In addition to sorting data with XSL, you can filter XML elements by the data they contain, which allows for precise output based on the data that is desired. *Element value queries* can be built using standard operators such as the following:

- equal (*EQ* or =)
- not equal (*NE* or *!=*)
- less than (*&LT&*)
- greater than (*&GT&*)

This type of query is shown in Code Listing 8-12 (Chap08\Lst8_12.xsl on the companion CD). Here the style sheet template contains a query that filters for Name elements where the Common element contains the value *Bloodroot*.

```
<?xml version="1.0"?>
<xsl:stylesheet xmlns:xsl="uri:xsl">
  <xsl:template match="/">
```

Code Listing 8-12.

```
<HTML>
  <BODY>
    <H1>Plant Selection</H1>
    <TABLE CELLSPACING="4" CELLPADDING="2">
      <TR STYLE="font-weight:bold; font-size:18">
        <TD>Name</TD>
      </TR>
      <xsl:for-each select="CATALOG/PLANT" order-by="+ NAME/COMMON">
        <TR>
          <xsl:apply-templates/>
        </TR>
      </xsl:for-each>
    </TABLE>
  </BODY>
</HTML>
  </xsl:template>

<xsl:template match="NAME[COMMON='Bloodroot']">
  <TD STYLE="font-style:italic; font-size:20">
    <xsl:value-of select="COMMON"/>
  </TD>
</xsl:template>
</xsl:stylesheet>
```

When the style sheet is processed, only the data that matches the query is output. The result is shown below.

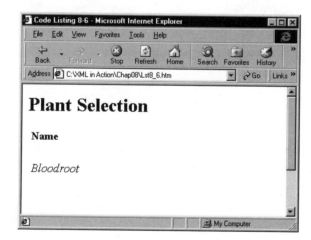

USING ATTRIBUTE VALUES IN A QUERY

In addition to element values, you can use attribute values as the criteria for queries. Attribute values work in the same way as element values, except that the attribute name must be preceded by the @ symbol. Code Listing 8-13 (Chap08\Lst8_13.xsl on the companion CD) queries for Plant elements that contain *BESTSELLER* attributes with the value *yes*.

```
<?xml version="1.0"?>
<xsl:stylesheet xmlns:xsl="uri:xsl">
  <xsl:template match="/">
    <HTML>
      <BODY>
        <H1>Best Sellers</H1>
        <TABLE CELLSPACING="4" CELLPADDING="2">
          <TR STYLE="font-weight:bold; font-size:18">
            <TD>Name (Sorted Alphabetically)</TD>
          </TR>
          <xsl:for-each select="CATALOG/PLANT[@BESTSELLER='yes']"
            order-by="+ NAME/COMMON">
            <TR>
              <xsl:apply-templates/>
            </TR>
          </xsl:for-each>
        </TABLE>
      </BODY>
    </HTML>
  </xsl:template>

<xsl:template match="NAME">
  <TD STYLE="font-style:italic; font-size:20">
    <xsl:value-of select="COMMON"/>
  </TD>
</xsl:template>
</xsl:stylesheet>
```

Code Listing 8-13.

In this code listing, only the elements that match the attribute criteria are output, regardless of any element data. This listing could also be written to check just for the existence of an attribute and ignore any associated value. For example, if we change the query in the above example to this,

```
<xsl:for-each select="CATALOG/PLANT[@BESTSELLER]"
    order-by="+ NAME/COMMON">
```

the output is a much longer list because the query returns any element that contains the *BESTSELLER* attribute.

The results from Code Listing 8-13 are shown here.

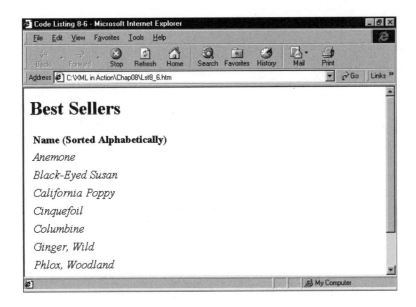

QUERYING USING CONDITIONAL STATEMENTS

In addition to sorting and filtering in XSL, you can perform conditional tests on data using the xsl:if, xsl:choose, xsl:when, and xsl:otherwise elements.

USING xsl:if   The xsl:if element is combined with the *match* attribute to allow for conditional testing and subpatterns. The *match* attribute accepts an XSL Patterns query as a value. To demonstrate this, Code Listing 8-13 has been modified to test for the existence of the *BESTSELLER* attribute. The new style sheet is shown in Code Listing 8-14 (Chap08\Lst8_14.xsl on the companion CD).

```
<?xml version="1.0"?>
<xsl:stylesheet xmlns:xsl="uri:xsl">
  <xsl:template match="/">
    <HTML>
      <BODY>
        <H1>Bestsellers</H1>
        <TABLE CELLSPACING="4" CELLPADDING="2">
          <TR STYLE="font-weight:bold; font-size:18">
            <TD>Name (Sorted Alphabetically)</TD>
          </TR>
          <xsl:for-each select="CATALOG/PLANT" order-by="+ NAME/COMMON">
            <xsl:if match=".[@BESTSELLER]">
              <TR>
                <xsl:apply-templates/>
              </TR>
```

Code Listing 8-14.

(continued)

```
                </xsl:if>
            </xsl:for-each>
         </TABLE>
      </BODY>
   </HTML>
 </xsl:template>

 <xsl:template match="NAME">
   <TD STYLE="font-style:italic; font-size:20">
     <xsl:value-of select="COMMON"/>
   </TD>
 </xsl:template>
</xsl:stylesheet>
```

USING xsl:choose   You can test for multiple conditions and control output based on the result using the xsl:choose element. You can combine this element with the xsl:when and xsl:otherwise elements to set up conditional branching that is similar to the if-then-else statement in some programming languages. Using this type of branching allows authors to set up sophisticated, data-driven style sheets that provide output based on the data being processed.

Code Listing 8-15 (Chap08\Lst8_15.xsl on the companion CD) demonstrates the use of *xsl:choose* to modify the output element when the *BESTSELLER* attribute is equal to *yes*.

```
<?xml version="1.0"?>
<xsl:stylesheet xmlns:xsl="uri:xsl">
  <xsl:template match="/">
    <HTML>
      <BODY>
        <H1>Bestsellers</H1>
        <TABLE CELLSPACING="4" CELLPADDING="2">
          <TR STYLE="font-weight:bold; font-size:18">
            <TD>Name (Sorted Alphabetically)</TD>
          </TR>
          <xsl:for-each select="CATALOG/PLANT" order-by="+ NAME/COMMON">
            <xsl:choose>
              <xsl:when match=".[@BESTSELLER='yes']">
                <TR BGCOLOR="#CC0000"><xsl:apply-templates/></TR>
              </xsl:when>
              <xsl:otherwise>
                <TR><xsl:apply-templates/></TR>
              </xsl:otherwise>
            </xsl:choose>
          </xsl:for-each>
```

Code Listing 8-15.

PART 3 PUTTING XML TO WORK

```
          </TABLE>
        </BODY>
      </HTML>
    </xsl:template>

    <xsl:template match="NAME">
      <TD STYLE="font-style:italic; font-size:20">
        <xsl:value-of select="COMMON"/>
      </TD>
    </xsl:template>
  </xsl:stylesheet>
```

Scripting in XSL

As with other XML technologies, XSL supports the use of scripting languages to allow authors to go beyond the native functionality. XSL is not tied to any particular scripting language and is designed to be scripting language neutral. The language is specified by assigning the name of the scripting language to the *language* attribute, which is similar to how language specification occurs in HTML. Several elements in XSL support the *language* attribute, including xsl:stylesheet, xsl:script, xsl:template, and xsl:eval. If no value is specified, the attribute default is *JavaScript*.

Code Listing 8-16 (Chap08\Lst8_16.xsl on the companion CD) includes a script function that generates a random number from 1 to 10. The function is called from the template in an xsl:eval element, and the result is included in the output, shown below:

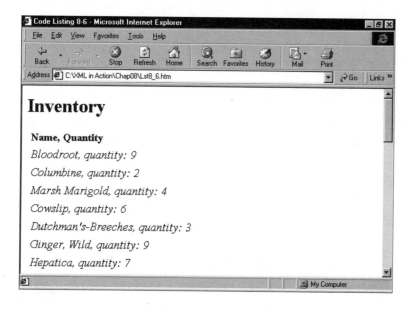

```
<?xml version="1.0"?>
<xsl:stylesheet xmlns:xsl="uri:xsl">
  <xsl:template match="/">
    <HTML>
      <BODY>
        <H1>Inventory</H1>
        <TABLE CELLSPACING="4" CELLPADDING="2">
          <TR STYLE="font-weight:bold; font-size:18">
            <TD>Name, Quantity</TD>
          </TR>
          <xsl:for-each select="CATALOG/PLANT">
            <TR>
              <xsl:apply-templates/>
            </TR>
          </xsl:for-each>
        </TABLE>
      </BODY>
    </HTML>
  </xsl:template>

  <xsl:script language="JavaScript">
    function numCalc()
      {
      rndNum = (Math.round(Math.random() * 9) + 1);
      return rndNum;
      }
  </xsl:script>

  <xsl:template match="NAME">
    <TD STYLE="font-style:italic; font-size:20">
      <xsl:value-of select="COMMON"/>,
        quantity:
        <xsl:eval language="JavaScript">
          numCalc();
        </xsl:eval>
    </TD>
  </xsl:template>
</xsl:stylesheet>
```

Code Listing 8-16.

NOTE

Scripting languages typically allow the use of global variables. Scripts can change the value of these variables or address objects through global variables. Due to the nature of how XSL works with style sheets and renders data, the use of global variables and other constructs that produce "side effects" were restricted in XSL.

Script code can also be directly included in the xsl:eval element, as opposed to being accessed via a function call. For example, the following template is equivalent to the one used previously.

```
<xsl:template match="NAME">
  <TD STYLE="font-style:italic; font-size:20">
    <xsl:value-of select="COMMON"/>,
      quantity:
      <xsl:eval language="JavaScript">
        rndNum = (Math.round(Math.random() * 9) + 1);
      </xsl:eval>
  </TD>
</xsl:template>
```

Script code can be used just as it would in other Web environments, such as HTML. Since XSL is language neutral, you can use a language that is familiar to do your scripting.

XSL Elements

Throughout this chapter, we have used several XSL elements. XSL elements act like commands, telling the XSL processor what to do with the data. Below is a complete list of the XSL elements currently supported and a description of what they do.

XSL Element	Description
xsl:apply-templates	Directs the XSL processor to find the correct template to apply based on the specified pattern.
xsl:attribute	Generates an attribute node and applies it to the output element.
xsl:cdata	Outputs a *CDATA* section in the output.
xsl:choose	Allows for conditional testing. This element is used in conjunction with the *xsl:otherwise* and *xsl:when* elements.
xsl:comment	Creates a comment in the output structure.
xsl:copy	Makes a copy of the target node from the source to include in the output.
xsl:define-template-set	Defines a set of templates at a specific level of scope.
xsl:element	Generates an element in the output with the specified name.
xsl:entity-ref	Generates an entity reference in the output with the specified name.
xsl:eval	Evaluates a string of text, usually script code.
xsl:for-each	Applies the same template to multiple document nodes.
xsl:if	Allows for conditional tests in a template.

(continued)

XSL Element	Description
xsl:node-name	Inserts the name of the current node into the output as a text string.
xsl:otherwise	Provides for conditional testing. This element is used in conjunction with the *xsl:choose* and *xsl:when* elements.
xsl:pi	Generates a processing instruction in the output.
xsl:script	Defines global variable declarations and functions.
xsl:stylesheet	Defines the set of templates that are to be applied to the source document tree to generate the output document.
xsl:template	Defines a template for output based on a specific pattern.
xsl:value-of	Evaluates an XSL pattern specified in the *select* attribute and returns the value of the identified node as text, which is then inserted into the template.
xsl:when	Provides for conditional testing. This element is used in conjunction with the *xsl:choose* and *xsl:otherwise* elements.

XSL Methods

In addition to the XSL elements described above, XSL comes with some built-in methods. These methods can be called from the xsl:eval element as well as from regular script code. For example, the *formatIndex* method could be used as shown below:

```
<xsl:template match="NAME">
  <TD STYLE="font-style:italic; font-size:20">
    <xsl:value-of select="COMMON"/>,
      item number:
    <xsl:eval>
        formatIndex(childNumber(this), "1")
    </xsl:eval>
  </TD>
</xsl:template>
```

The table below describes the currently supported built-in methods. These and other methods will be discussed further in Chapter 9.

XSL Method	Description
absoluteChildNumber	Returns the number of the specified node relative to all its siblings.
ancestorChildNumber	Returns the number of the nearest ancestor of a node with the specified name.
childNumber	Returns the number of the node relative to siblings of the same name.

XSL Method	Description
depth	For the specified node, returns the hierarchical depth within the document tree.
elementIndexList	Returns an array of child numbers for the specified node and for all parent nodes. This is recursive up to the root node.
formatDate	Formats the date provided using the specified formatting options.
formatIndex	Formats the integer provided using the specified numerical system.
formatNumber	Formats the number provided using the specified format.
formatTime	Formats the time provided using the specified formatting options.
uniqueID	Returns the unique identifier for the specified node.

Built-In Templates

In XSL, every element *must* have a template so that the document can be processed properly. In fact, if the processor tried to process an element without a template, an error would result and the remainder of the document processing would be halted. In our examples, we did not explicitly specify a template for every element, and since the documents seemed to be getting processed, something must have been going on behind the scenes. That something is the *built-in template*. Basically, built-in templates act as a safety net for your code. They assure that your document will be processed even if templates are missing or empty.

When the processor recognizes that an element does not have a template, it uses a built-in default template for that element. The default template simply targets the element in question and specifies no formatting for it. The default element template is shown below:

```
<xsl:template>
  <xsl:apply-templates/>
</xsl:template>
```

Conflicts

You might have noticed that it could be possible to create a conflict, by which two templates should act on the same data. XSL has a built-in conflict resolution mechanism known as the *specificity test*. Using specificity for conflict resolution involves testing the conflicting patterns and then using the more specific pattern. For example, examine the two templates below:

```
<xsl:template match="NAME">
  <TD STYLE="font-style:italic; font-size:10">
    <xsl:value-of select="COMMON"/>
  </TD>
</xsl:template>
```

(continued)

```
<xsl:template match="PLANT/NAME">
  <TD STYLE="font-weight:bold; font-style:italic; font-size:20">
    <xsl:value-of select="COMMON"/>
  </TD>
</xsl:template>
```

In this case, the second template would "win" because it is more specific in how it determines the target element, in this case *PLANT/NAME* as opposed to just *NAME* used in the first template. While the XSL processor does this work automatically, it is useful to know how conflict resolution works in case style sheets are not acting in ways that you would expect.

Part 4
Advanced Topics

Chapter 9
Addressing Data
with XSL Patterns

The value of using XML as a data source in applications is entirely dependent on the ability of the application, and ultimately the user, to access that data. So far we have looked at three ways to access data in an XML document. The first way is to walk the XML document tree and pull out information as we come across what we are looking for. This method, while obvious and straightforward to use, requires relatively complex coding and can be a big drain on performance in complex documents.

The second method is to use the XML Data Source Object (DSO) to populate a table with XML data. While this method provides more flexibility, it can be an all-or-nothing approach, including much more data than might be desired. Also, the DSO does not afford a high degree of flexibility when it comes to formatting the data.

We also looked at using XSL to apply rules to a document that describe how the data should be presented. While the document can be filtered and rearranged with XSL, we only scratched the surface of how XSL can be used for pinpointing specific data in a document or in a series of documents.

Where all three of these methods fall short is in their inability to address data by using specific criteria, similar to the way that data is addressed with a database query language such as Structured Query Language (SQL). XSL Patterns (an extension of XSL) solves this and other problems with a specific syntax that's built around filtering and addressing data in an XML document. In this chapter, you will learn what XSL Patterns is, find out why XSL Patterns was created, understand the basic syntax and structure of XSL Patterns, and look at examples of how to use XSL Patterns with XML documents. Finally, we will look at some specifics of the language syntax.

> **NOTE**
>
> XSL Patterns is a version of Extensible Query Language (XQL). As of this writing, XQL is still in the proposal stage with the World Wide Web Consortium (W3C). XSL Patterns is how XQL is implemented in Microsoft Internet Explorer 5. Because of this, some areas of the final XQL specification might differ from the version of XSL Patterns used to write this chapter.

What Is XSL Patterns?

Because XML is about data, and data is useful only if it is available, XSL Patterns was created to make XML document data more accessible. XSL Patterns is a general purpose language that is suited to many different applications. It was created to solve several types of problems. Some of these include:

- Performing queries within an XML document

- Performing queries across a collection of documents

- Addressing segments of data within a document or across documents

- Querying within XSL style sheets

Some Goals of XSL Patterns

To solve the problems identified above, the creators of XSL Patterns had a rather lengthy list of goals driving the process of developing the language. While all of the goals are not listed here, some of the more notable ones appear below to give you the "flavor" of how the language was developed:

- XSL Patterns shall be easily parsed.

- XSL Patterns shall be expressed in strings that can fit naturally in URLs.

- XSL Patterns shall be able to specify any path that can occur in an XML document and any set of conditions for the nodes in the path.

- XSL Patterns shall be able to uniquely identify any node in an XML document.

- XSL Patterns queries are declarative, not procedural. They say what should be found, not how it should be found. (This is important because a query optimizer must be free to use indexes or other structures to find results efficiently.)

- XSL Patterns query syntax is language-independent and does not imply use of a particular implementation language in the query engine.

- XSL Patterns query conditions can be evaluated at any level of a document and are not expected to navigate from the root of a document (which would make querying inefficient by requiring navigation).

- XSL Patterns query conditions should be allowed for any part of a document. Query conditions can be combined to indicate hierarchy or references.

- XSL Patterns queries return results in document order with no repeats of nodes.

One especially noteworthy goal is *XSL Patterns shall be expressed in strings that can fit naturally in URLs*. This goal was a big factor in creating the actual syntax of the XSL Patterns language. As you will see, a query looks similar to a path that you would type to locate a file. In fact, the idea is that a query should specify a "path" within a document. Because the form of XSL Patterns expressions was modeled after the URL syntax, it should be familiar to anyone who has used file paths or World Wide Web addresses.

What, Not How

Just like XSL, XSL Patterns is a declarative, not a procedural, language. That is, XSL Patterns queries specify *what* should be found in an XML document, not *how* to find it. This provides the application with much more flexibility to determine the most efficient method to use to find a piece of data.

> **NOTE**
>
> You might notice that the declarative nature of XSL Patterns follows the same philosophy of XML itself. XML is a declarative language, in that it indicates what the data *is* but does not specify how it should *look* in a document. XSL Patterns, like XML, is a general language that can be used in many different ways, depending on the application.

Let's look at a brief example of an XSL Patterns query. Suppose we want to find all the Chapter elements within the Book element. The XSL Patterns query might look like this:

```
BOOK/CHAPTER
```

That's really all there is to this query! You will notice that the format of the query, in addition to being very simple, looks similar to a file path or an Internet address in that the address elements are separated by a forward slash (/). You will also notice that the query simply identifies what is to be found. Nothing in this query specifies *how* the data is to be found. It is up to the processing application to determine the best way to find the data based on the parameters in the query.

WHAT GETS RETURNED?

The next logical question you might have after thinking about the query is, "What kind of result will I get?" The result of an XSL Patterns query will be a set of nodes from the XML document or documents on which the query was performed. And not only will XML document nodes be returned, but the relationships among those nodes will remain intact. This is important for you to know: instead of getting back just raw data, XSL Patterns returns full XML tree data that can be worked with just as you would with any other XML data.

The XSL Patterns Advantage

Before we jump in to see how XSL Patterns works, let's take a practical look at why XSL Patterns is a better solution for getting at XML data. If you have been following the examples in this book, you might have noticed that we have been working with small XML documents and that we are using them to demonstrate specific features. This is, of course, due to the size and other limitations of a book format, but in the real world, your documents will not always be so small and targeted. Let's look at some sample code that we worked with earlier to see how learning and reality can sometimes conflict and to see how XSL Patterns helps solve the problem. Recall our example from Chapter 4, in which we used an HTML file to display an XML email file. The code for the two files is reproduced here.

In Code Listing 9-1 is the Lst4_1.xml file (also included as Chap09\Lst9_1.xml on the companion CD):

```xml
<?xml version="1.0"?>

<!DOCTYPE EMAIL [
  <!ELEMENT EMAIL (TO, FROM, CC, SUBJECT, BODY)>
  <!ELEMENT TO (#PCDATA)>
  <!ELEMENT FROM (#PCDATA)>
  <!ELEMENT CC (#PCDATA)>
  <!ELEMENT SUBJECT (#PCDATA)>
  <!ELEMENT BODY (#PCDATA)>
]>

<EMAIL>
  <TO>Jodie@msn.com</TO>
  <FROM>Bill@msn.com</FROM>
  <CC>Philip@msn.com</CC>
  <SUBJECT>My First DTD</SUBJECT>
  <BODY>Hello, World!</BODY>
</EMAIL>
```

Code Listing 9-1.

And here is the Lst4_1.htm file:

```html
<!DOCTYPE HTML PUBLIC "-//W3C//DTD HTML 3.2 Final//EN">
<HTML>

  <HEAD>

    <SCRIPT LANGUAGE="JavaScript" FOR=window EVENT=onload>
      loadDoc();
    </SCRIPT>

    <SCRIPT LANGUAGE="JavaScript">
      var xmlDoc = new ActiveXObject("microsoft.xmldom");
      xmlDoc.load("Lst4_1.xml");

      function loadDoc()
        {
        if (xmlDoc.readyState == "4")
          start();
        else
          window.setTimeout("loadDoc()", 4000);
        }
```

(continued)

```
    function start()
      {
      var rootElem = xmlDoc.documentElement;
      var rootLength = rootElem.childNodes.length;

      for (cl=0; cl<rootLength; cl++)
        {
        currNode = rootElem.childNodes.item(cl);
        switch (currNode.nodeName)
          {
          case "TO":
            todata.innerText=currNode.text;
            break;
          case "FROM":
            fromdata.innerText=currNode.text;
            break;
          case "CC":
            ccdata.innerText=currNode.text;
            break;
          case "SUBJECT":
            subjectdata.innerText=currNode.text;
            break;
          case "BODY":
            bodydata.innerText=currNode.text;
            break;
          }
        }
      }
  </SCRIPT>

  <TITLE>Untitled</TITLE>
</HEAD>

<BODY>
  <DIV ID="to" STYLE="font-weight:bold;font-size:16">
    To:
    <SPAN ID="todata" STYLE="font-weight:normal"></SPAN>
  </DIV>
  <BR>

  <DIV ID="from" STYLE="font-weight:bold;font-size:16">
    From:
    <SPAN ID="fromdata" STYLE="font-weight:normal"></SPAN>
  </DIV>
  <BR>
```

```
<DIV ID="cc" STYLE="font-weight:bold;font-size:16">
  Cc:
  <SPAN ID="ccdata" STYLE="font-weight:normal"></SPAN>
</DIV>
<BR>

<DIV ID="subject" STYLE="font-weight:bold;font-size:16">
  Subject:
  <SPAN ID="subjectdata" STYLE="font-weight:normal"></SPAN>
</DIV>
<BR>

<HR>
<SPAN ID="bodydata" STYLE="font-weight:normal"></SPAN>
<P>
</BODY>

</HTML>
```

To make this example work, we had to know a lot about the XML file and to make some assumptions about what data would be there. Let's take a closer look at the code and examine some of these assumptions.

The *start* function gathers the data from the nodes in the XML document and puts that data into specific elements in the HTML document. To do this, the function walks every node in the tree, one by one, and determines whether the node contains any needed data. Basically, the code goes to every node in the document tree, asking, "Do you contain data I want?" Whenever the answer is "Yes," it grabs the data and stores it in an HTML element. To enable our code to walk through the document tree and pull out the data we want, we have to know the following:

◆ The kind of data each node contains

◆ The names of the nodes so that they can be accessed directly

◆ That the data actually applies (or not) to our application

And this document contains only one level in its document tree! While this approach might be fine for small documents like the one in our example, it could involve a lot of complicated code for large documents.

Suppose that we could just tell the XML processor what we wanted and it would return the appropriate data? Although we would still need to know some information about the document and its structure, we would not need to walk the entire tree looking for the data. Using XSL Patterns, we can do this, and this ability is one of the main advantages of XSL Patterns. To show you how XSL Patterns dramatically changes the process, let's rewrite the code using XSL Patterns queries to pull the data from the tree. The XML file remains unchanged. The new HTML page is shown in Code Listing 9-2 (Chap09\Lst9_2.htm on the companion CD).

```
<!DOCTYPE HTML PUBLIC "-//W3C//DTD HTML 3.2 Final//EN">
<HTML>

  <HEAD>
    <SCRIPT LANGUAGE="JavaScript" FOR=window EVENT=onload>
      loadDoc();
    </SCRIPT>

    <SCRIPT LANGUAGE="JavaScript">
      var xmlDoc = new ActiveXObject("microsoft.xmldom");
      xmlDoc.load("Lst9_1.xml");

      function loadDoc()
        {
        if (xmlDoc.readyState == "4")
          start();
        else
          window.setTimeout("loadDoc()", 4000);
        }

      function start()
        {
        todata.innerText =
          xmlDoc.selectSingleNode("EMAIL/TO").text;
        fromdata.innerText =
          xmlDoc.selectSingleNode("EMAIL/FROM").text;
        ccdata.innerText =
          xmlDoc.selectSingleNode("EMAIL/CC").text;
        subjectdata.innerText =
          xmlDoc.selectSingleNode("EMAIL/SUBJECT").text;
        bodydata.innerText =
          xmlDoc.selectSingleNode("EMAIL/BODY").text;
        }
    </SCRIPT>

    <TITLE>The First XSL Patterns Example</TITLE>
  </HEAD>

<BODY>
  <DIV ID="to" STYLE="font-weight:bold;font-size:16">
    To:
    <SPAN ID="todata" STYLE="font-weight:normal"></SPAN>
  </DIV>
  <BR>
```

Code Listing 9-2.

```
<DIV ID="from" STYLE="font-weight:bold;font-size:16">
  From:
  <SPAN ID="fromdata" STYLE="font-weight:normal"></SPAN>
</DIV>
<BR>

<DIV ID="cc" STYLE="font-weight:bold;font-size:16">
  Cc:
  <SPAN ID="ccdata" STYLE="font-weight:normal"></SPAN>
</DIV>
<BR>

<DIV ID="from" STYLE="font-weight:bold;font-size:16">
  Subject:
  <SPAN ID="subjectdata" STYLE="font-weight:normal"></SPAN>
</DIV>
<BR>

<HR>
<SPAN ID="bodydata" STYLE="font-weight:normal"></SPAN><P>
</BODY>

</HTML>
```

In the modified code above, the *start* function addresses the desired node by specifying the node's path within the document structure. The function is saying, "Find the node that matches this pattern, and get the data from it." It doesn't have to walk the entire document tree looking for what we want. This simple example shows some of the power of XSL Patterns. Now let's take a closer look at the language and how it can be used to create more complex queries.

XSL Patterns Language Syntax

As you saw in the last example, XSL Patterns matches data in an XML document to a specified *pattern*, and then it returns the result of the pattern match through the XSL Patterns object model (which will be discussed later). In Code Listing 9-2, each result was the actual data, but as you will see, a result can be much more than just a single node's worth of data. In fact, a result can be a complex collection of nodes that all contain data.

Providing Context

For an XSL Patterns query to work, you must give it the *context* in which it will operate. Context is the node or range of nodes on which the query will be focused. Remember that an XML document is structured in the form of a tree, and XSL Patterns can operate at the root level of that tree or at any branch level. Obviously, the context in which a query operates can vastly change the results.

To see an example of this, let's look back at one of the query patterns used in Code Listing 9-2 beginning on page 202.

```
EMAIL/TO
```

This query specifies that the processor should find the node named TO that's located under the node named EMAIL, which in this case is the root node. The XML document Lst9_1.xml includes only one element with the name TO, so the result is that only one node is returned.

But what if the document had more than one node by that name? Let's build another example using a more complex document. Code Listing 9-3 is a wildflower plant catalog, which is similar to the one we used in previous chapters. This document contains many nodes with the same name so we can see how the query reacts in that scenario.

```
<CATALOG>
  <PLANT>
    <COMMON>Bloodroot</COMMON>
    <BOTANICAL>Sanguinaria canadensis</BOTANICAL>
    <ZONE>4</ZONE>
    <LIGHT>Mostly Shady</LIGHT>
    <PRICE>$7.05</PRICE>
    <AVAILABILITY USONLY="true">02/01/99</AVAILABILITY>
  </PLANT>

  <PLANT>
    <COMMON>Columbine</COMMON>
    <BOTANICAL>Aquilegia canadensis</BOTANICAL>
    <LIGHT>Mostly Shady</LIGHT>
    <PRICE>$3.20</PRICE>
    <AVAILABILITY>04/08/99</AVAILABILITY>
  </PLANT>

  <PLANT>
    <COMMON>Marsh Marigold</COMMON>
    <BOTANICAL>Caltha palustris</BOTANICAL>
    <ZONE>4</ZONE>
    <LIGHT>Mostly Sunny</LIGHT>
    <PRICE>$2.90</PRICE>
    <AVAILABILITY>01/09/99</AVAILABILITY>
  </PLANT>

  <PLANT>
    <COMMON>Cowslip</COMMON>
    <LIGHT>Mostly Shady</LIGHT>
    <PRICE>$3.83</PRICE>
    <AVAILABILITY USONLY="true">05/19/99</AVAILABILITY>
  </PLANT>

  <PLANT>
    <COMMON>Dutchman's-Breeches</COMMON>
```

Code Listing 9-3.

```
      <BOTANICAL>Diecentra cucullaria</BOTANICAL>
      <ZONE>3</ZONE>
      <LIGHT>Mostly Shady</LIGHT>
      <PRICE>$7.63</PRICE>
      <AVAILABILITY>01/09/99</AVAILABILITY>
   </PLANT>

   <PLANT>
      <COMMON>Ginger, Wild</COMMON>
      <BOTANICAL>Asarum canadense</BOTANICAL>
      <ZONE>3</ZONE>
      <LIGHT>Mostly Shady</LIGHT>
      <PRICE>$8.90</PRICE>
      <AVAILABILITY>03/01/99</AVAILABILITY>
   </PLANT>

   <PLANT>
      <COMMON>Hepatica</COMMON>
      <BOTANICAL>Hepatica americana</BOTANICAL>
      <ZONE>4</ZONE>
      <LIGHT>Mostly Shady</LIGHT>
      <PRICE>$7.75</PRICE>
      <AVAILABILITY>12/16/98</AVAILABILITY>
   </PLANT>

   <PLANT>
      <COMMON>Liverleaf</COMMON>
      <BOTANICAL>Hepatica americana</BOTANICAL>
      <ZONE>4</ZONE>
      <LIGHT>Mostly Shady</LIGHT>
      <PRICE>$3.64</PRICE>
      <AVAILABILITY>12/29/98</AVAILABILITY>
   </PLANT>

   <PLANT>
      <COMMON>Jack-In-The-Pulpit</COMMON>
      <BOTANICAL>Arisaema triphyllum</BOTANICAL>
      <ZONE>4</ZONE>
      <LIGHT>Mostly Shady</LIGHT>
      <PRICE>$2.87</PRICE>
      <AVAILABILITY>02/12/99</AVAILABILITY>
   </PLANT>

   <PLANT>
      <COMMON>Mayapple</COMMON>
      <BOTANICAL>Podophyllum peltatum</BOTANICAL>
      <ZONE>3</ZONE>
      <LIGHT>Mostly Shady</LIGHT>
      <PRICE>$3.99</PRICE>
```

(continued)

```
      <AVAILABILITY>02/04/99</AVAILABILITY>
   </PLANT>

   <PLANT>
      <COMMON>Phlox, Woodland</COMMON>
      <BOTANICAL>Phlox divaricata</BOTANICAL>
      <ZONE>3</ZONE>
      <LIGHT>Sun or Shade</LIGHT>
      <PRICE>$8.82</PRICE>
      <AVAILABILITY>05/21/99</AVAILABILITY>
   </PLANT>

   <PLANT>
      <COMMON>Phlox, Blue</COMMON>
      <BOTANICAL>Phlox divaricata</BOTANICAL>
      <ZONE>3</ZONE>
      <LIGHT>Sun or Shade</LIGHT>
      <PRICE>$9.65</PRICE>
      <AVAILABILITY>02/11/99</AVAILABILITY>
   </PLANT>

   <PLANT>
      <COMMON>Spring-Beauty</COMMON>
      <BOTANICAL>Claytonia Virginica</BOTANICAL>
      <ZONE>7</ZONE>
      <LIGHT>Mostly Shady</LIGHT>
      <PRICE>$3.44</PRICE>
      <AVAILABILITY>03/11/99</AVAILABILITY>
   </PLANT>

   <PLANT>
      <COMMON>Trillium</COMMON>
      <BOTANICAL>Trillium grandiflorum</BOTANICAL>
      <ZONE>5</ZONE>
      <LIGHT>Sun or Shade</LIGHT>
      <PRICE>$8.97</PRICE>
      <AVAILABILITY>05/22/99</AVAILABILITY>
   </PLANT>

   <PLANT>
      <COMMON>Wake Robin</COMMON>
      <BOTANICAL>Trillium grandiflorum</BOTANICAL>
      <ZONE>5</ZONE>
      <LIGHT>Sun or Shade</LIGHT>
      <PRICE>$6.76</PRICE>
      <AVAILABILITY>03/14/99</AVAILABILITY>
   </PLANT>
</CATALOG>
```

Code Listing 9-3 has been condensed to save space. For the full document, refer to Chap09\Lst9_3.xml on the companion CD.

Next we'll need an HTML page to display the results. Code Listing 9-4 (Chap09\ Lst9_4.htm on the companion CD) loads the XML document, performs a query on the data, and then displays the results.

```html
<!DOCTYPE HTML PUBLIC "-//W3C//DTD HTML 3.2 Final//EN">
<HTML>

  <HEAD>
    <SCRIPT LANGUAGE="JavaScript" FOR=window EVENT=onload>
      loadDoc();
    </SCRIPT>

    <SCRIPT LANGUAGE="JavaScript" SRC="Lst9_5.js">
    </SCRIPT>

    <SCRIPT LANGUAGE="JavaScript">
      var rootElem;
      var xmlDoc = new ActiveXObject("microsoft.xmldom");
      xmlDoc.load("Lst9_3.xml");

      function loadDoc()
        {
        if (xmlDoc.readyState == 4)
          start();
        else
          window.setTimeout("loadDoc()", 250);
        }

      function start()
        {
        var qry = xmlDoc.selectNodes("CATALOG");
        var bt;
        var hTank = "";

        for (bt = qry.nextNode(); bt != null; bt = qry.nextNode())
          {
          hTank += buildTree(bt);
          }
        document.body.innerHTML = hTank
        }
    </SCRIPT>
```

Code Listing 9-4.

(continued)

```
    <TITLE>Code Listing 9-4</TITLE>
  </HEAD>

  <BODY>
  </BODY>

</HTML>
```

The output of Code Listing 9-4 is shown in Figure 9-1 on page 210. Since the XSL Patterns object model does not return raw XML code, Code Listing 9-4 uses a linked script to build the XML code from the returned data. This script is shown in Code Listing 9-5, and can also be found in Chap09\Lst9_5.js on the companion CD.

```
function buildTree(qNode, i)
  {
  var output = "<DL CLASS=xml><DD>";

  if (qNode != null)
    {
    type = qNode.nodeType;

    if (type == 6)
      {
      output += "<SPAN>" + qNode.nodeValue + "</SPAN></DD></DL>";
      return output;
      }

    output += "<SPAN CLASS=tag>&lt;" + qNode.nodeName + "</SPAN>";

    var hasChildren = qNode.childNodes.length > 0;
    if (!hasChildren)
      output += "<SPAN CLASS=tag>/&gt;</SPAN>";
    else
      output += "<SPAN CLASS=tag>&gt;</SPAN>";

    if (hasChildren > 0)
      {
      if (isMixed(qNode) > 0)
        {
        output += qNode.text;
        }
      else
        {
        var child;
```

Code Listing 9-5.

```
            var children = qNode.childNodes;
            for (child = children.nextNode();
             child != null;
             child = children.nextNode())
             {
             output += "\n";
             output += buildTree(child, i + 1);
             }
            }
        output += "<SPAN CLASS=tag>&lt;/" + qNode.nodeName +
          "&gt;</SPAN>\n";
        }

    }
    output += "</DD></DL>"
    return output;
  }

function isMixed(qNode,num)
  {
  var child;
  var children = qNode.childNodes;
  for (child = children.nextNode();
    child != null;
    child = children.nextNode())
    {
    var type = child.nodeType;
    if (type == 3 || type == 4 || type == 5)
      {
      return 1;
      }
    }

  return 0;
  }
```

The key line in Code Listing 9-4 is the query found at the beginning of the *start* function:

```
var qry = xmlDoc.selectNodes("CATALOG");
```

To demonstrate how this query works, we'll change the query context and see how the result changes. Notice that the result from Code Listing 9-4 included the entire XML document because the context of the query was CATALOG, which is the root node. Let's modify the query so that it searches one level deeper in the tree, to the PLANT level:

```
var qry = xmlDoc.selectNodes("CATALOG/PLANT");
```

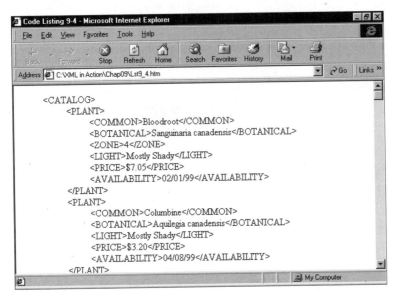

Figure 9-1. *The result of an XSL Patterns query.*

The query now says, "Give me all the data that is contained in the PLANT node when the PLANT node is contained within the CATALOG node." The result is shown in Figure 9-2.

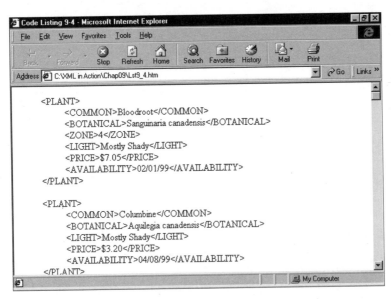

Figure 9-2. *The result of an XSL Patterns query with a limited context.*

Now let's take the query one level deeper and look at the result. Since several different types of nodes are located at this level, we'll just pick one at random.

```
var qry = xmlDoc.selectNodes("CATALOG/PLANT/LIGHT");
```

This query requests only the nodes that match the pattern specified. The result, shown in Figure 9-3, is the set of all nodes named LIGHT that are contained within nodes named PLANT, which are in turn contained within nodes named CATALOG.

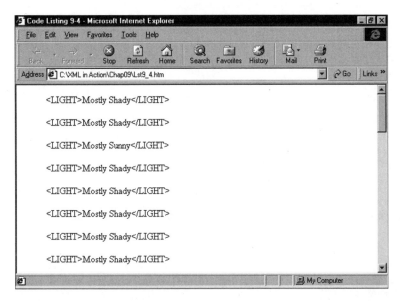

Figure 9-3. *The result of an XSL Patterns query with an even more limited context.*

COLLECTIONS

You might have noticed that the result of a query is a set of nodes that meets the query pattern. That set is called a *collection*. A collection is referenced by the name of a given element. So in the last example above, the query returned a LIGHT collection. The LIGHT collection was part of the PLANT collection, and so on. You can begin to see how a simple change to the query pattern causes dramatic changes to the query result.

So far we have looked at only the most simple kind of query—the node path. But XSL Patterns provides many different context operators that enable you to create more advanced queries.

SELECTION OPERATORS

You have already seen the basic selection operator in action in the last example. The forward slash (/) indicates the hierarchical relationship of a node to the other nodes in the pattern. The node can be identified as either a parent or child node, depending on which side of the slash it appears. For example, in the pattern CATALOG/PLANT, the item on the left side of the slash, CATALOG, is the parent and the item on the right side, PLANT, is the child of CATALOG. So in a query with this pattern, PLANT nodes will be returned only if they have the appropriate relationship to a CATALOG node.

You can use this selection operator in other ways to specify different contexts for a query. For example, you can use a single forward slash (/) prefix at the beginning of a query to specify that the context is relative to the root level of the document. (However, since the root level is implied if no prefix is present, this slash is not always needed.) Here's an example of how it might be used:

```
/CATALOG/PLANT/LIGHT
```

This tells the processor to begin searching for the pattern CATALOG/PLANT/LIGHT at the root level of the document. Since the root level is implied if no prefix exists, the same query could be executed with this pattern:

```
CATALOG/PLANT/LIGHT
```

Another selection operator is the double forward slash (//). This operator specifies *recursive descent*—that is, the query requests every instance in which the pattern that appears to the right of the operator is located below the pattern that appears to the left of the operator. For example, the query CATALOG//LIGHT finds all Light nodes that appear below a Catalog node. The query //LIGHT finds the Light node anywhere in which it appears in the document.

To try this, change the query in Code Listing 9-4 on page 207 to match the query below:

```
var qry = xmlDoc.selectNodes("//LIGHT");
```

When the page is opened, the result (shown in Figure 9-4) looks just like the previous result (shown on page 211 in Figure 9-3), even though the search pattern is different. That is because the LIGHT node exists in only one context in the XML document; we just approached the query in a different way in this case. If LIGHT nodes appeared in other levels of the hierarchy, the new query would have returned all of them, not just the ones in a specific context.

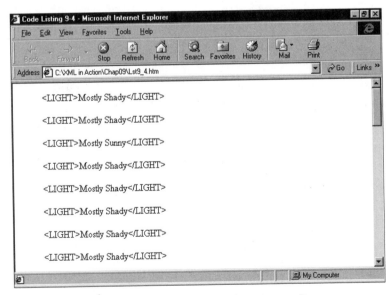

Figure 9-4. *Different queries can produce the same results.*

Two other selection operators are dot forward slash (./) and dot double-forward slash (.//). The ./ operator indicates that the pattern on the right side should be found in the current context, wherever that is. The .// operator indicates that the pattern on the right should be found recursively descending from the current context. Since these two operators are never used alone, they will make more sense later after you see them in use.

THE ALL OPERATOR

The all operator (*) finds all the children within a given context. For example, the query:

```
var qry = xmlDoc.selectNodes("CATALOG/PLANT/*");
```

returns the result shown below.

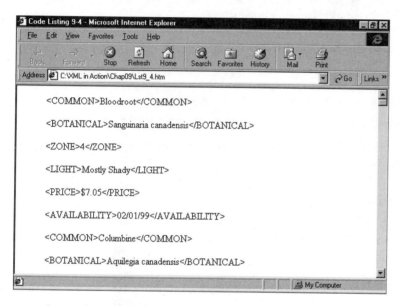

As another example, the pattern CATALOG/*/LIGHT finds all LIGHT nodes that are the grandchildren of the CATALOG node.

THE ATTRIBUTE OPERATOR

The attribute operator (@) identifies an attribute within the specified element. The attribute operator works by placing the @ symbol in front of the desired attribute name. For example, the following query finds all the Availability elements that contain the *USONLY* attribute:

```
var qry = xmlDoc.selectNodes("CATALOG/PLANT/AVAILABILITY/@USONLY");
```

Grouping and Precedence

Sometimes the normal query syntax will not provide enough clarity to allow a pattern match. To address this problem, XSL Patterns allows you to use grouping and subquery operators that have built-in precedence. The grouping operators are the open and close parentheses, (); the subquery operators are the open and close brackets, [].

The order of precedence, from highest to lowest, is as follows:

1. Grouping operators: ()

2. Subquery operators: []

3. Selection operators: /, //, ./, .//

SUBQUERIES

A subquery provides a mechanism to use for constraining a query. You can add a condition to a query pattern by inserting a pattern into the subquery operators. The result is the set of those elements that meet the subquery criteria. For example, the query pattern CATALOG/PLANT[ZONE] states, "Find all the Plant elements that are children of the Catalog element and that contain at least one Zone element."

NOTE

The subquery clause is similar to the SQL WHERE clause. So using that parlance, the query above states, "Find ANY Plant elements that are children of the Catalog element and WHERE the existence of the Zone element is TRUE."

Any number of subqueries can exist at any level of the pattern, and subqueries can be nested. Empty subqueries are not allowed.

Comparing Data

Most powerful database programming languages provide you with the ability to compare one set of data with another. XSL Patterns also provides a comparison capability that allows authors to create sophisticated query expressions.

BOOLEAN EXPRESSIONS (*AND/OR/NOT*)

Boolean expressions can be used within subqueries and follow the form *value $operator$ value*. These three Boolean operators are available:

♦ *and*

♦ *or*

♦ *not*

Let's build a query using some of these operators and combine them with the grouping operators to see how some relatively complex logical expressions can be created in XSL Patterns.

```
var qry = xmlDoc.selectNodes
   ("CATALOG/PLANT[$not$ (ZONE $or$ BOTANICAL) $and$ LIGHT]");
```

This query states, "Find all the Plant elements that are children of the Catalog element and that contain at least one Light element but do not contain Zone or Botanical elements." The result of the query is a single node from our XML document that matches the pattern, as shown below.

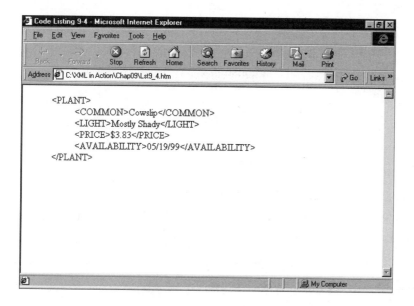

```
<PLANT>
    <COMMON>Cowslip</COMMON>
    <LIGHT>Mostly Shady</LIGHT>
    <PRICE>$3.83</PRICE>
    <AVAILABILITY>05/19/99</AVAILABILITY>
</PLANT>
```

EQUALITY

Some of you have been waiting for this section. You might have noticed that until now, we have not tested for the *value* of any element; we've tested only to determine that an element exists. In many cases, the ability to query a document structure will be truly valuable only if the content of the document can be searched. The equality expressions allow us to test the content of an element against a specified value.

Equality expressions come in four forms:

◆ Equality (*eq* or =)

◆ Case-insensitive equality (*ieq*)

◆ Inequality (*ne* or *!=*)

◆ Case-insensitive inequality (*ine*)

Let's see these expressions in action. The query below finds any Plant element in the document that contains a Light element with the value *Mostly Shady*.

```
var qry = xmlDoc.selectNodes("//PLANT[LIGHT = 'Mostly Shady']");
```

The expression can also be written as:

```
var qry = xmlDoc.selectNodes("//PLANT[LIGHT $eq$ 'Mostly Shady']");
```

String values must be contained inside single quotes.

OTHER COMPARISON OPERATORS (*ALL/ANY*)

The *all* and *any* comparison operators allow searches within a collection that specify how every element in the collection should be evaluated. In other words, search parameters can be applied to all of the elements in the collection or to any of the elements in the collection, depending on the operator used.

The *all* operator specifies that the entire collection will be returned as the result as long as the query pattern matches all the elements in the collection. If no match is found, the result is the empty set. The *all* operator is written like this: *all*.

The query below searches for CATALOG nodes in which all PLANT nodes have a ZONE child node with the value 4.

```
var qry = xmlDoc.selectNodes
    ("//CATALOG[$all$ PLANT/ZONE = '4']");
```

The result of this query is the empty set because not every PLANT node contains a ZONE child node with the value 4, as shown below.

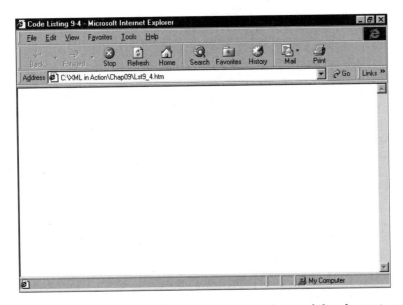

The *any* operator finds a pattern match if any of the elements match the conditions of the query. In other words, the entire collection is returned as the query result if at least one element in the collection matches the query pattern. The *any* operator is written as *any* and is used as shown below.

```
var qry = xmlDoc.selectNodes
    ("//CATALOG[$any$ PLANT/ZONE = '4']");
```

In this example, if any PLANT node contains a ZONE child node with the value 4, the entire collection will be returned as the result. This is shown below.

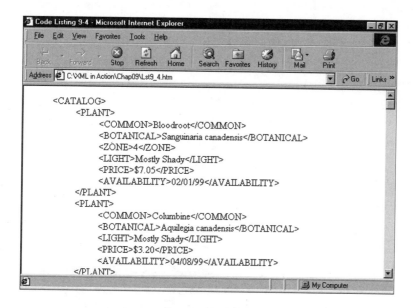

NUMERIC COMPARISONS

While all element and attribute values are strings in an XML document, XSL Patterns does support numeric comparisons, such as *2 < 45*. The list below identifies the numeric operators that are supported in XSL Patterns.

Numeric Operator	Shortcut	Description
lt	<	Less than
ilt		Case-insensitive less than
le	<=	Less than or equal to
ile		Case-insensitive less than or equal to
gt	>	Greater than
igt		Case-insensitive greater than
ge	>=	Greater than or equal to
ige		Case-insensitive greater than or equal to

To compare numeric values, XSL Patterns changes, or casts, text values to numeric types for comparisons where appropriate. Various kinds of comparisons apply, depending on the nature of the comparison value—the value on the right side of the expression.

Type of Comparison Value	Kind of Comparison
string	A string-to-string comparison will take place.
integer	The comparison value will be cast as a long integer.
real	The comparison value will be cast as a double number.

Using Methods

In addition to providing operators for building expressions, XSL Patterns provides functions, or methods, that can be used to manipulate collections or to get information about nodes and elements. Methods take the form *method(arguments)* and are case-sensitive. In code, a method is appended to the context name and an exclamation point, as shown here:

```
context!method(arguments)
```

THE *text* METHOD

Use the *text* method to return the text of a node, without including any document structure. Note that the method returns text to the query, which then uses the text as part of the query pattern. The result of the query is still a node or collection. For example, the query below finds every PLANT node for which *Mostly Sunny* is the text of its LIGHT node.

```
var qry = xmlDoc.selectNodes
    ("//PLANT[LIGHT!text() = 'Mostly Sunny']");
```

The result of this query is the only PLANT node in the document that matches the criteria, as shown below.

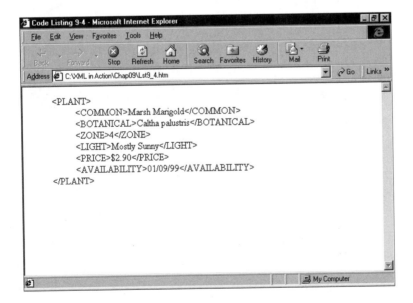

```
<PLANT>
        <COMMON>Marsh Marigold</COMMON>
        <BOTANICAL>Caltha palustris</BOTANICAL>
        <ZONE>4</ZONE>
        <LIGHT>Mostly Sunny</LIGHT>
        <PRICE>$2.90</PRICE>
        <AVAILABILITY>01/09/99</AVAILABILITY>
</PLANT>
```

A *long integer* is an integer that supports numbers from 2,147,483,648 through 2,147,483,647. A double number is a decimal number.

THE *nodeType* METHOD

The *nodeType* method returns a number that indicates the type of node. The table below identifies each different node type and its corresponding number.

Type of Node	Value Returned by *nodeType*
element	1
attribute	2
text	3
cdata	4
entity reference	5
entity	6
processing instruction	7
comment	8
document	9
document type	10
document fragment	11
notation	12

The following example returns a collection of nodes of the type *attribute*:

```
var qry = xmlDoc.selectNodes
   ("//PLANT/AVAILABILITY/@USONLY[nodeType() = '2']");
```

THE *nodeName* METHOD

The *nodeName* method returns the name of the node specified in the context. The query below, for example, returns a collection of nodes with the name PRICE.

```
var qry = xmlDoc.selectNodes("//PLANT /*[nodeName() = 'PRICE']");
```

THE *value* METHOD

Use *value* to retrieve the value of the node indicated in the context. In many cases, this value will be the same as the text returned by the *text* method, but the *value* method will return a type-casted value when casting is supported. The query below returns a collection of nodes in which the value of the Zone element is 4:

```
var qry = xmlDoc.selectNodes("//PLANT[ZONE!value() = 4]");
```

THE *index* METHOD

The *index* method returns the index number of a node in relationship to its parent. Note that 0-based numbering is used, so the first child node will have an index number of 0. The example query below finds the child nodes within PLANT nodes that have an index number of 2.

```
var qry = xmlDoc.selectNodes("//PLANT/*[index() = 2]");
```

The result of the query is shown below.

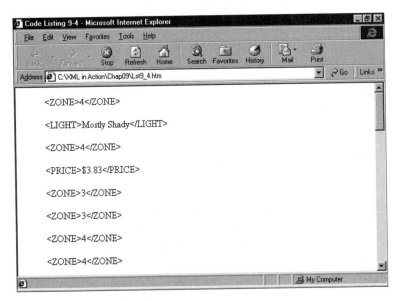

The following query finds the third node within the entire collection of PLANT children:

```
var qry = xmlDoc.selectNodes("(//PLANT/*)[index() = 2]");
```

Finally, this query finds the third child node within the fourth PLANT node:

```
var qry = xmlDoc.selectNodes("//PLANT[index() = 3]/*[index() = 2]");
```

THE *end* METHOD

The *end* method returns *true* for the last element in a collection and *false* otherwise. The following query finds the last PLANT node in the collection of all PLANT nodes in the document:

```
var qry = xmlDoc.selectNodes("//PLANT[end()]");
```

The result of the query is the last PLANT node, as shown here:

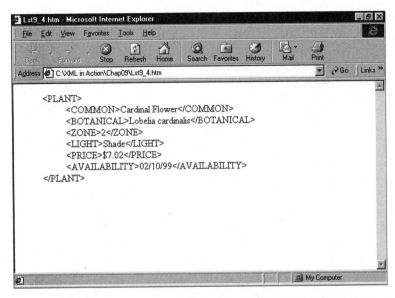

```
<PLANT>
    <COMMON>Cardinal Flower</COMMON>
    <BOTANICAL>Lobelia cardinalis</BOTANICAL>
    <ZONE>2</ZONE>
    <LIGHT>Shade</LIGHT>
    <PRICE>$7.02</PRICE>
    <AVAILABILITY>02/10/99</AVAILABILITY>
</PLANT>
```

In addition to the methods discussed above, XSL Patterns supports other methods, including the built-in XSL methods discussed in Chapter 8. Additional XSL Patterns methods can be categorized as information methods and collection methods. The following three tables identify the complete set of XSL Patterns methods.

XSL Method	Description
absoluteChildNumber	Returns the number of the specified node relative to all its siblings.
ancestorChildNumber	Returns the number of the nearest ancestor of a node with the specified name.
childNumber	Returns the number of the node relative to siblings of the same name.
depth	For the specified node, returns the hierarchical depth within the document tree.
elementIndexList	Returns an array of child numbers for the specified node and for all parent nodes. This is recursive up to the root node.
formatDate	Formats the date provided using the specified formatting options.
formatIndex	Formats the integer provided using the specified numerical system.
formatNumber	Formats the number provided using the specified format.
formatTime	Formats the time provided using the specified formatting options.
uniqueID	Returns the unique identifier for the specified node.

Information Method	Description
date	Casts values to date format.
end	Returns *true* for the last element in a collection and *false* otherwise.
index	Returns the index number of the node relative to the parent.
nodeName	Specifies the tag name of the node, including the namespace prefix.
nodeType	Returns a number to indicate the type of element.
text	Specifies the text contained within an element.
value	Returns a type-cast version of the value of an element.

Collection Method	Description
ancestor	Finds the nearest ancestor matching the pattern. Returns either a single element or *null*.
attribute	Returns the collection of all attributes. If the optional text parameter is provided, it returns only attributes matching that particular text.
comment	Returns a collection of comment nodes.
element	Returns the collection of all element nodes. If the optional text parameter is provided, it returns only child elements matching that particular text.
node	Returns the collection of all nonattribute nodes.
pi	Returns the collection of all processor instruction nodes for this document.
textnode	Returns the collection of all text nodes for the current document.

The XSL Patterns Object Model

For XSL Patterns to be usable in script code, it must include an object model that is accessible to the outside world. Fortunately, the XSL Patterns object model is very simple. In fact, the object model includes only one object and two methods. The XSL Patterns object is the *nodeList* object, and XSL Patterns provides two methods that can be used on the *nodeList* object to execute queries: the *selectNodes* method and the *selectSingleNode* method.

The *nodeList* Object

The XSL Patterns object model is simple because a query always returns an XML *nodeList* object. Because the node list that is returned is an ordinary XML object, the regular XML object model can take over. The node list can be processed just as any other XML data is processed. All the XML object model properties and methods are now available.

The *selectNodes* Method

If you have been following the examples in this chapter, you should be familiar with the *selectNodes* method by now. The *selectNodes* method returns a *nodeList* object that can then be processed for its content. All of the samples in this chapter have processed the results of the queries so that we could see the content. Code Listing 9-6 (Chap09\Lst9_6.htm on the companion CD) displays an alert box, shown in Figure 9-5, with a query result that hasn't been processed for display.

```
<!DOCTYPE HTML PUBLIC "-//W3C//DTD HTML 3.2 Final//EN">
<HTML>

  <HEAD>
    <SCRIPT LANGUAGE="JavaScript" FOR=window EVENT=onload>
      loadDoc();
    </SCRIPT>

    <SCRIPT LANGUAGE="JavaScript" SRC="Lst9_5.js">
    </SCRIPT>

    <SCRIPT LANGUAGE="JavaScript">
      var rootElem;
      var xmlDoc = new ActiveXObject("microsoft.xmldom");
      xmlDoc.load("Lst9_3.xml");

      function loadDoc()
        {
        if (xmlDoc.readyState == 4)
          start();
        else
          window.setTimeout("loadDoc()", 250);
        }

      function start()
        {
        var qry = xmlDoc.selectNodes("CATALOG/PLANT");
        alert(qry);
        }
    </SCRIPT>
```

Code Listing 9-6.

(continued)

```
    <TITLE>Code Listing 9-6</TITLE>
  </HEAD>

  <BODY>
  </BODY>

</HTML>
```

Figure 9-5. *A* nodeList *object is returned from an XSL Patterns query.*

The *selectSingleNode* Method

We looked at this method briefly at the beginning of the chapter. Whereas the *selectNodes* method returns all the nodes that match a given pattern, the *selectSingleNode* method returns only the first node that matches the pattern. If we modify the start function in Code Listing 9-4 to use the *selectSingleNode* method, the result would be just the first matching node instead of a collection of matching nodes:

```
function start()
  {
  var qry = xmlDoc.selectSingleNode("CATALOG/PLANT");
  var hTank = "";
  hTank += buildTree(qry);
  document.body.innerHTML = hTank;
  }
```

More on XSL Patterns

This chapter has covered the basics of working with XSL Patterns. For more information about XQL, visit the W3C Web site at *http://www.w3.org/Style/XSL/Group/1998/09/XQL-proposal.html*. Note that at the time of this writing this is a secure location for W3C members only, but it should be available to the public in the near future.

Chapter 10
XML-Data

ou might notice that the title of this chapter closely resembles the title of Chapter 6, "XML As Data." However, the two chapters are in fact very different. While Chapter 6 provides a high-level view of how XML can be used as a data source for many different applications, this chapter discusses a specific application of XML named *XML-Data*. XML-Data is a language used to create a *schema,* which identifies the structure and constraints of a particular XML document. In this chapter, you will learn what XML-Data is about and why it was created. You'll also learn the basics of creating a document using an XML-Data schema.

The Need for a Schema Language

You'll recall from Chapter 4 that a Document Type Definition, or DTD, is an expression of an XML document structure and a description of the rules that govern the data it contains. You might also remember that the DTD mechanism was carried over into XML from SGML. Many corporate application developers, including Microsoft, believed that the language of the DTD would not be adequate for the needs of current and future applications of XML. As a result, it was proposed by several corporate and educational organizations, including Microsoft, DataChannel, and the University of Edinburgh, that a new mechanism was needed to carry out the same basic tasks accomplished by a DTD—one that also provided more power and flexibility.

The Goals of XML-Data

As with many of the other XML-based languages covered in this book, XML-Data was created with several goals in mind. As mentioned above, XML-Data was developed to help avoid some of the limitations involved in using DTDs. The following sections identify the goals of XML-Data. As you work through the specifics of the language, you will see how XML-Data reaches these goals.

GOAL 1: SPECIAL TOOLS SHOULD NOT BE REQUIRED FOR MAINTAINING SCHEMA DOCUMENTS.   DTDs are written using a special syntax that is meant only for DTDs. Because of this, the ability of XML documents to use DTDs requires not only DTD authors who have the knowledge of that syntax, but special tools (that can read and write DTDs) for every XML authoring tool that is developed. This first goal of XML-Data is to avoid the need for such special tools, and this is accomplished simply by having XML-Data use XML syntax for its language.

GOAL 2: XML AND HTML AUTHORS SHOULD NOT HAVE TO LEARN A NEW SYNTAX TO EXPRESS SCHEMA INFORMATION.   This goal is closely related to Goal 1 in that the schema language should be usable without requiring knowledge of a new language or syntax. Again, this is accomplished by the use of XML syntax.

GOAL 3: SCHEMAS SHOULD BE EXTENSIBLE.   A schema should be flexible enough to be adapted to a specific application without requiring application-specific constraints. In other words, the application should not be required to provide extensibility to the schema. This flexibility is accomplished through an open schema definition syntax, whereby a schema can be specialized by authors adding elements or attributes. The way authors achieve this specialization is covered in more detail later in this chapter.

GOAL 4: THE SCHEMA LANGUAGE SHOULD BE SIMPLE ENOUGH TO ENCOURAGE IMPLEMENTATION IN ALL XML PROCESSORS.   Here again is the theme that a standard must be widely implemented to be used. To that end, this goal is included to help ensure that the XML-Data language is not so prohibitively complex that it will not be implemented by most XML processor developers. This goal can be accomplished by using the XML syntax to define the schema language. Doing so simplifies implementation and eliminates the need for a special processor to parse the schema.

GOAL 5: XML-DATA SHOULD MEET THE NEEDS OF WEB-BASED APPLICATIONS THAT REQUIRE ADDITIONAL DATA VALIDATION BEYOND WHAT CAN BE EXPRESSED IN XML DTDs TODAY (SUCH AS E-COMMERCE APPLICATIONS).   While DTDs can define document structure and rules, the mechanism is limited when defining data types and performing data validation. The XML-Data language defines primitive data types and can express ranges in data values, for example, by allowing the author to define minimum and maximum values. These kinds of features are typically found in relational database languages, such as Structured Query Language (SQL), and most modern programming languages.

GOAL 6: XML-DATA SHOULD MEET THE NEEDS OF WEB-BASED APPLICATIONS THAT REQUIRE STANDARD ENCODINGS TO FACILITATE DOCUMENT INTERCHANGE.   The form that data takes is called its *encoding scheme*. One of XML's features that presents great opportunities is its ability to act as an interchange format for disparate data formats. To help accomplish this, XML-Data defines standard encoding schemes for the data types it supports. For example, a floating point number in XML-Data takes the same standard form that it would take in a programming or database language such as Microsoft Visual Basic or SQL.

GOAL 7: THE SCHEMA LANGUAGE MUST SUPPORT THE ABILITY OF INDIVIDUAL DOCUMENTS TO COMPRISE PARTS DEFINED IN SEVERAL SOURCES.   As you'll recall from Chapter 4, XML documents can comprise other documents or pieces of other documents that are located in different places by using pointers in the DTD. This goal states that XML-Data must provide similar functionality, which is accomplished by the use of namespace support in XML-Data schemas.

GOAL 8: REUSE OF CONTENT MODEL DEFINITIONS SHOULD BE EASIER THAN WHEN USING PARAMETER ENTITIES. Recall again from Chapter 4 that parameter entities provide a "shorthand" for organizing DTDs and help make them more concise. The problem with parameter entities, however, is that they can quickly become complex and difficult to manage. One of the goals of XML-Data is to minimize these problems. This is accomplished by the support of class-based content model inheritance. As you will see, content model inheritance allows authors to reuse content model definitions in a way that is less cumbersome and easier to manage than parameter entities.

GOAL 9: XML-DATA MUST BE UPWARDLY COMPATIBLE WITH XML 1.0. This goal's purpose is to help minimize the problem of "technology churn," in which older technology is outdated as soon as a new implementation or update is available. As stated in Goal 4, the hope is that XML-Data will be widely implemented, aided by the fact that XML-Data uses XML syntax. This goal adds further weight to that idea by requiring that XML-Data be upwardly compatible with XML 1.0.

The XML-Data Schema Language

It is important to note that any XML-Data schema is a well-formed XML document and, as such, might also be a valid XML document. The XML-Data language is based on the XML-Data DTD. A document can be validated if it refers to this DTD, but simply complying with the XML-Data specification will result in well-formed XML, even if no DTD reference is made in the prolog.

> **NOTE**
>
> As of this writing, it has not been decided by any standards body where (or if) the XML-Data DTD will be posted. This will not prevent individual documents from being validated against a schema, however, even though the schema itself is not validated.

Schema Document Structure

In Chapter 3, you learned that a basic XML document is made up of a prolog and a document element. An XML-Data schema document also contains these components. The major difference between the two is that a schema document contains no DTD. Instead, the structure for the document is defined inside a Schema element, which is the document, or root, element in a schema definition. The basic usage is as shown below:

```
<?xml version="1.0"?>
<Schema name="schemaname" xmlns="urn:schemas-microsoft-com:xml-data">
  <!-- Declarations go here -->
  <ElementType name="elementname" content="contenttype"/>
</Schema>
```

> **NOTE**
>
> The Schema element must be derived from the *xml-data* namespace *urn:schemas-microsoft-com:xml-data*. It is not necessary to declare the namespace in the schema prolog.

While it is generally preferred to make the *xml-data* namespace the default namespace, it is not required. However, by making the *xml-data* namespace the default, you can avoid having to prefix all the definitions in a schema document. The schema document below, for example, does not assume that the *xml-data* namespace is the default. Using the prefix declared in the namespace declaration, the following schema document is equivalent to the previous schema example.

```
<?xml version="1.0"?>
<?xml:namespace ns="urn:schemas-microsoft-com:xml-data" prefix="s"?>
<s:Schema name="schemaname">
  <!-- Declarations go here -->
  <s:ElementType name="elementname" content="contenttype"/>
</s:Schema>
```

In this chapter, we will assume that the *xml-data* namespace is the default namespace. However, we must keep in mind that schema declarations can have different scopes. That is, they might come in the form of both top-level declarations and local-level declarations. The *scope* of a declaration identifies where and how the declared item can be used in the schema document.

TOP-LEVEL DECLARATIONS

Top-level declarations include any element types or attribute types declared within the Schema element. Element or attribute types declared at top-level scope can be referenced in the content declaration of other element types in the same schema. For example, in the schema that follows, the element type *name* is declared at the top level and is referenced in the *plant* element type declaration.

```
<Schema name="wildflowers"
  xmlns="urn:schemas-microsoft-com:xml-data">
  <ElementType name="name" content="textonly"/>

  <ElementType name="plant">
    <element type="name"/>
  </ElementType>
</Schema>
```

LOCAL-LEVEL DECLARATIONS

A declaration that appears inside another declaration that is not at the top level is considered local-level in scope. A local-level declaration can be referenced only within the declaration in which it is declared. For example, let's add a local-level attribute declaration to the *plant* element type declaration.

```
<Schema name="wildflowers"
  xmlns="urn:schemas-microsoft-com:xml-data">
  <ElementType name="name" content="textOnly"/>

  <ElementType name="plant">
    <element type="name"/>
    <attribute name="bestseller" values="yes no"/>
  </ElementType>
</Schema>
```

In this example, the attribute *bestseller* can be used only in the *plant* element type declaration.

NOTE

You have probably seen several new concepts in the examples above that we have not discussed before. Don't worry. This brief introduction is included here to give you some context for what comes next.

Element Type Declarations

An element type is declared in an ElementType element. Each element type declaration must include a *name* attribute, which identifies the element type. For example, the element type declaration below declares an element type by the name of *plant*.

```
<ElementType name="plant"/>
```

The type of content that an element can contain can be declared with the *content* attribute. This constrains the element content only to the type specified.

CONTENT TYPE

Each type of element can contain one of four content categories: empty, text only, subelements only, or a mixture of text and subelements. The category is expressed as the value of the *content* attribute in the element type declaration. Here are the possible values:

♦ *empty*—cannot contain any content

♦ *textOnly*—can contain text content only

♦ *eltOnly*—can contain subelements only

♦ *mixed*—can contain a mixture of text and subelements

In the example below, the *plant* element type can contain text content only:

```
<ElementType name="plant" content="textOnly"/>
```

In addition to content constraints, an element type declaration can also specify the pattern in which the elements in the declaration can appear. This is done using the *order* attribute.

CONTENT ORDER

The *order* attribute constrains the pattern for the types of elements declared in an element type declaration. These are the possible values:

♦ *seq*—Elements must appear in the same sequential order as the elements referenced in the element type declaration. This is the default pattern for *eltOnly* content.

♦ *one*—One subelement of the type declared in the element type declaration must appear in the parent element.

- *all*—An element of each type declared in the element type declaration must appear as a subelement, but the subelements can appear in any order.

- *many*—Any of the subelements declared in the element type declaration can appear and in any order. This is the default pattern for *mixed* content.

The example below shows the *plant* element type declaration, containing subelements that must appear in sequential order.

```
<ElementType name="name" content="textOnly"/>
<ElementType name="growth" content="mixed"/>
<ElementType name="salesinfo" content="mixed"/>

<ElementType name="plant" content="eltOnly" order="seq">
  <element type="name"/>
  <element type="growth"/>
  <element type="salesinfo"/>
</ElementType>
```

Note that the content type of the *plant* element was constrained to *eltOnly*. We did not have to explicitly declare the value of the *order* attribute because *seq* is the default content order for *eltOnly* content. The *order* attribute was included for illustrative purposes only.

Element content can be further constrained by grouping element references via the Group element. The Group element supports the *order* attribute with the same values used for the ElementType element. Now let's create a new content model that uses a Group element.

```
<ElementType name="name" content="textOnly"/>
<ElementType name="zone" content="textOnly"/>
<ElementType name="light" content="textOnly"/>
<ElementType name="price" content="textOnly"/>

<ElementType name="plant" content="eltOnly" order="seq">
  <element type="name"/>
  <group order="one">
    <element type="zone"/>
    <element type="light"/>
    <element type="price"/>
  </group>
</ElementType>
```

Here the *plant* element type must contain a name, and then following the name, only one of the elements Zone, Light, or Price. Note that if an order constraint is not declared for the group, the default value will be the order for the enclosing element type declaration. So in the example above, if an order was not specified for the group, the default order value would have been *seq*.

ELEMENT AND GROUP QUANTITIES

As with XML DTDs, constraints can be placed on how many times an element or a group may or may not appear in a document. The *minOccurs* and *maxOccurs* attributes can be specified in Element and Group elements. The *minOccurs* attribute specifies the minimum number of times an element can appear. The *maxOccurs* attribute specifies the maximum number of times an element can appear. Table 10-1 shows the possible value combinations for the *minOccurs* and *maxOccurs* attributes and what they mean.

TABLE 10-1
Meanings of Various Combinations of *minOccurs* and *maxOccurs*

minOccurs	*maxOccurs*	Number of times element or group can appear
1 or unspecified	1 or unspecified	1 (Required)
0	1 or unspecified	0 or 1 (Optional)
greater than 1	greater than n	At least *minOccurs* times, but not more than *maxOccurs* times
greater than 1	less than 1	0
0	"*"	Any number of times
1	"*"	At least once
greater than 0	"*"	At least *minOccurs* times
any value	0	0

The default value for both the *minOccurs* and *maxOccurs* attributes is 1. That is, unless otherwise specified, elements must appear exactly once inside any given element type. Let's look at an example of how this might work. (Here the group must appear at least once, but it can appear more often than that.)

```
<ElementType name="name" content="textOnly"/>
<ElementType name="zone" content="textOnly"/>
<ElementType name="light" content="textOnly"/>
<ElementType name="price" content="textOnly"/>

<ElementType name="plant" content="eltOnly" order="seq">
  <element type="name"/>
  <group minOccurs="1" maxOccurs="*" order="one">
    <element type="zone"/>
    <element type="light"/>
    <element type="price"/>
  </group>
</ElementType>
```

Attribute Type Declarations

An attribute type is declared in an AttributeType element. XML-Data supports the same attribute types that are available in the XML 1.0 DTD. XML-Data also supports other data types that are more like those found in programming or database languages—as you'll see below.

AttributeType ELEMENTS

As with the ElementType element, each AttributeType element must specify a name. The example below declares an attribute type named *bestseller*.

```
<AttributeType name="bestseller"/>
```

Attribute type declarations are made at the top level, independent of element type declarations. They can then be referenced in any element type declaration that the author wants. For example, we'll use our *bestseller* attribute in an element type declaration named *plant*.

```
<AttributeType name="bestseller"/>
<ElementType name="plant">
  <attribute type="bestseller"/>
</ElementType>
```

In this example, the attribute can now appear as part of the Plant element in a document.

DEFAULT VALUES

An attribute type declaration or reference can also include a *default* attribute, which indicates the default attribute value. For example, in the schema below, the *default* attribute is included in the attribute type declaration.

```
<AttributeType name="bestseller" default="yes"/>
<ElementType name="plant">
  <attribute type="bestseller"/>
</ElementType>
```

This specifies that the value of the *default* attribute will apply everywhere that the attribute type is used in an element. If we change the example as shown here

```
<AttributeType name="bestseller"/>
<ElementType name="plant">
  <attribute type="bestseller" default="no"/>
</ElementType>
```

the value of the *default* attribute will apply to the attribute only when it is used inside the Plant element. If *default* attributes are specified in both places, as shown here

```
<AttributeType name="bestseller" default="yes"/>
<ElementType name="plant">
  <attribute type="bestseller" default="no"/>
</ElementType>
```

the *default* attribute specified at the declaration level takes precedence. So, using the above example, the default value *yes* would apply everywhere the *bestseller* attribute is used, except when it appears in the Plant element, where the default value *no* would apply.

required ATTRIBUTE

An attribute type declaration or reference can contain a *required* attribute that identifies whether the attribute must have a value.

```
<ElementType name="plant">
  <attribute type="bestseller" default="no" required="yes"/>
</ElementType>
```

Here the *bestseller* attribute in the Plant element must have a value. Since it is combined with the *default* attribute, *bestseller* will always contain that value if no other is specified.

Data Types

Values for attributes and elements can be constrained as instances of a specific data type. XML-Data supports a wider range of data types than XML's 10 or so data types. In the same way that schemas are defined from the *xml-data* namespace, data types are defined from the *datatypes* namespace. This might appear in the prolog as shown below:

```
<Schema name="wildflowers" xmlns="urn:schemas-microsoft-com:xml-data"
  xmlns:dt="uuid:C2F41010-65B3-11d1-A29F-00AA00C14882">
  <AttributeType name="dateordered"/>
  <ElementType name="plant">
    <attribute type="dateordered"/>
  </ElementType>
</Schema>
```

NOTE

To use the *datatypes* namespace, the namespace must be declared as shown above. We will use the *dt:* prefix in our examples, but you could use any other prefix and get the same result.

type ATTRIBUTE

A data type is designated by referencing it using the *type* attribute from the *datatypes* namespace. In the example below, we specify a data type for the *dateordered* attribute type.

```
<AttributeType name="dateordered" dt:type="dateTime"/>
<ElementType name="plant">
  <attribute type="dateordered"/>
</ElementType>
```

The *dateTime* data type conforms to one of the supported data types for attributes.

ATTRIBUTE DATA TYPES

Table 10-2 shows the supported data types for attributes.

TABLE 10-2
Supported Attribute Data Types

Data Type Name	XML Equivalent	Meaning
id	ID	Attribute value must be a unique identifier. If a document contains more than one *id* attribute with the same value, the processor should generate an error.
string	PCDATA	Only character data can be used in the attribute.
entity	ENTITY	The attribute value must refer to an entity.
entities	ENTITIES	Same as entity, but allows multiple values separated by white space.
idref	IDREF	Value must be a reference to an *id* attribute declared elsewhere in the document.
idrefs	IDREFS	Same as *idref*, but allows multiple values separated by white space.
nmtoken	NMTOKEN	Attribute value is any mixture of name token characters, which must be letters, numbers, periods, dashes, colons, or underscores.
nmtokens	NMTOKENS	Same as *nmtoken*, but allows multiple values separated by white space.
enumeration	ENUMERATION	Attribute value must match one of the included values.
notation	NOTATION	Attribute value must refer to a notation.

ELEMENT DATA TYPES

Table 10-3 identifies some of the more common supported element data types. For a complete list of supported XML-Data element data types, see Appendix B.

TABLE 10-3
Supported Element Data Types

Data Type Name	Meaning
boolean	1 or 0.
string	Character data.
float	A signed, unsigned, whole, or fractional number. Essentially no limit on number of digits. Can contain an exponent.

(continued)

Table 10-3 continued

Data Type Name	Meaning
int	An unsigned whole number, no exponent.
number	A signed, unsigned, whole, or fractional number. Essentially no limit on number of digits. Can contain an exponent.
uri	Universal Resource Identifier.
uuid	Hexadecimal digits that represent octets. Optional hyphens should be ignored.

DATA TYPE CONSTRAINTS

Constraints can be placed on data type values. Use these constraints to help further identify the nature of the data that an element or attribute can contain.

min and max The *min* and *max* attributes define inclusive lower and upper limits for the data in an element or attribute. For example, the attribute below can contain a minimum value of 0 and a maximum value of 50.

```
<attribute type="inventory" dt:type="int" dt:min="0" dt:max="50"/>
```

enumeration At times it might be necessary to enumerate values in an element or attribute. This is defined with the *enumeration* data type and the *values* attribute.

```
<ElementType name="growinginfo">
   <datatype dt:type="enumeration" dt:values="sun partialsun shade"/>
</ElementType>
```

The values to be enumerated are separated by white space.

maxLength The *maxLength* attribute specifies the length of a value in number of characters. In the example below, the value for the Name element can be no more than 30 characters in length.

```
<ElementType name="name" dt:type="string" dt:maxLength="30"/>
<ElementType name="plant">
  <element type="name"/>
</ElementType>
```

Schemas at Work

We have covered a lot of information so far, but we haven't really put it all together. So to follow the message in the title of this book, let's put a schema into action. Since one of the primary purposes of XML-Data is to provide an alternative to DTDs, let's jump way back to Chapter 4, take our sample DTD, and rework it as an XML-Data schema. This should give you a good idea of how DTDs and schemas match up.

The Email Document

If you recall, the sample XML document we used (shown in Code Listing 4-5) was an email message that contained the header information and document content. Reprinted below is the XML code for that document:

```
<?xml version="1.0"?>
<!DOCTYPE EMAIL SYSTEM "Lst4_4.dtd">

<EMAIL LANGUAGE="Western" ENCRYPTED="128" PRIORITY="HIGH">
  <TO>Jodie@msn.com</TO>
  <FROM>&SIGNATURE;@msn.com</FROM>
  <CC>Philip@msn.com</CC>
  <BCC>Naomi@msn.com</BCC>
  <SUBJECT>Sample Document with External DTD</SUBJECT>

  <BODY>
    Hello, this is &SIGNATURE;.
    Take care, -&SIGNATURE;
  </BODY>
</EMAIL>
```

Note that the document contains attributes, internal entities, and a DTD reference in the prolog.

The DTD

One of the things we'll do is replace the DTD with a schema. First let's look again at the DTD from Code Listing 4-4:

```
<?xml version="1.0"?>

<!ELEMENT EMAIL (TO+, FROM, CC*, BCC*, SUBJECT?, BODY?)>
<!ATTLIST EMAIL
  LANGUAGE (Western|Greek|Latin|Universal) "Western"
  ENCRYPTED CDATA #IMPLIED
  PRIORITY (NORMAL|LOW|HIGH) "NORMAL">

<!ELEMENT TO (#PCDATA)>
<!ELEMENT FROM (#PCDATA)>
<!ELEMENT CC (#PCDATA)>

<!ELEMENT BCC (#PCDATA)>
<!ATTLIST BCC
  HIDDEN CDATA #FIXED "TRUE">
```

(continued)

```
<!ELEMENT SUBJECT (#PCDATA)>
<!ELEMENT BODY (#PCDATA)>

<!ENTITY SIGNATURE "Bill">
```

You should note some important items in the DTD that we'll need to incorporate into our schema. In addition to defining the overall structure of an email document, the DTD contains these other specific items.

- The To element is declared with a plus sign (+), indicating that it must appear one or more times.

- The From element is declared without a symbol, indicating that exactly one must appear.

- The Cc and Bcc elements are each declared with an asterisk (*), indicating that the elements are optional, but can appear more than once.

- The Subject and Body elements are each declared with a question mark (?), indicating that the elements are optional but can appear only once.

- The Email and Bcc elements have associated attributes with default values.

- Most elements are declared as text elements (*#PCDATA*).

- The entity *Signature* is declared and contains a value.

These items tell us everything we need to know to make a schema document that meets the criteria needed to match the DTD. The final piece we needed to work with the sample in Chapter 4 was an HTML page used as a template to display the data.

The HTML Page

The HTML page we used to display the XML content is shown below:

```
<!DOCTYPE HTML PUBLIC "-//W3C//DTD HTML 3.2 Final//EN">
<HTML>

  <HEAD>

    <SCRIPT LANGUAGE="JavaScript" FOR=window EVENT=onload>
      loadDoc();
    </SCRIPT>

    <SCRIPT LANGUAGE="JavaScript">
      var xmlDoc = new ActiveXObject("microsoft.xmldom");
      xmlDoc.load("Lst4_5.xml");

      function loadDoc()
        {
```

```
        if (xmlDoc.readyState == "4")
          start();
        else
          window.setTimeout("loadDoc()", 4000);
        }

    function start()
        {
      var rootElem = xmlDoc.documentElement;
      var rootLength = rootElem.childNodes.length;

      for (cl=0; cl<rootLength; cl++)
        {
        currNode = rootElem.childNodes.item(cl);
        switch (currNode.nodeName)
          {
          case "TO":
            todata.innerText=currNode.text;
            break;
          case "FROM":
            fromdata.innerText=currNode.text;
            break;
          case "CC":
            ccdata.innerText=currNode.text;
            break;
          case "SUBJECT":
            subjectdata.innerText=currNode.text;
            break;
          case "BODY":
            bodydata.innerText=currNode.text;
            break;
          }
        }
      }
  </SCRIPT>

  <TITLE>Untitled</TITLE>
</HEAD>

<BODY>
  <DIV ID="to" STYLE="font-weight:bold;font-size:16">
    To:
    <SPAN ID="todata" STYLE="font-weight:normal"></SPAN>
  </DIV>
  <BR>

  <DIV ID="from" STYLE="font-weight:bold;font-size:16">
    From:
    <SPAN ID="fromdata" STYLE="font-weight:normal"></SPAN>
  </DIV>
```

(continued)

```
    <BR>

    <DIV ID="cc" STYLE="font-weight:bold;font-size:16">
      Cc:
      <SPAN ID="ccdata" STYLE="font-weight:normal"></SPAN>
    </DIV>
    <BR>

    <DIV ID="from" STYLE="font-weight:bold;font-size:16">
      Subject:
      <SPAN ID="subjectdata" STYLE="font-weight:normal"></SPAN>
    </DIV>
    <BR>

    <HR>
    <SPAN ID="bodydata" STYLE="font-weight:normal"></SPAN>
    <P>
  </BODY>

</HTML>
```

The resulting displayed document is shown in Figure 10-1.

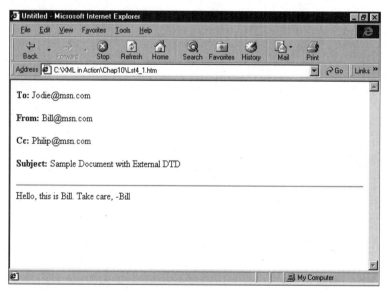

Figure 10-1. *The email document using a DTD and an HTML page.*

The Schema

Now let's create our schema version. First we will create the schema document. Remember that we need to provide the same semantic and structural rules that were used in our DTD. Code Listing 10-1 (Chap10\Lst10_1.xml on the companion CD) shows the schema code.

Entities are not supported in the current version of XML-Data in Microsoft Internet Explorer 5. As such, we will not be able to duplicate the entity functionality in our schema document. Also note that entities are accounted for in the specification submitted to the W3C, and it is expected that entities will be supported in future versions of XML-Data.

```xml
<?xml version="1.0"?>

<Schema name="email" xmlns="urn:schemas-microsoft-com:xml-data"
  xmlns:dt="urn:schemas-microsoft-com:datatypes">

  <AttributeType name="language"
    dt:type="enumeration" dt:values="Western Greek Latin Universal"/>
  <AttributeType name="encrypted"/>
  <AttributeType name="priority"
    dt:type="enumeration" dt:values="NORMAL LOW HIGH"/>
  <AttributeType name="hidden" default="true"/>

  <ElementType name="to" content="textOnly"/>
  <ElementType name="from" content="textOnly"/>
  <ElementType name="cc" content="textOnly"/>

  <ElementType name="bcc" content="mixed">
    <attribute type="hidden" required="yes"/>
  </ElementType>

  <ElementType name="subject" content="textOnly"/>
  <ElementType name="body" content="textOnly"/>

  <ElementType name="email" content="eltOnly">
    <attribute type="language" default="Western"/>
    <attribute type="encrypted"/>
    <attribute type="priority" default="NORMAL"/>
    <element type="to" minOccurs="1" maxOccurs="*"/>
    <element type="from" minOccurs="1" maxOccurs="1"/>
    <element type="cc" minOccurs="0" maxOccurs="*"/>
    <element type="bcc" minOccurs="0" maxOccurs="*"/>
    <element type="subject" minOccurs="0" maxOccurs="1"/>
    <element type="body" minOccurs="0" maxOccurs="1"/>
  </ElementType>

</Schema>
```

Code Listing 10-1.

The schema looks a bit different from the DTD! Fortunately, it is all just XML code, so the syntax and constructs should look familiar. Let's go through our requirements checklist and make sure we have everything covered.

THE TO ELEMENT IS DECLARED SUCH THAT IT MUST APPEAR ONE OR MORE TIMES.
Check. Notice that the To element is referenced with the attributes *minOccurs="1"* and *maxOccurs="*"*, which indicates that the element must appear at least once but there is no limit to how many times it can appear.

THE FROM ELEMENT IS DECLARED SUCH THAT ONLY ONE MUST APPEAR. Okay here. The From element is referenced with the attributes *minOccurs="1"* and *maxOccurs="1"*, which indicates that the element must appear exactly one time.

THE CC AND BCC ELEMENTS ARE DECLARED SUCH THAT THE ELEMENTS ARE OPTIONAL BUT CAN APPEAR MORE THAN ONCE. Got it covered. Both contain the attributes *minOccurs ="0"* and *maxOccurs="*"*, which indicates that they are optional and that there is no limit to how many can appear.

THE SUBJECT AND BODY ELEMENTS ARE DECLARED SUCH THAT THE ELEMENTS ARE OPTIONAL BUT CAN APPEAR NO MORE THAN ONCE. Yes. The *minOccurs="0"* and *maxOccurs="1"* attributes indicate that the elements are optional, but if they do appear, each one can only appear once.

THE EMAIL AND BCC ELEMENTS HAVE ASSOCIATED ATTRIBUTES, WITH DEFAULT VALUES WHERE APPROPRIATE. Check. You can see that the attribute types are declared at the top level of the document and referenced in their respective element type declarations. Note that it is not required to declare the attribute types at the top level—we could have just made the attribute declarations at the local level. But since this is a pretty small document, we included the declarations at the top level for demonstration purposes.

MOST ELEMENTS ARE DECLARED AS TEXT ELEMENTS. Yes. Most element type declarations include the *content="textOnly"* attribute, which indicates that they can contain text only. The exceptions to this are the Email element, which can contain only subelements, and the Bcc element, which contains an attribute in addition to text.

THE ENTITY SIGNATURE IS DECLARED AND CONTAINS A VALUE. Entities are not yet supported in XML-Data schemas, so there is nothing to add here.

Well, it looks like our schema meets all of the requirements that we need for the email document type. Now let's modify the XML document to work with the schema, as shown in Code Listing 10-2 (Chap10\Lst10_2.xml on the companion CD).

```
<?xml version="1.0"?>

<em:email xmlns:em="x-schema:Lst10_1.xml"
    language="Western" encrypted="128" priority="HIGH">
  <em:to>Jodie@msn.com</em:to>
  <em:from>Bill@msn.com</em:from>
```

Code Listing 10-2.

```
    <em:cc>Philip@msn.com</em:cc>
    <em:subject>My first schema</em:subject>
    <em:body>Hello, this is Bill. XML is cool! Take care, -Bill.</em:body>
</em:email>
```

You will notice two major changes from the DTD version of the XML document. First, instead of a DTD reference in the prolog, we have a schema namespace reference in the em:email element. Second, all the element tags in the document contain the *em* prefix, identifying them as part of the associated namespace. Other than those two small but important changes, this is basically the same document as the one used in our Chapter 4 sample. Again, we can have a document with the same structure rules because functionally our schema matches the DTD we created earlier.

Now we need a way to display the XML document. While we could just use the HTML page from Chapter 4, we will do things a bit differently and use some display methods we have learned since then. To format the XML document, we'll use an XSL style sheet, as shown in Code Listing 10-3 (Chap10\Lst10_3.xsl on the companion CD).

```
<?xml version="1.0"?>
<xsl:template xmlns:xsl="uri:xsl">

  <DIV STYLE="font-weight:bold;font-size:16">
    To:
    <SPAN STYLE="font-weight:normal">
      <xsl:value-of select="em:email/em:to"/>
    </SPAN>
  </DIV>
  <BR></BR>

  <DIV STYLE="font-weight:bold;font-size:16">
    From:
    <SPAN STYLE="font-weight:normal">
      <xsl:value-of select="em:email/em:from"/>
    </SPAN>
  </DIV>
  <BR></BR>

  <DIV STYLE="font-weight:bold;font-size:16">
    Cc:
    <SPAN STYLE="font-weight:normal">
      <xsl:value-of select="em:email/em:cc"/>
    </SPAN>
  </DIV>
  <BR></BR>
```

Code Listing 10-3.

(continued)

```
<DIV STYLE="font-weight:bold;font-size:16">
  Subject:
  <SPAN STYLE="font-weight:normal">
    <xsl:value-of select="em:email/em:subject"/>
  </SPAN>
</DIV>
<HR></HR>

<SPAN STYLE="font-weight:normal">
  <xsl:value-of select="em:email/em:body"/>
</SPAN>

</xsl:template>
```

Remember that this style sheet is designed specifically for the email document type. It will not work for just any document. This is beneficial because it *is* specific to a certain document type, and the formatting and even the structure of the output can be changed, enhanced, and modified without ever having to touch the data itself. In addition, any other document that conforms to the email schema could work with that same style sheet.

The final piece is an HTML page we'll use to run the whole thing. The page is much simpler than the one from Chapter 4, because a great deal of the display code is now in the style sheet. The HTML code is shown in Code Listing 10-4 (Chap10\Lst10_4.htm on the companion CD).

```
<!DOCTYPE HTML PUBLIC "-//W3C//DTD HTML 3.2 Final//EN">
<HTML>

  <HEAD>
    <TITLE>Code Listing 10-4</TITLE>
  </HEAD>

  <SCRIPT LANGUAGE="JavaScript" FOR="window" EVENT="onload">
    var source = new ActiveXObject("Microsoft.XMLDOM");
    source.load("Lst10_2.xml");

    var style = new ActiveXObject("Microsoft.XMLDOM");
    style.load("Lst10_3.xsl");

    document.all.item("dataContainer").innerHTML =
      source.transformNode(style.documentElement);
  </SCRIPT>
```

Code Listing 10-4.

```
<BODY>
  <DIV ID="dataContainer"></DIV>
</BODY>
</HTML>
```

The result of running this page is shown in Figure 10-2. You can see that even though the code is very different from the original documents, the result is much the same. In addition, we get a validated document with the added benefits of a schema instead of a DTD and the power and flexibility of XSL for formatting.

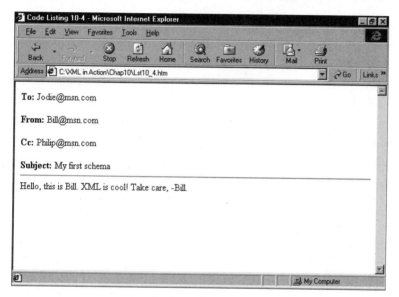

Figure 10-2. *The email document using a schema and an XSL style sheet.*

Advanced Topics

In addition to the supported features covered so far, XML-Data supports other features that extend its capability beyond DTDs. In this section, we will look at topics that could be interesting for more advanced uses, such as different content model options, inheritance, and subclassing with XML-Data.

Open and Closed Content Models

In XML-Data, if an element type declaration sets the *content* attribute to anything other than *empty* or *textOnly*, elements of that type can contain attributes and subelements that were not referred to in the declaration. This is known as an *open* content model. The open content model provides more freedom to add pieces to a document without having to declare them, but it also can make for very unstable content if many people are adding information to document types that are outside of the declared content model.

The alternative is a *closed* content model. As you might guess, in a closed content model, only those attributes and subelements referred to in the element type declaration can actually appear in a document. This is done using the *model* attribute in the element type declaration, as shown below:

```
<ElementType name="plant" model="closed">
  <attribute type="dateordered"/>
  <attribute type="classification"/>
  <attribute type="inventory" dt:type="int"/>
</ElementType>
```

Here, the Plant element can contain only the three attributes referenced.

NOTE

The Schema element's *model* attribute defaults to *open* and thus causes all its child elements to use the same default. This can be altered by changing the value of the *model* attribute in the Schema element, or it can be overridden locally, as we have shown in our example above.

Element Inheritance and Subclassing

An element type can be declared to reuse the content model of other element types. This again brings up the notion of object-oriented design that we briefly explored in Chapter 4. When a content model is reused in other element types, the new element type inherits all of the features of the first element's content model. This means that work done in one area can be leveraged in other areas, and it provides more consistency in the schema or schemas because the same content model can be used in several different places. Reusing a content model is known as *subclassing* that element type. This is done by using the Extends element.

THE EXTENDS ELEMENT

Using the Extends element, not only can you reuse the content model of an element type but you can expand on it in the new element type. Consider the following example:

```
<ElementType name="book">
  <attribute type="language" required="yes"/>
  <attribute type="coverColor"/>
  <element type="title"/>
  <element type="index"/>
</ElementType>

<ElementType name="textBook">
  <element type="glossary"/>
  <extends type="book"/>
</ElementType>

<ElementType name="cookBook">
  <element type="recipe"/>
```

```
    <extends type="book"/>
  </ElementType>
```

Here we have a "base" element type named *book*. The extending element type named *textBook* includes a new element of type *glossary*. The extending element type named *cookBook* contains a new element of type *recipe*. Because they both extend *book*, they also include the attributes *language* and *coverColor*, as well as Title and Index elements. Now any time *book* is changed, *textBook* and *cookBook* will reflect the same changes. Let's add to this example:

```
<ElementType name="scienceBook">
  <element type="diagram"/>
  <element type="formula"/>
  <extends type="textBook"/>
</ElementType>
```

The *scienceBook* element type now includes all the pieces of the *textBook* element type and the *book* element type. This is because *scienceBook* subclasses *textBook*, and as we know, *textBook* subclasses *book*. So the element below would be legal per the schema:

```
<scienceBook language="English" coverColor="blue">
  <diagram>ch05d1.eps</diagram>
  <index>index.xml</index>
  <title>The Complete Book of Science</title>
</scienceBook>
```

In addition to the fact that an extending element type allows the base element type's content model, the reverse is true. In other words, any element type that allows the base element type automatically allows the extending element type. In the example above, this means that any element type that allows *book* automatically allows *textBook* and *scienceBook*. For example, this element type declaration

```
<ElementType name="library">
  <element type="book" minOccurs="1" maxOccurs="*"/>
</ElementType>
```

could result in the following element:

```
<library language="multiple">
  <scienceBook language="Italian" coverColor="red"></scienceBook>
  <cookBook language="French"></cookBook>
</library>
```

SOME RULES

As you might suspect, all this subclassing and extending element types could get kind of sticky for situations in which the "merger" was not clear. For example, you might try to extend an element type with a closed content model, but this wouldn't work. Because of this, a few rules governing the use of extending elements were created, as identified here:

1. Either the base element type must have an open content model or the extending element type must not have any content. These element type characteristics can either be explicit or inherited from other base element types.

2. The values of the *order* attribute must be consistent. The table below shows the *order* values that are allowed:

Base Element Type	Extending Element Type
seq	*seq*
all	*all; seq*
many	*seq; one; all; many*

NOTE

For cases in which a base element type has an *order* value of *one*, an extension cannot occur.

3. The values of the *content* attribute must be consistent, as described in the table that follows:

Base Element Type	Extending Element Type
empty	*empty*
textOnly	*textOnly; empty*
eltOnly	*eltOnly*
mixed	*mixed; textOnly; eltOnly*

4. Attributes and data type constraints apply to all merged element types. Problems can occur if merged data types are not able to combine appropriately.

Including Other Schemas by Using Namespaces

In your schema, you can include declarations from other schemas by using namespaces. For example, in the element type declaration below, a namespace prefix is used to reference an element type declared in another schema.

```
<?xmlns:ann="uri:http://www.plants.com/schemas/annuals.xml"?>

<ElementType name="plant">
  <element type="ann:flower"/>
</ElementType>
```

This allows the author to have access to an entirely separate content model simply by referencing it in the current document.

Only the Beginning

In this chapter, I have only skimmed the surface of what can be done with XML-Data. You are encouraged to look at what others are doing with schemas and come up with your own ways to use this powerful technology.

Chapter 11
XML Today
and Tomorrow

O ne advantage of living on the "bleeding edge" of technology is the constant exposure it offers to new products that provide the potential to improve the way we live and work. Of course, a disadvantage of this exposure is that we are also the first to catch the bugs that come with every new technology. New products typically go through initial development cycles before they run smoothly enough to be put on the consumer market. This book was written as Microsoft Internet Explorer 5 was being developed. Over the months, changes were constantly being made to the XML technologies covered here (XSL, XSL Patterns, and XML-Data), and XML and many other XML technologies are still under development.

This chapter looks at some of the most promising XML products under development and consideration. Hopefully, this discussion will spark your interest enough to try them out.

XML for the (Serious) Programmer

One implementation under consideration is using XML for serialization. *Serialization* is a modern programming technique used to keep object data persistent. An object can maintain its current state, or *persist*, if a "serializable" code object that represents an object's structure and maintains the value of its member variables is created and then contained in a persistent storage mechanism such as in a file on a hard disk. The object can re-create itself from that store by reading in, or *deserializing*, the data from storage. In programming languages such as C++ or Java, serialization is done with specialized technology, in the form of a serialization protocol, which allows object classes to be serialized. When applied, this protocol produces a *closed* binary file that represents the serialized object. That is, its contents are available only to the program written specifically to deserialize the object. Further, it is language dependent. For example, you could not easily serialize an object in C++ and deserialize it in Java. This type of work is relatively complex and has been traditionally reserved for the serious programmer.

Object Persistence with XML

Considering the purpose of serialization—to maintain persistence of object data—work is being done to use XML as the data format. This would make the serialized data language independent and, in turn, ease the work required for serialization and deserialization. Objects could be exchanged between different object architectures, such as Microsoft COM (Component Object Model) and the Object Management Group's CORBA (Common Object Request Broker Architecture). The code below shows what a simple serialized data structure looks like.

```
<OBJECT>
  <DATA>
    <STRING>Hello, World!</STRING>
  </DATA>
</OBJECT>
```

These few lines of just plain old XML might not look impressive, but this simplicity is really what makes it such a breakthrough. Plain XML can be used to describe complex object data that can then be used by applications in place of binary data. Obviously, for this to work, the application has to understand what the structure of the data is. There are several companies and organizations working on XML-based serialization technologies, some of which are described below.

WEB DISTRIBUTED DATA EXCHANGE

XML serialization technologies can either be directly read into an application or object (where XML is the native format) or function as a translation layer between two incompatible formats. Web Distributed Data Exchange (WDDX) is intended to do the latter. Developed by Allaire Corporation, WDDX is a technology that was created specifically for use by Web applications. It consists of a proposed standard for representing application-level data and serialization/deserialization modules for each language or technology that uses WDDX. For example, there is a deserializer written entirely in JavaScript, which enables WDDX-data representations to be deserialized in a JavaScript environment such as a Web browser. For more information, visit Allaire at *http://www.allaire.com* or *http://www.codebits.com/wddx*.

KOALA OBJECT MARKUP LANGUAGE

Koala Object Markup Language (KOML) is a serialization technology for Java objects. The serialization/deserialization modules are built in Java, and they use XML documents as their persistent store. For more information, visit *http://www.inria.fr/koala/XML/serialization*.

XML METADATA OBJECT PERSISTENCE

XML Metadata Object Persistence (XMOP) is another XML-based serialization technology that allows interoperability between different object technologies such as COM and Java. Because object technologies use different methods of serialization, one goal of XMOP is to provide a common, or cross-technology, serialization mechanism. For more information, visit *http://jabr.ne.mediaone.net/documents/xmop.htm*.

COINS

Coins is an XML serialization alternative to JavaBeans. While the Java language is considered by many to be a very good language for developing components, JavaBeans, a Java-based component architecture, is dependent on Java serialization. This means that any changes in the Java classes that make up a serialized component could negatively impact that component. Coins is designed to replace JavaBeans serialization with an XML-based scheme. More information on Coins can be found at *http://www.jxml.com/coins/index.html*.

XML-based serialization models may provide a whole new mechanism for data exchange between applications and on the Internet. For this to happen, more standardization of the serialization scheme is needed. The groundwork for these standards is being laid now with the proposals described above.

XML Data Islands

Throughout this book, we have worked with XML as the data source and HTML as the display mechanism. The data source and the display page are separate documents that are merged. To get our XML data into an HTML page, the data is parsed and inserted into the HTML code by using JavaScript, the XML DSO, XSL, or XSL Patterns. Microsoft Internet Explorer 5 users have another option—XML data islands. Data islands allow authors to insert XML fragments directly into an HTML document. These fragments can be either inline XML or linked XML documents. There are pros and cons to using XML data islands, but the advantages include:

◆ You don't need a separate XML file.

◆ You don't need to load the XML data through script code.

◆ You don't need to explicitly instantiate the ActiveX control with an Object element.

Depending on how a data island is used, is also has disadvantages such as:

◆ The XML data is no longer really independent of the HTML file.

◆ The XML data is not very portable to other applications or HTML pages.

◆ The XML data may be more difficult to manage if it is interspersed with HTML code.

Working with Inline XML Data Islands

With inline XML data islands, you simply insert XML code directly into an HTML page. The XML "document" is contained inside a set of <XML></XML> tags. To demonstrate this, we'll take our familiar email document used in previous chapters and embed it into an HTML page.

```
<!DOCTYPE HTML PUBLIC "-//W3C//DTD HTML 3.2 Final//EN">
<HTML>

  <HEAD>
    <TITLE>Data Island</TITLE>
  </HEAD>

  <BODY>
    <XML ID="email">
      <EMAIL LANGUAGE="Western" ENCRYPTED="128" PRIORITY="HIGH">
        <TO>Jodie@msn.com</TO>
        <FROM>Bill@msn.com</FROM>
        <CC>Philip@msn.com</CC>
        <SUBJECT>My First DTD</SUBJECT>
        <BODY>Hello, World!</BODY>
      </EMAIL>
    </XML>
  </BODY>

</HTML>
```

Note that although the document is enclosed in the Xml element, that element is *not* the root node, or document element. The browser recognizes that whatever is contained inside an Xml element is XML code. Notice also that the Xml element has an ID assigned to it. That is so it may be referenced elsewhere in the HTML page, for instance in script code. We can now work with the XML code just as we would if it were contained in a separate document and we had instantiated the XML parser object in our HTML page. Code Listing 11-1 (Chap11\Lst11_1.htm on the companion CD) includes all the display mechanisms and script code for the XML document.

```
<!DOCTYPE HTML PUBLIC "-//W3C//DTD HTML 3.2 Final//EN">
<HTML>

  <HEAD>
    <SCRIPT LANGUAGE="JavaScript" FOR=window EVENT=onload>
      start();
    </SCRIPT>

    <SCRIPT LANGUAGE="JavaScript">
      function start()
        {
        var rootElem = email.documentElement;
        var rootLength = rootElem.childNodes.length;
        for (cl=0; cl<rootLength; cl++)
          {
          currNode = rootElem.childNodes.item(cl)
          switch (currNode.nodeName)
            {
            case "TO":
              todata.innerText=currNode.text;
              break;
            case "FROM":
              fromdata.innerText=currNode.text;
              break;
            case "CC":
              ccdata.innerText=currNode.text;
              break;
            case "SUBJECT":
              subjectdata.innerText=currNode.text;
              break;
            case "BODY":
              bodydata.innerText=currNode.text;
              break;
            }
          }
        }
    </SCRIPT>
```

Code Listing 11-1.   *(continued)*

```
      <TITLE>Untitled</TITLE>
   </HEAD>

   <BODY>
     <XML ID="email">
       <EMAIL LANGUAGE="Western" ENCRYPTED="128" PRIORITY="HIGH">
         <TO>Jodie@msn.com</TO>
         <FROM>Bill@msn.com</FROM>
         <CC>Philip@msn.com</CC>
         <SUBJECT>My first DTD</SUBJECT>
         <BODY>Hello, World!</BODY>
       </EMAIL>
     </XML>

     <DIV ID="to" STYLE="font-weight:bold;font-size:16">
       To:
       <SPAN ID="todata" STYLE="font-weight:normal"></SPAN>
     </DIV>
     <BR>

     <DIV ID="from" STYLE="font-weight:bold;font-size:16">
       From:
       <SPAN ID="fromdata" STYLE="font-weight:normal"></SPAN>
     </DIV>
     <BR>

     <DIV ID="cc" STYLE="font-weight:bold;font-size:16">
       Cc:
       <SPAN ID="ccdata" STYLE="font-weight:normal"></SPAN>
     </DIV>
     <BR>

     <DIV ID="from" STYLE="font-weight:bold;font-size:16">
       Subject:
       <SPAN ID="subjectdata" STYLE="font-weight:normal"></SPAN>
     </DIV>
     <BR>

     <HR>
     <SPAN ID="bodydata" STYLE="font-weight:normal"></SPAN><P>

   </BODY>
</HTML>
```

In this document, the XML Email document is referenced by its ID, and we are able to perform all the same functions on it that we did when it was explicitly called from the ActiveX control. In fact, the same processor is being used; Internet Explorer 5 just uses it in a different way. In addition to the inline data island, there is another way to use the Xml element—by linking it to an external document.

Working with Linked XML Data Islands

To link an Xml element to an external document, the first thing we need, obviously, is the external document. For this example, let's just cut the XML code from the previous example and put it into its own document, as shown in Code Listing 11-2 (Chap11\Lst11_2.xml on the companion CD).

```
<?xml version="1.0"?>

<EMAIL LANGUAGE="Western" ENCRYPTED="128" PRIORITY="HIGH">
  <TO>Jodie@msn.com</TO>
  <FROM>Bill@msn.com</FROM>
  <CC>Philip@msn.com</CC>
  <SUBJECT>My first DTD</SUBJECT>
  <BODY>Hello, World!</BODY>
</EMAIL>
```

Code Listing 11-2.

To link the Xml element to this external document, simply change the Xml element in the HTML page to the following: (The entire listing for this can be found in Chap11\Lst11_3.htm on the companion CD.)

```
<XML ID="email" SRC="Lst11_2.xml"></XML>
```

This works exactly like the previous example. The advantage to this method is that the XML data remains separate from the HTML document. Essentially, it works much like the ActiveX control method, except that here the browser takes the responsibility for instantiating the control and loading the document.

Attributes for the Xml Element

The Xml element includes some additional attributes that provide more control over what happens when the document is loaded.

The *VALIDATEONPARSE* attribute indicates whether or not the document should be validated when it is parsed. It is used as shown below:

```
<XML ID="xmlDoc" SRC="xmlDoc.xml" VALIDATEONPARSE="false"></XML>
```

The default value is *true* if the attribute is not included in the element.

The *ASYNC* attribute indicates whether or not the document should be downloaded asynchronously. A sample element is shown below:

```
<XML ID="xmlDoc" SRC="xmlDoc.xml" ASYNC="false"></XML>
```

The default value for the *ASYNC* attribute is *true*.

Multimedia Description Languages

Computer-based multimedia has evolved considerably over the past five to seven years. However, one of the constants within the multimedia industry is the battle over whether to standardize a system for the delivery of multimedia content. Today there are many commercial multimedia authoring systems on the market (Macromedia Director, Asymmetrix Toolbook, and Microsoft Liquid Motion to mention a few) that provide content developers with a complete system for creating and delivering multimedia content. Many more developers create custom multimedia engines in C++ or Java, for instance, to perform tasks that the commercial packages don't. What all these multimedia delivery systems have in common is their proprietary approach to delivering content. Usually, content developed in one system is not portable to another system—at least, not easily portable. Since the advent of XML, efforts have been underway to develop a multimedia description language that would provide authors with a standard way to describe multimedia content for playback on any system that understands the language. The two proposals currently getting the most "traction" are the Synchronized Multimedia Integration Language (SMIL, pronounced "smile") and HTML Timed Interactive Multimedia Extensions (HTML+TIME).

SMIL

SMIL 1.0 was recently released as a W3C recommendation. SMIL is an XML-based, stand-alone multimedia presentation language. Its purpose is to provide a standardized format for describing multimedia that can be used by multiple authoring and display systems, such as a Web browser, or by an authoring tool such as Macromedia Flash. In a general sense, SMIL models itself after a page-based presentation. SMIL documents define regions on a page, allow authors to provide temporal information about the objects on the page, and support the hyperlinking of those objects. The code below shows an example of what a SMIL document might look like.

```
<SMIL>
  <HEAD>
    <LAYOUT>

      <ROOT-LAYOUT WIDTH="640" HEIGHT="480"
        BACKGROUND-COLOR="black"/>
```

```
    <!-- Logo -->
    <REGION ID="logo" LEFT="20" TOP="5" WIDTH="100" HEIGHT="50"
      FIT="fill"/>

    <!-- Video -->
    <REGION ID="vidbk" LEFT="200" TOP="50" WIDTH="150" HEIGHT="76"
      BACKGROUND-COLOR="#330033" Z-INDEX="1"/>
    <REGION ID="video" LEFT="210" TOP="55" WIDTH="100" HEIGHT="70"
      FIT="fill" BACKGROUND-COLOR="#000000" Z-INDEX="3" />

    <!-- Closed Caption -->
    <REGION ID="ccbk" LEFT="20" TOP="200" WIDTH="400" HEIGHT="30"
      BACKGROUND-COLOR="#666600" Z-INDEX="2"/>
    <REGION ID="ccscroll" LEFT="21" TOP="210" WIDTH="350"
      HEIGHT="25" FIT="fill" Z-INDEX="2" />

  </LAYOUT>
</HEAD>

<BODY>
  <PAR>
    <!-- Blocks below play one after the other (in parallel) -->
    <SEQ>
      <PAR>
        <IMG SRC="logo.gif" REGION="logo" FILL="freeze"/>
      </PAR>
      <PAR>
        <VIDEO SRC="video.asx" REGION="video" FILL="freeze" />
        <TEXT SRC="cctext.txt" REGION="ccscroll" FILL="freeze" />
      </PAR>
    </SEQ>
  </PAR>
</BODY>
</SMIL>
```

NOTE

Although neither Microsoft Internet Explorer nor Netscape Navigator have plans to support SMIL directly, several vendors are providing browser support for SMIL. This is being done through the use of a separate playback utility or plug-in. RealPlayer G2 from RealNetworks is one such player.

The sample above is intended to simply show what SMIL code looks like, not to provide instructions on its use. For detailed information on SMIL and the tools currently available for authoring SMIL documents, visit the W3C site at *http://www.w3.org/AudioVideo*. The current SMIL recommendation can be found at *http://www.w3.org/TR/REC-smil*.

One perceived shortcoming of SMIL is that although it is an XML-based language, it does not integrate well with current Web-based multimedia solutions, such as DHTML and

CSS. To address this problem, Microsoft has teamed up with Compaq Computer and Macromedia to extend SMIL into a new XML-based multimedia language called HTML+TIME.

HTML+TIME

HTML+TIME addresses the SMIL shortcomings with two solutions. First, it supports the ability to apply time attributes to any HTML element so that effects on a Web page can be timed, or scheduled. That is, instead of just displaying, for example, a Div element on a page, the author can specify *when* it should appear based on the timing of the presentation. Support includes the ability to access the temporal properties of media elements, such as streaming media files. You could retrieve the duration of a video, for example. HTML+TIME uses HTML for display and CSS for positioning and style.

The second solution HTML+TIME provides is support for the use of common attributes across all elements in the presentation. This feature allows all the elements on a page to interact during a presentation. The code below shows a simple example of HTML+TIME attributes.

```
<DIV t:begin="1">
  This Div element appears after one second.
</DIV>

<IMG SRC="pic.gif t:begin="2">
  This image appears after two seconds.
</IMG>

<P t:begin="3">
  This text appears after three seconds.
</P>
```

NOTE

HTML+TIME was not developed to replace SMIL. Rather, its purpose is to fill SMIL gaps with regard to Web-based multimedia. In fact, the W3C note located at *http://www.w3.org/TR/NOTE-HTMLplusTIME* is subtitled "Extending SMIL into the Web Browser." It is understood by the creators of HTML+TIME that SMIL is a good solution for describing multimedia outside of a Web environment.

Also note that the HTML+TIME attributes are applied to standard HTML elements. Like SMIL, HTML+TIME supports the sequencing of media elements, as shown in the sample code below:

```
<DIV HEIGHT=200 WIDTH=300>
  <t:seq ID="presentation" t:beginEvent="none">
    <IMG SRC="image1.gif" t:dur="5" t:timeAction="display"
      onclick="this.endElement()">
    <IMG SRC="image2.gif" t:dur="5" t:timeAction="display"
      onclick="this.endElement()">
  </t:seq>
```

```
<IMG SRC="showOver.gif" t:beginAfter="presentation"
  t:timeAction="display">

<P ALIGN=center onclick="presentation.beginElement()">
  Click here to begin the slide show. It will play automatically.
</P>
<P ALIGN=center>
  Click an image to manually advance the presentation.
</P>
</DIV>
```

At this time, HTML+TIME is still a proposal and more changes to its language are expected before it becomes a full recommendation. The general concepts and functions should remain about the same.

HTML+TIME will make it easier to integrate XML-based multimedia on a Web page. Since it is based on familiar standards, the only task is learning the new attributes.

Vector Images with XML

One of the great things about the Web is its ability to integrate graphics into text pages for display over the Internet. However, one problem graphics still present to the Web developer is their size. Because Web graphics files are large and take a long time to download, they have become the main cause of Web bottlenecks for users. Before we discuss XML solutions to graphics formatting and downloading problems, it might be helpful to review and compare the current raster and vector formats, just in case you have not kept up with the latest and greatest in image formatting.

Raster Image Format

Raster images (also called bitmapped images) store information, such as color information, for every pixel in the image. For example, suppose you had a raster image of a blue line that is 10 pixels long. In English it would look like this:

1. Pixel 1: x-coordinate:20, y-coordinate:20, rgb value:0,0,255

2. Pixel 2: x-coordinate:21, y-coordinate:20, rgb value:0,0,255

3. Pixel 3: x-coordinate:22, y-coordinate:20, rgb value:0,0,255

4. Pixel 4: x-coordinate:23, y-coordinate:20, rgb value:0,0,255

5. Pixel 5: x-coordinate:24, y-coordinate:20, rgb value:0,0,255

6. Pixel 6: x-coordinate:25, y-coordinate:20, rgb value:0,0,255

7. Pixel 7: x-coordinate:26, y-coordinate:20, rgb value:0,0,255

8. Pixel 8: x-coordinate:27, y-coordinate:20, rgb value:0,0,255

9. Pixel 9: x-coordinate:28, y-coordinate:20, rgb value:0,0,255

10. Pixel 10: x-coordinate:29, y-coordinate:20, rgb value:0,0,255

What makes the image files so large compared to other file formats is this required pixel-level information. In addition, because raster images are binary files, they always require an editing tool that understands the format before any changes or modifications can be made. To help reduce the size of raster images, and make them download to the Web faster, the files are compressed. Over the years, progress has been made toward improving image compression, but raster images must still be handled with care to prevent long download times. The most common image formats used on the Web, GIF and JPEG, are raster formats.

Vector Image Format

Another graphics format that is becoming increasingly popular is the *vector* format. This format stores image information in a very different way from the raster format. Instead of storing information about every pixel in an image, the vector format stores mathematical descriptions of objects in the image. In other words, because an image is a combination of lines, ovals, arcs, rectangles, and other shapes, the vector format can recognize and describe their individual geometry. The vector rendering engine can then interpret each description and draw the shapes, reproducing the entire image. Because this formatting does not require drawing a line or a circle pixel by pixel, the graphics files are much smaller. Notice that our blue, 10-pixel line described above in raster format requires only three lines of English in the vector format.

1. Line Start Point: x-coordinate:20, y-coordinate:20

2. Line End Point: x-coordinate:29, y-coordinate:20

3. RGB: 0,0,255

This simple but effective example makes the difference between raster and vector formatting obvious. Besides shrinking the file size substantially, the vector format also makes the image scalable, which can't be done with raster-formatted images.

NOTE

While it is possible to "scale" a raster image, more often than not it is distorted, or "pixelized," in the process because the display program has to interpolate the image based on the original pixel information. A vector image can just be redrawn without distortion using new vector information.

Vector Images with VML

Because of the compact, highly descriptive nature of the vector format, several companies including Autodesk, Hewlett-Packard, Macromedia, Microsoft, and Visio thought that XML would make an ideal language on which to base a vector encoding scheme. The proposed name for this vector language is Vector Markup Language, or VML. Although VML is not yet a standard, a proposal to make it one was recently submitted to the W3C. For more information on this proposal, visit *http://www.w3.org/TR/NOTE-VML*.

BENEFITS OF AN XML-BASED VECTOR FORMAT

If you are familiar with other vector formats such as Microsoft Windows Metafile or Macromedia Flash or FreeHand, or with structured graphics, you may be wondering why anyone would want to bother using XML to describe vector images. The significant improvements XML offers over these vector graphics formats might make XML worth your while.

◆ VML is based on an open standard—XML. This simple, text-based language can be used to describe small, scalable graphics which can then be included in XML applications.

◆ VML includes support for other W3C standards such as CSS and DOM. This provides interoperability with other elements on a Web page.

◆ VML images are small and therefore download faster than images in other formats.

◆ Because VML is a text-based description language, VML images are downloaded with XML or HTML data and are fully integrated with the other objects on a Web page. This contrasts with current image formats which must be downloaded separately and usually do not integrate well with other page objects.

◆ Because of its standards-based design, VML should simplify authoring and facilitate interchangeability between different tools and platforms.

Let's look at an example of some VML code taken from the VML proposal. VML allows an author to describe a basic shape, such as the arrow shown below.

The VML code used to describe the image is listed below:

```
<v:shapetype id="downArrow" coordsize="21600, 21600" adj="16200,
5400"
   path="m0@0l1@0@1,0@2,0@2@0,21600@0,10800,21600xe">
<v:stroke joinstyle="miter"/>
<v:formulas>
   <v:f eqn="sum #0 0 0"/>
   <v:f eqn="sum #1 0 0"/>
   <v:f eqn="sum height 0 #1"/>
   <v:f eqn="sum 10800 0 #1"/>
   <v:f eqn="sum width 0 #0"/>
   <v:f eqn="prod @4 @3 10800"/>
   <v:f eqn="sum width 0 @5"/>
</v:formulas>
<v:path textboxrect="@1, 0, @2, @6"/>
```

(continued)

```
<v:handles>
  <v:h position="#1, #0" xrange="0, 10800" yrange="0, 21600"/>
</v:handles>
</v:shapetype>
```

To get the arrows shown below, this basic shape was repeated and modified:

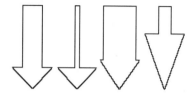

The following VML code could be used:

```
<v:shape type="#downArrow"
  style='position: absolute; left: 77; top: 16;
  width: 64; height: 128'/>
<v:shape type="#downArrow"
  style='position: absolute; left: 149; top: 16;
  width: 64; height: 128'
  adj=", 9450"/>
<v:shape type="#downArrow"
  style='position: absolute; left: 219; top: 16;
  width: 64; height: 128'
  adj="14175, 2025"/>
<v:shape type="#downArrow"
  style='position: absolute; left: 292; top: 16;
  width: 64; height: 128'
  adj="7088, 7425"/>
```

Notice that the original shape name is used, but different shapes are produced when CSS attributes are applied and other adjustments are made. Vector Markup Language, combined with other XML technologies, such as SMIL or HTML+TIME, can produce small, integrated, interactive presentations that are based on a common syntax.

Document Object Model

As noted earlier in this book, the W3C recently approved the Document object model (DOM) Level 1 specification as a recommendation. Even though by this point in the book you are familiar with DOM, it might be helpful to look at what it does and does not currently offer, and what plans are being made for future versions.

What Is DOM and Where Did It Come From?

The Document object model grew out of a need for a standardized way to (1) define the logical structure of a document and (2) define how a document is accessed and manipulated.

The term *document* refers specifically to HTML and XML documents, and DOM provides an application programming interface (API) for those documents. You may recall that when Internet Explorer 4 and Netscape Navigator 4 arrived, each had a different implementation of a technology called *Dynamic HTML*. At its most basic level, Dynamic HTML provides authors with access to various HTML elements and a way to manipulate those elements through properties, methods, and events. The problem with this technology is the lack of an implementation standard, which caused cross-browser compatibility problems for users of Dynamic HTML. DOM was developed to resolve the compatibility problems. Note, however, that while DOM was influenced by Dynamic HTML, it is not a full implementation of it. For instance, events are not included in the Level 1 specification. DOM is so named because it is an object model in the true sense, in that it provides a structure and behavior model for document objects.

DOCUMENT STRUCTURE WITH DOM

As stated above, DOM provides a model for the structure of an HTML or XML document. DOM identifies a logical, tree-like structure for a document, but does not specify how that structure must be implemented. Let's take a basic HTML document and examine how its structure would be represented by DOM.

```
<HTML>
  <HEAD>
    <TITLE>DOM Test</TITLE>
  </HEAD>

  <BODY>
    <P>Some text</P>
    <DIV>
      <SPAN>More text</SPAN>
    </DIV>
  </BODY>

</HTML>
```

The DOM representation of the code is shown in the diagram below:

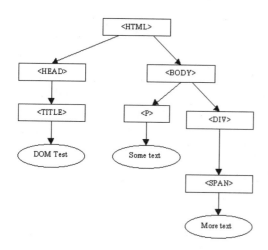

Notice that the document is represented in a hierarchical structure. If more elements were added to the document, they could be integrated into the same hierarchy. This model can also be applied to XML documents. We have discussed many times how to use XML to represent data. But in terms of DOM, a document does not represent a data structure. From a technical standpoint, DOM looks at documents as being made up of individual objects.

DOCUMENT BEHAVIOR WITH DOM

With the understanding that, as far as DOM is concerned, documents are made up of objects and not just data, we can then understand that each object has properties, such as an ID, and methods. For each object, DOM represents:

- the interfaces used to manipulate the object
- the meaning (semantics) of the object in relationship to the rest of the document, including its behavior and attributes
- the collaboration between interfaces and objects

This ability to work with the document object structure, semantics, and behavior provides a powerful mechanism for developing sophisticated document-based applications.

What DOM Is Not

To help clarify what DOM is, it might be helpful to point out what it does not do and how it differs from other similar-looking object models. The differences are worth noting.

1. As stated above, DOM represents the semantics of the objects in the object model. Understand, however, that DOM does not *define* the semantics of an XML or HTML document. The semantics are defined by the specifications for those languages. DOM simply represents those semantics.

2. DOM is not a replacement for, and does not compete with, other object systems such as COM or CORBA. While these models are language independent, DOM is a way to manage objects and interfaces in HTML and XML. In fact, DOM can be used within an object-based system like COM or CORBA.

3. DOM does not define a set of data structures. It is a model that defines objects and interfaces. Although a document can be represented by a parent/child hierarchy of data elements, this is simply a representation of the logical relationships defined by the object model. Understand that a document is represented by DOM and can be authored using HTML or XML.

4. Earlier in this chapter, we discussed how XML can be used to structure data in a serialized, persistent storage mechanism. However, it is not DOM that provides this persistence. Rather than identifying how objects can be represented by HTML or XML, DOM specifies how HTML and XML are represented by objects. These document objects can then be used in object-oriented systems.

The Future of DOM

As we have been discussing throughout this section, DOM is a representation of an HTML or XML document's objects and interfaces. This is really the limit of DOM in the Level 1 specification. Plans for future versions of DOM include some of the following: (Note that most of these can be accomplished today without DOM.)

◆ Making it a standard event model. Today events are supported through nonstandard interfaces.

◆ Schema validation. Today schema validation is done at the processor level. There is currently no specification for how to do this at the DOM level.

◆ Document rendering via style sheets. Today the use of style sheets is external to DOM.

For more information on DOM, visit the W3C DOM Web site at *http://www.w3.org/TR/REC-DOM-Level-1*.

Document Content Description

Chapter 10 detailed XML-Data, a method for describing the structure of an XML document by using a schema. In reality, XML-Data is much more than just a document structure model. The aspects of XML-Data that we covered are really a subset of XML-Data as it is currently implemented in Internet Explorer. This implementation corresponds to functionality as described in the Document Content Description (DCD) specification. Document Content Description is a subset of XML-Data that is designed specifically for defining the rules and structure of XML documents.

> **NOTE**
>
> It may interest some readers to know that DCD is expressed in a way that is consistent with the Resource Description Framework (RDF) syntax. RDF is not covered here, but more information can be found at *http://www.w3.org/TR/PR-rdf-syntax*.

DCD provides the same functionality as a traditional DTD, and adds additional functionality such as support for basic data types. You will notice in the example below that the DCD code looks very similar to the schema we created in Chapter 10 even though the syntax is a bit different.

```
<DCD>
  <AttributeDef name="language" dt:type="enumeration"
    dt:values="Western Greek Latin Universal"/>
  <AttributeDef name="encrypted"/>
  <AttributeDef name="priority" dt:type="enumeration"
    dt:values="NORMAL LOW HIGH"/>
  <AttributeDef name="hidden" default="true"/>
  <ElementDef name="TO" content="textOnly"/>
  <ElementDef name="FROM" content="textOnly"/>
  <ElementDef name="CC" content="textOnly"/>
```

(continued)

```
<ElementDef name="BCC" content="mixed">
  <attribute type="hidden" required="yes"/>
</ElementDef>
<ElementDef name="SUBJECT" content="textOnly"/>
<ElementDef name="BODY" content="textOnly"/>
</DCD>
```

Currently, the DCD specification is in the proposal stage with the W3C. It is not the purpose of this section to detail the DCD vocabulary and usage, as we have covered similar functionality in Chapter 10. But DCD could eventually become the method of choice for describing an XML document's structure and content. For more information on DCD and the current proposal, visit *http://www.w3.org/TR/NOTE-dcd*.

Cross-Platform XML

A common question posed to XML developers, especially Web-based developers, is how much cross-platform and cross-browser compatibility does XML offer? If your intent is to use XML to find solutions for the Web, you will undoubtedly run into browser compatibility problems. As XML exists today, the answer to the compatibility question is both simple and complex.

The simple answer is that cross-platform compatibility can occur on any platform that implements XML according to the published (W3C) standards. For example, Msxml in Internet Explorer is XML 1.0 compliant. If the Netscape processor is also XML 1.0 compliant, documents authored for one browser should be parsable by the other browser. One problem is that there are many XML-based technologies being implemented in current browsers before they have the W3C stamp of approval as recommendations. This is because software companies typically move faster than the W3C. Another difficulty is that as technology advances, it often is no longer compatible with the published specifications.

This scenario becomes even more complex when different software vendors introduce features and functionality on the software side that do not exist on other platforms. For example, XML data island functionality covered earlier in this chapter is specific to Internet Explorer. It is not part of the XML specification, nor is it part of the DOM specification. Let's look at what this means. The XML code below is a well-formed XML 1.0 document.

```
<?xml version="1.0"?>
<INVENTORY>

  <ITEM>
    <NAME>Brandenburg Concerto No. 2</NAME>
    <AUTHOR>Bach, J.S.</AUTHOR>
    <PRICE>17.95</PRICE>
  </ITEM>

  <ITEM>
    <NAME>Piano Sonata in A</NAME>
    <AUTHOR>Mozart, W.A.</AUTHOR>
    <PRICE>16.95</PRICE>
  </ITEM>

</INVENTORY>
```

This document could be parsed by any browser or application that understands XML 1.0 documents. Exactly how the document is loaded into the processor and what is done with the data once it is parsed is up to the application, but the document itself would be cross-platform. Now let's take that same XML document and implement it as a data island in an HTML page as shown below.

```
<!DOCTYPE HTML PUBLIC "-//W3C//DTD HTML 3.2 Final//EN">
<HTML>

  <HEAD>
    <TITLE>Music Inventory</TITLE>
  </HEAD>

  <BODY>
    <XML ID=music>
      <INVENTORY>

        <ITEM>
          <NAME>Brandenburg Concerto No. 2</NAME>
          <AUTHOR>Bach, J.S.</AUTHOR>
          <PRICE>17.95</PRICE>
        </ITEM>

        <ITEM>
          <NAME>Piano Sonata in A</NAME>
          <AUTHOR>Mozart, W.A.</AUTHOR>
          <PRICE>16.95</PRICE>
        </ITEM>

      </INVENTORY>
    </XML>

    <TABLE DATASRC=#music CELLSPACING="10" CELLPADDING="2">
      <THEAD STYLE="font-weight:bold">
        <TD>Name</TD>
        <TD>Author</TD>
        <TD>Price</TD>
      </THEAD>

      <TR>
        <TD><DIV DATAFLD="NAME"></TD>
        <TD><DIV DATAFLD="AUTHOR"></TD>
        <TD><DIV DATAFLD="PRICE"></TD>
      </TR>
    </TABLE>
  </BODY>

</HTML>
```

Currently, this page is viewable only in Internet Explorer 5. Does this mean that data islands and similar technologies are bad for XML and bad for users? Not at all. It just means that software developers are often ahead of the curve when it comes to solutions based on a standard such as XML. In fact, what often occurs is that a specific technology, such as data islands, is included in some form in the next version of a formal recommendation.

The message here is that when you are creating XML-based applications or Web pages, it is important to understand clearly what technologies you are using and who your intended audience is.

Some Conclusions

Is XML the solution to all the problems that have plagued the Web, or is it just more hype? We hope that after reading this book you will realize that it is neither. There is no one software solution to all the problems. However, in looking at the solutions that have been developed using XML so far, and the industry-wide support for the technology, it is obvious that XML is more than just a passing fad. It has been said that the World Wide Web phenomenon was built around HTML. For XML to be as successful as HTML, several things must occur industry-wide.

◆ People and organizations have to see the value of XML. Just as HTML was adopted because it provided a standard format in which to display rich content on the Internet, XML should be recognized as a valuable tool for structuring and delivering data, not only on the Web, but in other applications as well.

◆ Tools must be made available to allow people access to the technology. Tools can include anything from an XML editing application, to a Software Development Kit (SDK), to a book like this one. For any new technology to be adopted, it has to be introduced, taught, and supported.

◆ Standardization needs to continue. One reason XML is being chosen over other data formats and solutions is because it is based on a standard recommended by an independent body, the W3C, which is not controlled by any one company or organization. Standardization ensures that everyone, including individual vendors, has access to the language and can contribute to its implementation and development. For XML to be successful, new XML technologies must continue to go through the standards process and implementers must abide by the standards.

The goal of this book is to give you the information you need to develop your own XML-based applications and Web solutions. The best way for any technology to gain acceptance is for people like you and me to use it.

Appendix A
The XML Object Model

C hapter 5 discussed how authors can use scripting to interact with elements on an HTML page and to work with the XML object model. This appendix explores the XML object model in more detail, including the objects that make up the model, their properties and methods, and how they are used in an application.

The Object Model Structure

As you learned in Chapter 3, objects are organized in a tree structure. The "trunk" of the tree is the *document* object. Other objects branch from the *document* object. The XML object model consists of four basic objects:

- ◆ *document* object—the XML data source

- ◆ *node* object—a parent node or one of its child nodes

- ◆ *nodeList* object—a list of "sibling" nodes

- ◆ *parseError* object—a non–content-bearing object used for retrieving parsing error information

Figure A-1 shows the relationships among these objects.

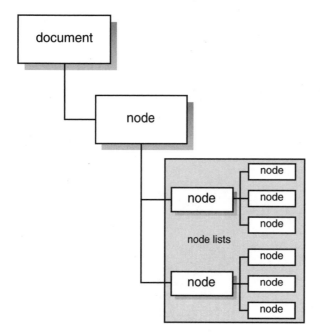

Figure A-1. *The XML object model.*

Each object in the object model possesses specific properties or methods or both. Using script code, content authors can access these properties and methods to get information and act on the XML data directly. This appendix will walk through the XML object model and survey the objects and their associated properties and methods.

Since this book is about putting XML in action, you'll get to see the object model at work! Later in this appendix, there are examples of how objects in the object model can be used. To work with these examples, you'll need the XML document shown in Code Listing A-1 and found in the AppxA\LstA_1.xml file on the companion CD.

```
<?xml version="1.0"?>

<!DOCTYPE EMAIL SYSTEM "LstA_2.dtd">
<EMAIL PRIORITY="HIGH">
  <TO>Jodie@msn.com</TO>
  <FROM>Bill@msn.com</FROM>
  <CC>Philip@msn.com</CC>
  <BCC>Naomi@msn.com</BCC>
  <SUBJECT>My document is a tree.</SUBJECT>
  <BODY>This is an example of a tree structure.</BODY>
</EMAIL>
```

Code Listing A-1.

As you can see from the document type declaration, this document uses a Document Type Definition (DTD). The DTD, which you can find in the AppxA\LstA_2.dtd file on the companion CD, is shown in Code Listing A-2.

```
<!-- This is an XML document that could be used as an email template. -->

<!ELEMENT EMAIL (TO+, FROM, CC*, BCC*, SUBJECT?, BODY?)>
<!ATTLIST EMAIL
  LANGUAGE  (Western|Greek|Latin|Universal) "Western"
  ENCRYPTED CDATA #IMPLIED
  PRIORITY (NORMAL|LOW|HIGH) "NORMAL">
<!ELEMENT TO (#PCDATA)>
<!ELEMENT FROM (#PCDATA)>
<!ELEMENT CC (#PCDATA)>
<!ELEMENT BCC (#PCDATA)>
<!ATTLIST BCC
  HIDDEN CDATA #FIXED "TRUE">
<!ELEMENT SUBJECT (#PCDATA)>
<!ELEMENT BODY (#PCDATA)>
```

Code Listing A-2.

Finally, the XML document will be displayed by the HTML page shown in Code Listing A-3 (AppxA\LstA_3.htm on the companion CD).

```
<!DOCTYPE HTML PUBLIC "-//W3C//DTD HTML 3.2 Final//EN">
<HTML>

  <HEAD>
    <SCRIPT LANGUAGE="JavaScript" FOR=window EVENT=onload>
      showMe();
    </SCRIPT>

    <SCRIPT LANGUAGE="JavaScript">
      var xmlDoc = new ActiveXObject("microsoft.xmldom");
      xmlDoc.load("LstA_1.xml");

      function showMe()
        {
        // Insert sample code here.
        }
    </SCRIPT>

    <TITLE>Code Listing A-3</TITLE>
  </HEAD>

  <BODY>
  </BODY>

</HTML>
```

Code Listing A-3.

Notice in Code Listing A-3 that the function *showMe* contains no code. This is because it will be up to you to insert the snippets of code throughout the rest of this appendix. The snippets are designed to just "snap" into place in the *showMe* function.

NOTE

To use the samples in this appendix, you can either type the snippets of code into the *showMe* function in LstA_3.htm, or you can use the complete set of HTML files that are included in the AppxA folder on the companion CD.

The *document* Object

As noted previously, the *document* object represents the document's data source. The object model allows the author to load an XML document via script code, using any XML processor supported by the browser or the application. For example, a document can be loaded by creating an instance of the Microsoft ActiveX control and calling the *load* method (discussed later), as shown in this sample HTML code:

```
var xmlDoc = new ActiveXObject("microsoft.xmldom");
xmlDoc.load("LstA_1.xml");
```

Loading could also be accomplished using a Java applet, as shown here:

```
<SCRIPT>
  xmldso.load("LstA_1.xml");
</SCRIPT>

<BODY>
  <APPLET CODE=com.ms.xml.dso.XMLDSO.class
    WIDTH=100% HEIGHT=0 ID=xmldso MAYSCRIPT=true>
  </APPLET>
</BODY>
```

Since the object model expects the *load* method to be used, the code is the same after the control is loaded. It's important to note that once the data source is established, the object model provides a consistent way to navigate and manipulate the XML data.

NOTE

Msxml extends the basic Document object model (DOM) to include XML-specific interfaces. It is beyond the scope of this book to discuss the entire DOM. As a result, the following sections focus only on the more commonly used XML DOM extensions.

document Object Properties

The list below shows the properties available for the *document* object:

- *async*
- *attributes*
- *childNodes*
- *doctype*
- *documentElement*
- *firstChild*
- *implementation*
- *lastChild*
- *nextSibling*
- *nodeName*
- *nodeType*
- *nodeValue*
- *ondataavailable*
- *onreadystatechange*
- *ownerDocument*
- *parentNode*
- *parseError*
- *previousSibling*
- *readyState*
- *url*
- *validateOnParse*
- *xml*

THE *async* PROPERTY

The *async* property specifies whether asynchronous download is allowed.

Basic Syntax	`boolValue = XMLDocument.async;` `XMLDocument.async = boolValue;`
Details	Boolean value is read/write. Value is *true* if asynchronous download is permitted, *false* if not.

USAGE EXAMPLE The following example can be found in AppxA\LstA_4.htm on the companion CD:

```
xmlDoc.async = "false";
alert(xmlDoc.async);
```

THE *attributes* PROPERTY

Returns the list of attributes for the current node.

Basic Syntax	`objAttributeList = xmlNode.attributes;`
Details	Returns an object. If the node cannot contain attributes, *null* is returned.

USAGE EXAMPLE The following example can be found in AppxA\LstA_5.htm on the companion CD:

```
objAttList = xmlDoc.documentElement.attributes;
alert(objAttList);
```

NOTE

The example above returns *[object]* as a result. This is because an object is returned that can't be represented as text without using other properties of the object. This is the case for several examples in this appendix. While many object properties may not be very useful by themselves, you will see throughout this appendix how combining properties and methods will give you a result you can work with.

THE *childNodes* PROPERTY

Returns a node list containing all the available children of the current node.

Basic Syntax	`objNodeList = node.childNodes;`
Details	Returns an object. If the node does not contain children, *null* is returned.

USAGE EXAMPLE The following example can be found in AppxA\LstA_6.htm on the companion CD:

```
objNodeList = xmlDoc.childNodes;
alert(objNodeList);
```

THE *doctype* PROPERTY

Returns the document type node that contains the DTD for the current document. This node is typically the document type declaration. For example, for the node *<!DOCTYPE EMAIL SYSTEM "LstA_2.dtd">*, a node object with the name *EMAIL* would be returned.

Basic Syntax	*objDocType = xmlDocument*.doctype;
Details	Returns an object. This property is read-only. If the document does not contain a DTD, *null* is returned.

USAGE EXAMPLE The following example can be found in AppxA\LstA_7.htm on the companion CD:

```
objDocType = xmlDoc.doctype;
alert(objDocType.nodeName);
```

THE *documentElement* PROPERTY

Identifies the root node of an XML document.

Basic Syntax	*objDoc = xmlDocument*.documentElement;
Details	Returns an object that contains the data in the single root document element. This property is read/write. If the document does not contain a root, *null* is returned.

USAGE EXAMPLE The following example can be found in AppxA\LstA_8.htm on the companion CD:

```
objDocRoot = xmlDoc.documentElement;
alert(objDocRoot);
```

THE *firstChild* PROPERTY

Identifies the first child element in the current node.

Basic Syntax	*objFirstChild = xmlDocNode*.firstChild;
Details	Returns an object. This property is read-only. If the node does not contain a first child element, *null* is returned.

USAGE EXAMPLE   The following example can be found in AppxA\LstA_9.htm on the companion CD:

```
objFirstChild = xmlDoc.documentElement.firstChild;
alert(objFirstChild);
```

THE *implementation* PROPERTY

DOM applications can use objects from other implementations. The *implementation* property identifies the DOM implementation object for the current XML document.

Basic Syntax	*objImplementation* = *xmlDocument*.implementation;
Details	Returns an object. This property is read-only.

USAGE EXAMPLE   The following example can be found in AppxA\LstA_10.htm on the companion CD:

```
objImp = xmlDoc.implementation;
alert(objImp);
```

THE *lastChild* PROPERTY

Identifies the last child element in the current node.

Basic Syntax	*objLastChild* = *xmlDocNode*.lastChild;
Details	Returns an object. This property is read-only. If the node does not contain a last child element, *null* is returned.

USAGE EXAMPLE   The following example can be found in AppxA\LstA_11.htm on the companion CD:

```
objLastChild = xmlDoc.documentElement.lastChild;
alert(objLastChild);
```

THE *nextSibling* PROPERTY

Returns the next sibling in the child list of the current document node.

Basic Syntax	*objNextSibling* = *xmlDocNode*.nextSibling;
Details	Returns an object. This property is read-only. If the node does not contain a next sibling node, *null* is returned.

USAGE EXAMPLE   The following example can be found in AppxA\LstA_12.htm on the companion CD:

```
objSibling = xmlDoc.documentElement.childNodes.item(1).nextSibling;
alert(objSibling);
```

THE *nodeName* PROPERTY

Returns a string representing the name of the current node.

Basic Syntax	`strNodeName = xmlDocNode.nodeName;`
Details	Returns a string. This property is read-only. This property returns the qualified name for an element, attribute, or entity reference.

USAGE EXAMPLE The following example can be found in AppxA\LstA_13.htm on the companion CD:

```
strNodeName = xmlDoc.documentElement.nodeName;
alert(strNodeName);
```

THE *nodeType* PROPERTY

Identifies the DOM type for the given node.

Basic Syntax	`numNodeType = xmlDocNode.nodeType;`
Details	Returns a number. This property is read-only. The available numbers correspond to the following types: 1—*ELEMENT* 2—*ATTRIBUTE* 3—*TEXT* 4—*CDATA* 5—*ENTITY REFERENCE* 6—*ENTITY* 7—*PI* (processing instruction) 8—*COMMENT* 9—*DOCUMENT* 10—*DOCUMENT TYPE* (as found in the document type declaration) 11—*DOCUMENT FRAGMENT* (can contain a node or subtree of a document) 12—*NOTATION*

NOTE

The data types in the preceding table are covered in more depth in Appendix B.

USAGE EXAMPLE The following example can be found in AppxA\LstA_14.htm on the companion CD:

```
numNodeType = xmlDoc.documentElement.nodeType;
alert(numNodeType);
```

THE *nodeValue* PROPERTY

Returns the text associated with a specified node. This is not the value of the data in an element, but rather unparsed text that might be associated with a node, such as an attribute or a processing instruction.

Basic Syntax	*varNodeValue* = *xmlDocNode*.nodeValue;
Details	Text returned represents a typed value based on the *nodeType* property of the node. (See the *nodeType* property in this appendix for more information.) Because the node type can be one of several data types, the return value is considered a variant. Returns *null* for nodes of type *DOCUMENT, ELEMENT, DOCUMENT TYPE, DOCUMENT FRAGMENT, ENTITY, ENTITY REFERENCE,* and *NOTATION*. This property is read/write.

USAGE EXAMPLE   The following example can be found in AppxA\LstA_15.htm on the companion CD:

```
varNodeValue = xmlDoc.documentElement.nodeValue;
alert(varNodeValue);
```

THE *ondataavailable* PROPERTY

Specifies an event handler for the *ondataavailable* event. (For information on the *ondataavailable* event, see the section entitled document Object Events later in this appendix.)

Basic Syntax	*xmlDocNode*.ondataavailable = *value*;
Details	This property is write-only. This property allows the author to start working with data as soon as it is available.

USAGE EXAMPLE   The following example can be found in AppxA\LstA_16.htm on the companion CD:

```
xmlDoc.ondataavailable = alert("Data is now available.");
```

THE *onreadystatechange* PROPERTY

Specifies an event handler for the *onreadystatechange* event. This event identifies when the *readyState* property changes. (For information on the *onreadystatechange* event, see the section entitled document Object Events later in this appendix.)

Basic Syntax	*xmlDocNode*.onreadystatechange = *value*;
Details	This property is write-only. This property allows the author to specify an event handler to be called when the *readyState* property changes.

USAGE EXAMPLE The following example can be found in AppxA\LstA_17.htm on the companion CD:

```
xmlDoc.onreadystatechange =
    alert("The readyState property has changed.");
```

THE *ownerDocument* PROPERTY

Returns the root node of the document that contains the current node.

Basic Syntax	*objOwnerDoc* = *xmlDocument*.ownerDocument;
Details	This property is read-only. This property returns an object containing the root node for the document that contains the specified node.

USAGE EXAMPLE The following example can be found in AppxA\LstA_18.htm on the companion CD:

```
objOwnerDoc = xmlDoc.childNodes.item(2).ownerDocument;
alert(objOwnerDoc);
```

THE *parentNode* PROPERTY

Returns the parent node of the current node. Applies only to those nodes that can have parents.

Basic Syntax	*objParentNode* = *xmlDocumentNode*.parentNode;
Details	This property is read-only. This property returns an object containing the parent node for a specified node. If the node does not exist in the tree, *null* is returned.

USAGE EXAMPLE The following example can be found in AppxA\LstA_19.htm on the companion CD:

```
objParentNode = xmlDoc.childNodes.item(1).parentNode;
alert(objParentNode);
```

THE *parseError* PROPERTY

Returns a DOM parse error object that describes the last parse error.

Basic Syntax	*objParseErr* = *xmlDocument*.parseError;
Details	This property is read-only. If no error has occurred, *0* is returned.

USAGE EXAMPLE The following example can be found in AppxA\LstA_20.htm on the companion CD:

```
objParseErr = xmlDoc.parseError;
alert(objParseErr);
```

THE *previousSibling* PROPERTY

Returns the sibling node that occurs just before the current node.

Basic Syntax	`objPrevSibling = xmlDocument.previousSibling;`
Details	Returns an object. This property is read-only. If the node does not contain a previous sibling node, *null* is returned.

USAGE EXAMPLE The following example can be found in AppxA\LstA_21.htm on the companion CD:

```
objPrevSibling =
    xmlDoc.documentElement.childNodes.item(3).previousSibling
alert(objPrevSibling);
```

THE *readyState* PROPERTY

Returns the current state of the XML document data.

Basic Syntax	`intState = xmlDocument.readyState;`
Details	This property is read-only. One of the following numbers is returned: 0—UNINITIALIZED. XML object is created but no document is loaded. 1—LOADING. The load is in progress, but the document has not yet started to be parsed. 2—LOADED. Some of the document is loaded and parsing has begun, but the object model is not yet available. 3—INTERACTIVE. The object model is available for the portions of the document that are loaded. The object model is read-only in this state. 4—COMPLETED. The document has been completely loaded. This does not necessarily mean that the load was successful.

USAGE EXAMPLE The following example can be found in AppxA\LstA_22.htm on the companion CD:

```
alert("The readyState property is " + xmlDoc.readyState);
```

THE *url* PROPERTY

Returns the URL of the most recently loaded XML document.

Basic Syntax	`strDocUrl = xmlDocument.url;`
Details	This property is read-only. Returns the URL for the last document that was loaded successfully. If the document exists only in memory (it was not loaded from an external file), *null* is returned.

USAGE EXAMPLE The following example can be found in AppxA\LstA_23.htm on the companion CD:

```
alert(xmlDoc.url);
```

THE *validateOnParse* PROPERTY

Indicates to the parser whether the document should be validated.

Basic Syntax	`boolValidate = xmlDocument.validateOnParse;` `xmlDocument.validateOnParse = boolValidate;`
Details	This property is read/write. If *true*, the document is validated when it is parsed. If *false*, the document is not validated and is expected only to be well formed.

USAGE EXAMPLE The following example can be found in AppxA\LstA_24.htm on the companion CD:

```
xmlDoc.validateOnParse = true;
alert(xmlDoc.validateOnParse);
```

THE *xml* PROPERTY

Returns the XML representation of the specified node and any descendants.

Basic Syntax	`xmlValue = xmlDocumentNode.xml;`
Details	This property is read-only.

USAGE EXAMPLE The following example can be found in AppxA\LstA_25.htm on the companion CD:

```
xmlValue = xmlDoc.documentElement.xml;
alert(xmlValue);
```

document Object Methods

The list below shows the methods available for the *document* object:

- *abort*
- *appendChild*
- *cloneNode*
- *createAttribute*
- *createCDATASection*
- *createComment*
- *createDocumentFragment*
- *createElement*
- *createEntityReference*
- *createNode*
- *createProcessingInstruction*
- *createTextNode*
- *getElementsByTagName*
- *hasChildNodes*

- *insertBefore*
- *load*
- *loadXML*
- *nodeFromID*
- *parsed*

- *removeChild*
- *replaceChild*
- *selectNodes*
- *selectSingleNode*
- *transformNode*

THE *abort* METHOD

The *abort* method cancels an asynchronous download that is in progress.

Basic Syntax	`xmlDocument.abort();`
Details	If this method is called during an asynchronous download, all parsing is stopped and any portion of the document in memory is discarded.

THE *appendChild* METHOD

Appends a node as the last child of a specified node.

Basic Syntax	`xmlDocumentNode.appendChild(newChild);`
Details	*newChild* is the address of the child node to be appended.

USAGE EXAMPLE The following example can be found in AppxA\LstA_26.htm on the companion CD:

```
docObj = xmlDoc.documentElement;
alert(docObj.xml);
objNewNode = docObj.appendChild(xmlDoc.documentElement.firstChild);
alert(docObj.xml);
```

THE *cloneNode* METHOD

Creates an exact replica of a specified node.

Basic Syntax	`xmlDocumentNode.cloneNode(deep);`
Details	*deep* is a Boolean value. If *true*, the node is cloned with all of its descendants. If *false*, only the specified node and its attributes are cloned.

USAGE EXAMPLE The following example can be found in AppxA\LstA_27.htm on the companion CD:

```
currNode = xmlDoc.documentElement.childNodes.item(1);
objClonedNode = currNode.cloneNode(1);
alert(objClonedNode.xml);
```

THE *createAttribute* METHOD

Creates an attribute with a specified name.

Basic Syntax	*xmlDocument*.createAttribute(*name*);
Details	*name* is the name of the attribute to be created.

USAGE EXAMPLE The following example can be found in AppxA\LstA_28.htm on the companion CD:

```
objNewAtt = xmlDoc.createAttribute("encryption");
alert(objNewAtt.xml);
```

THE *createCDATASection* METHOD

Creates a *CDATA* section that contains the specified data.

Basic Syntax	*xmlDocument*.createCDATASection(*data*);
Details	*data* is a string containing the data to be placed in the *CDATA* section.

USAGE EXAMPLE The following example can be found in AppxA\LstA_29.htm on the companion CD:

```
objNewCDATA = xmlDoc.createCDATASection("This is a CDATA Section");
alert(objNewCDATA.xml);
```

THE *createComment* METHOD

Creates a comment that contains the specified data.

Basic Syntax	*xmlDocument*.createComment(*data*);
Details	*data* is a string containing the data to be placed in the comment.

USAGE EXAMPLE The following example can be found in AppxA\LstA_30.htm on the companion CD:

```
objNewComment = xmlDoc.createComment("This is a comment");
alert(objNewComment.xml);
```

THE *createDocumentFragment* METHOD

Creates an empty document fragment object.

Basic Syntax	*xmlDocument*.createDocumentFragment();
Details	A new document fragment is created but not added to the document tree. To add the fragment to the tree, one of the insert methods must be used, such as *insertBefore*, *replaceChild*, or *appendChild*.

USAGE EXAMPLE   The following example can be found in AppxA\LstA_31.htm on the companion CD:

```
objNewFragment = xmlDoc.createDocumentFragment();
alert(objNewFragment.xml);
```

THE *createElement* METHOD

Creates an element with the specified name.

Basic Syntax	*xmlDocument*.createElement(*tagName*);
Details	*tagName* is a case-sensitive string specifying the name of the new element.

USAGE EXAMPLE   The following example can be found in AppxA\LstA_32.htm on the companion CD:

```
objNewElement = xmlDoc.createElement("TO");
alert(objNewElement.xml);
```

THE *createEntityReference* METHOD

Creates an entity reference with the specified name.

Basic Syntax	*xmlDocument*.createEntityReference(*name*);
Details	*name* is a case-sensitive string specifying the name of the new entity reference. A new entity reference is created but not added to the document tree. To add the entity reference to the tree, one of the insert methods must be used, such as *insertBefore*, *replaceChild*, or *appendChild*.

USAGE EXAMPLE   The following example can be found in AppxA\LstA_33.htm on the companion CD:

```
objNewER = xmlDoc.createEntityReference("eRef");
alert(objNewER.xml);
```

THE *createNode* METHOD

Creates a new node with the specified type, name, and namespace.

Basic Syntax	*xmlDocument*.createNode(*type, name, nameSpaceURI*);
Details	*type* identifies the type of node being created.
	name is a string identifying the name of the new node. Optionally includes a namespace prefix.

nameSpaceURI is a string defining the namespace URI. If a prefix is included in the *name* parameter, the node is created with the specified prefix in the context of *nameSpaceURI*. If a prefix is not included, the specified namespace is treated as the default namespace.

USAGE EXAMPLE The following example can be found in AppxA\LstA_34.htm on the companion CD:

```
objNewNode = xmlDoc.createNode(1, "TO", "");
alert(objNewNode.xml);
```

THE *createProcessingInstruction* METHOD

Creates a new processing instruction containing the specified target and data.

Basic Syntax	*xmlDocument*.createProcessingInstruction(*target*, *data*);
Details	*target* is a string that identifies the target, or name, of the processing instruction.
	data is a string identifying the remainder, or value, of the processing instruction.
	A new processing instruction is created but not added to the document tree. To add the processing instruction to the tree, one of the insert methods must be used, such as *insertBefore*, *replaceChild*, or *appendChild*.

USAGE EXAMPLE The following example can be found in AppxA\LstA_35.htm on the companion CD:

```
objNewPI =
    xmlDoc.createProcessingInstruction('XML', 'version="1.0"');
alert(objNewPI.xml);
```

THE *createTextNode* METHOD

Creates a new text node containing the specified data.

Basic Syntax	*xmlDocument*.createTextNode(*data*);
Details	*data* is a string identifying the value of the new text node.
	A new text node is created but not added to the document tree. To add the node to the tree, one of the insert methods must be used, such as *insertBefore*, *replaceChild*, or *appendChild*.

The following example can be found in AppxA\LstA_36.htm on the companion CD:

```
objNewTextNode = xmlDoc.createTextNode("This is a text node.");
alert(objNewTextNode.xml);
```

THE *getElementsByTagName* METHOD

Returns a collection of elements with the specified name.

Basic Syntax	*objNodeList = xmlDocument*.getElementsByTagName(*tagname*);
Details	*tagname* is a string identifying the tag name of the element to be found. Using the tagname "*" returns all the elements found in the document.

USAGE EXAMPLE The following example can be found in AppxA\LstA_37.htm on the companion CD:

```
objNodeList = xmlDoc.getElementsByTagName("*");
alert(objNodeList.item(1).xml);
```

THE *hasChildNodes* METHOD

Returns *true* if the specified node has one or more children.

Basic Syntax	*boolValue = xmlDocumentNode*.hasChildNodes();
Details	Returns *true* if the node has children and *false* otherwise.

USAGE EXAMPLE The following example can be found in AppxA\LstA_38.htm on the companion CD:

```
boolValue = xmlDoc.documentElement.hasChildNodes();
alert(boolValue);
```

THE *insertBefore* METHOD

Inserts a child node before the specified node.

Basic Syntax	*objDocumentNode = xmlDocumentNode*.insertBefore(*newChild, refChild*);
Details	*newChild* is an object containing the address of the new child node.
	refChild is the address of the reference node. The new child is inserted before the reference node. If the *refChild* parameter is not included, the new child is inserted at the end of the child list.

The following example can be found in AppxA\LstA_39.htm on the companion CD:

```
objRefNode = xmlDoc.documentElement;
alert(xmlDoc.xml);
objNewNode = xmlDoc.createComment("This is a comment");
xmlDoc.insertBefore(objNewNode, objRefNode);
alert(xmlDoc.xml);
```

THE *load* METHOD

Loads the indicated document from the specified location.

Basic Syntax	*boolValue = xmlDocument*.load(*url*);
Details	*url* is a string containing the URL for the file to be loaded.
	If the document loads successfully, *true* is returned. If the load fails, *false* is returned.

USAGE EXAMPLE The following example can be found in AppxA\LstA_40.htm on the companion CD:

```
boolValue = xmlDoc.load("LstA_1.xml");
alert(boolValue);
```

THE *loadXML* METHOD

Loads an XML document or fragment from a string.

Basic Syntax	*boolValue = xmlDocument*.loadXML(*xmlString*);
Details	*xmlString* is a string containing XML code. The string can contain either an entire document or just a document fragment.
	If the document loads successfully, *true* is returned. If the load fails, *false* is returned.

USAGE EXAMPLE The following example can be found in AppxA\LstA_41.htm on the companion CD:

```
xmlString = "<GREETING><MESSAGE>Hello!</MESSAGE></GREETING>";
boolValue = xmlDoc.loadXML(xmlString);
alert(boolValue);
```

THE *nodeFromID* METHOD

Returns a node for which the node ID matches the specified value.

Basic Syntax	`xmlDocumentNode = xmlDocument.nodeFromID(idString);`
Details	*idString* is a string containing an ID value. The matching node must be of the type *ID*. If a match is found, an object is returned. If the operation fails, *null* is returned.

USAGE EXAMPLE The following example can be found in AppxA\LstA_42.htm on the companion CD:

```
objDocumentNode = xmlDoc.nodeFromID("TO");
alert(objDocumentNode);
```

THE *parsed* METHOD

Verifies whether the specified node and all its descendants have been parsed and instantiated.

Basic Syntax	`boolValue = xmlDocumentNode.parsed();`
Details	If the entire node has been parsed, *true* is returned. If any part of the node has not yet been parsed, *false* is returned.

USAGE EXAMPLE The following example can be found in AppxA\LstA_43.htm on the companion CD:

```
currNode = xmlDoc.documentElement.childNodes.item(0);
boolValue = currNode.parsed();
alert(boolValue);
```

THE *removeChild* METHOD

Removes the specified child node from the node list.

Basic Syntax	`objDocumentNode = xmlDocumentNode.removeChild(oldChild);`
Details	*oldChild* is an object containing the child node to be removed.

USAGE EXAMPLE The following example can be found in AppxA\LstA_44.htm on the companion CD:

```
objRemoveNode = xmlDoc.documentElement.childNodes.item(3);
alert(xmlDoc.xml);
xmlDoc.documentElement.removeChild(objRemoveNode);
alert(xmlDoc.xml);
```

THE *replaceChild* METHOD

Replaces the specified old child node with the supplied new child node.

Basic Syntax	*objDocumentNode* = *xmlDocumentNode*.replaceChild(*newChild*, *oldChild*);
Details	*newChild* is an object containing the new child. If this parameter is *null*, the old child is removed without a replacement.
	oldChild is an object containing the child node to be replaced.

USAGE EXAMPLE   The following example can be found in AppxA\LstA_45.htm on the companion CD:

```
objOldNode = xmlDoc.documentElement.childNodes.item(3);
objNewNode = xmlDoc.createComment("I've replaced the BCC element.");
alert(xmlDoc.xml);
xmlDoc.documentElement.replaceChild(objNewNode, objOldNode);
alert(xmlDoc.xml);
```

THE *selectNodes* METHOD

Returns the nodes that match the supplied pattern.

Basic Syntax	*objDocumentNodeList* = *xmlDocumentNode*.selectNodes(*patternString*);
Details	*patternString* is a string containing the XSL pattern to be matched.
	A node list object is returned that contains matching nodes. If no matches are found, an empty list is returned.

USAGE EXAMPLE   The following example can be found in AppxA\LstA_46.htm on the companion CD:

```
objNodeList = xmlDoc.selectNodes("/");
alert(objNodeList.item(0).xml);
```

THE *selectSingleNode* METHOD

Returns the first node that matches the supplied pattern.

Basic Syntax	*objDocumentNode* = *xmlDocumentNode*.selectSingleNode(*patternString*);
Details	*patternString* is a string containing the XSL pattern to be matched.
	A node object is returned that contains the first matching node. If no matches are found, *null* is returned.

USAGE EXAMPLE   The following example can be found in AppxA\LstA_47.htm on the companion CD:

```
objNode = xmlDoc.selectSingleNode("EMAIL/BCC");
alert(objNode.xml);
```

THE *transformNode* METHOD

Processes the node and its child nodes using the supplied style sheet.

Basic Syntax	*strTransformedDocument = xmlDocumentNode*`.transformNode(`*stylesheet*`);`
Details	*stylesheet* is an XML document or fragment containing XSL elements that conduct the transformation of the node. A string is returned that contains the result of the transformation.

USAGE EXAMPLE   The following example can be found in AppxA\LstA_48.htm on the companion CD:

```
var style = new ActiveXObject("Microsoft.XMLDOM");
style.load("LstA_49.xsl");
strTransform = xmlDoc.transformNode(style.documentElement);
alert(strTransform);
```

NOTE

For more details on XSL, see Chapters 8 and 9.

document Object Events

The list below shows the events available for the *document* object:

- ◆ *ondataavailable*
- ◆ *onreadystatechange*

THE *ondataavailable* EVENT

This event is triggered when the XML document data is available.

Basic Syntax	This event can be handled in any of three ways: ◆ Inline: *<element* ondataavailable = *handler>*; ◆ Event property: *object*.ondataavailable = *handler*; ◆ Named script: <SCRIPT FOR = *object* EVENT = *ondataavailable*>;
Details	The *ondataavailable* event is fired as soon as any data is available. This technique does not indicate how much of a given document is available.

USAGE EXAMPLE The following example can be found in AppxA\LstA_50.htm on the companion CD:

```
xmlDoc.ondataavailable = alert('Data is now available.');
```

THE *onreadystatechange* EVENT

This event is triggered when the *readyState* property changes.

Basic Syntax	This event can be handled in any of three ways: ◆ Inline: *<element* onreadystatechange = *handler>*; ◆ Event property: *object*.onreadystatechange = *handler*; ◆ Named script: <SCRIPT FOR = *object* EVENT = *onreadystatechange>*;
Details	The *onreadystatechange* event is fired when the *readyState* property changes, but the event does not indicate what the ready state is. Use the *readyState* property to get the current state.

USAGE EXAMPLE The following example can be found in AppxA\LstA_51.htm on the companion CD:

```
xmlDoc.onreadystatechange =
    alert("The readyState property is " + xmlDoc.readyState);
```

The *node* Object

The *node* object represents an individual "branch" of a document tree. You will see that the *node* object has many of the same properties, methods, and events as the *document* object. This is true because the *document* object is just another node on the tree in most respects. Because of this, we will list all of the properties, methods, and events for the *node* object, but we'll detail only the new ones.

node Object Properties

The list below shows the properties available for the *node* object:

◆ *attributes*	◆ *nameSpace*	◆ *ownerDocument*
◆ *baseName*	◆ *nextSibling*	◆ *parentNode*
◆ *childNodes*	◆ *nodeName*	◆ *prefix*
◆ *dataType*	◆ *nodeStringType*	◆ *previousSibling*
◆ *definition*	◆ *nodeType*	◆ *specified*
◆ *firstChild*	◆ *nodeTypedValue*	◆ *text*
◆ *lastChild*	◆ *nodeValue*	◆ *xml*

THE *baseName* PROPERTY

Returns the base name for a name that is qualified with a namespace.

Basic Syntax	*strValue = xmlDocumentNode.baseName;*
Details	This property is read-only. In a qualified name such as *ns:base*, the right side of the name is returned. In this example, *base* would be returned.

USAGE EXAMPLE The following example can be found in AppxA\LstA_52.htm on the companion CD:

```
strBaseName = xmlDoc.documentElement.childNodes.item(1).baseName;
alert(strBaseName);
```

THE *dataType* PROPERTY

Gets or sets the data type for a specified node.

Basic Syntax	*objValue = xmlDocumentNode.dataType;* *xmlDocumentNode.dataType = objValue;*
Details	This property is read/write. This property gets or sets rich data types only (or *null* if no data type is specified). See Appendix B for more information on rich data types.

USAGE EXAMPLE The following example can be found in AppxA\LstA_53.htm on the companion CD:

```
objNode = xmlDoc.documentElement.childNodes.item(1);
objNode.dataType = "string";
alert(objNode.dataType);
```

THE *definition* PROPERTY

Returns the definition of the node as specified in the DTD or schema.

Basic Syntax	*objDefinition = xmlDocumentNode.definition;*
Details	This property returns an object and is read-only. Applies only to entities that have a corresponding entity reference. For all other element types, *null* is returned.

USAGE EXAMPLE The following example can be found in AppxA\LstA_54.htm on the companion CD:

```
objNode = xmlDoc.documentElement.childNodes.item(1);
alert(objNode.definition);
```

Because this document does not contain any entity references, *null* is returned.

THE *nameSpace* PROPERTY

Returns the URI for a namespace.

Basic Syntax	*strURI* = *xmlDocumentNode*.nameSpace;
Details	This property returns a string and is read-only. The URI is returned, but the namespace name is not.

USAGE EXAMPLE The following example can be found in AppxA\LstA_55.htm on the companion CD:

```
objNode = xmlDoc.createNode(1, "bp:myNode", "bp/nodens");
alert(objNode.nameSpace);
```

THE *nodeStringType* PROPERTY

Returns the node type as a string.

Basic Syntax	*strTypeValue* = *xmlDocumentNode*.nodeStringType;
Details	This property returns a string and is read-only.

USAGE EXAMPLE The following example can be found in AppxA\LstA_56.htm on the companion CD:

```
objNode = xmlDoc.documentElement.childNodes.item(0);
alert(objNode.nodeStringType);
```

THE *nodeTypedValue* PROPERTY

Returns the node value in the form of its defined data type.

Basic Syntax	*objValue* = *xmlDocumentNode*.nodeTypedValue; *xmlDocumentNode*.nodeTypedValue = *objValue*;
Details	This property is read/write.

USAGE EXAMPLE The following example can be found in AppxA\LstA_57.htm on the companion CD:

```
objNode = xmlDoc.documentElement.childNodes.item(1);
alert(objNode.nodeTypedValue);
```

THE *prefix* PROPERTY

Returns the namespace prefix.

Basic Syntax	*strPrefixValue = xmlDocumentNode*.prefix;
Details	This property returns a string and is read-only. Only the namespace prefix is returned.

USAGE EXAMPLE The following example can be found in AppxA\LstA_58.htm on the companion CD:

```
objNode = xmlDoc.createNode(1, "bp:myNode", "bp/nodens");
alert(objNode.prefix);
```

THE *specified* PROPERTY

Indicates whether a node value is explicitly specified in the element or whether it is derived from a DTD or schema. This property is usually used for attribute values.

Basic Syntax	*boolSpecified = xmlDocumentNode*.specified;
Details	This property returns a Boolean value and is read-only. Returns *true* if the value is specified in the element. Returns *false* if the value comes from the DTD or schema.

USAGE EXAMPLE The following example can be found in AppxA\LstA_59.htm on the companion CD:

```
objNode = xmlDoc.documentElement.childNodes.item(0);
alert(objNode.specified);
```

THE *text* PROPERTY

Gets or sets the text for a node.

Basic Syntax	*strText = xmlDocumentNode*.text; *xmlDocumentNode*.text = *strText*;
Details	This property is a string value and is read/write.

USAGE EXAMPLE The following example can be found in AppxA\LstA_60.htm on the companion CD:

```
objNode = xmlDoc.documentElement.childNodes.item(0);
alert(objNode.text);
```

node Object Methods

The list below shows the methods available for the *node* object:

- *appendChild*
- *cloneNode*
- *hasChildNodes*
- *insertBefore*
- *parsed*

- *removeChild*
- *replaceChild*
- *selectNodes*
- *selectSingleNode*
- *transformNode*

THE *hasChildNodes* METHOD

Returns *true* if the specified node has one or more children.

Basic Syntax	`boolValue = xmlDocumentNode.hasChildNodes();`
Details	This method returns a Boolean value and is read-only.

USAGE EXAMPLE   The following example can be found in AppxA\LstA_61.htm on the companion CD:

```
objNode = xmlDoc.documentElement;
alert(objNode.hasChildNodes());
```

The *nodeList* Object

The *nodeList* object is an active collection of nodes in the document tree. It is "active" in the sense that any changes to the *nodeList* object are instantly reflected in the collection.

nodeList Object Property

The *length* property is the only property available for the *nodeList* object.

THE *length* PROPERTY

Returns the number of items in a collection.

Basic Syntax	`intValue = xmlNodeList.length;`
Details	This property returns a long integer value and is read-only.

USAGE EXAMPLE   The following example can be found in AppxA\LstA_62.htm on the companion CD:

```
objNodeList = xmlDoc.documentElement.childNodes;
alert(objNodeList.length);
```

nodeList Object Methods

The list below shows the methods available for the *nodeList* object:

- *item*
- *nextNode*
- *reset*

THE *item* METHOD

Accesses an individual node in a document tree.

Basic Syntax	*objDocumentNode* = *xmlNodeList*.item(*index*);
Details	*index* is a long integer specifying the numeric index (0-based) of the desired child node.

USAGE EXAMPLE The following example can be found in AppxA\LstA_63.htm on the companion CD:

```
objNode = xmlDoc.documentElement.childNodes.item(2);
alert(objNode.xml);
```

THE *nextNode* METHOD

Accesses the next node in the collection.

Basic Syntax	*objDocumentNode* = *xmlNodeList*.nextNode();
Details	Returns an object containing the next node. Returns *null* if a node is not available.

USAGE EXAMPLE The following example can be found in AppxA\LstA_64.htm on the companion CD:

```
objNode = xmlDoc.documentElement.childNodes;
objNextNode = objNode.nextNode();
alert(objNextNode.xml);
objNextNode = objNode.nextNode();
alert(objNextNode.xml);
```

THE *reset* METHOD

Resets the index pointer in the node list.

Basic Syntax	*objDocumentNode* = *xmlNodeList*.reset();
Details	Resets the pointer in the node list to just before the first node in the list.

The following example can be found in AppxA\LstA_65.htm on the companion CD:

```
objNode = xmlDoc.documentElement.childNodes;
objNextNode = objNode.nextNode();
alert(objNextNode.xml);
objNode.reset();
objNextNode = objNode.nextNode();
alert(objNextNode.xml);
```

The *parseError* Object

The *parseError* object returns information about the last parse error. To demonstrate how the *parseError* object works, we need to use an XML document with an error in it. Code Listing A-1a (AppxA\LstA_1a.xml on the companion CD) is the email document with the Cc and Bcc elements reversed, which is an error according to the DTD.

```
<?xml version="1.0"?>

<!DOCTYPE EMAIL SYSTEM "LstA_2.dtd">
<EMAIL PRIORITY="HIGH">
  <TO>Jodie@msn.com</TO>
  <FROM>Bill@msn.com</FROM>
  <BCC>Naomi@msn.com</BCC>
  <CC>Philip@msn.com</CC>
  <SUBJECT>My document is a tree.</SUBJECT>
  <BODY>This is an example of a tree structure.</BODY>
</EMAIL>
```

Code Listing A-1a.

parseError Object Properties

The list below shows the properties available for the *parseError* object:

- *errorCode*
- *filePos*
- *line*
- *linePos*
- *reason*
- *srcText*
- *url*

THE *errorCode* PROPERTY

Returns the error code of the last parse error.

Basic Syntax	`intErrorValue = xmlDocument.parseError.errorCode;`
Details	Returns a long integer. This property is read-only.

USAGE EXAMPLE   The following example can be found in AppxA\LstA_66.htm on the companion CD:

```
intParseValue = xmlDoc.parseError.errorCode;
alert(intParseValue);
```

THE *filePos* PROPERTY

Returns the position in the file where the error occurred.

Basic Syntax	`intErrorValue = xmlDocument.parseError.filePos;`
Details	Returns a long integer representing the absolute position (in number of characters) of the error. This property is read-only.

USAGE EXAMPLE   The following example can be found in AppxA\LstA_67.htm on the companion CD:

```
intParseValue = xmlDoc.parseError.filePos;
alert(intParseValue);
```

THE *line* PROPERTY

Returns the line number where the error occurred.

Basic Syntax	`intErrorValue = xmlDocument.parseError.line;`
Details	Returns a long integer representing the line number where the error occurred. This property is read-only.

USAGE EXAMPLE   The following example can be found in AppxA\LstA_68.htm on the companion CD:

```
intParseValue = xmlDoc.parseError.line;
alert(intParseValue);
```

THE *linePos* PROPERTY

Returns the position in the line where the error occurred.

Basic Syntax	`intErrorValue = xmlDocument.parseError.linePos;`
Details	Returns a long integer representing the character position in the line where the error occurred. This property is read-only.

USAGE EXAMPLE The following example can be found in AppxA\LstA_69.htm on the companion CD:

```
intParseValue = xmlDoc.parseError.linePos;
alert(intParseValue);
```

THE *reason* PROPERTY

Returns the reason for the last parse error.

Basic Syntax	*strErrorReason* = *xmlDocument*.parseError.reason;
Details	Returns a string containing a description of the reason for the last parse error. This property is read-only.

USAGE EXAMPLE The following example can be found in AppxA\LstA_70.htm on the companion CD:

```
strErrorReason = xmlDoc.parseError.reason;
alert(strErrorReason);
```

THE *srcText* PROPERTY

Returns the text of the line containing the error.

Basic Syntax	*strSrcText* = *xmlDocument*.parseError.srcText;
Details	Returns a string containing the full text of the line that contains the error, including white space. This property is read-only.

USAGE EXAMPLE The following example can be found in AppxA\LstA_71.htm on the companion CD:

```
strSrcText = xmlDoc.parseError.srcText;
alert(strSrcText);
```

Appendix B
Data Types in XML

his appendix contains three tables that identify various data types in XML: two tables focuses on XML content and one table focuses on the XML Document object model (DOM). The first table contains the primitive data types, the second table contains the supported rich data types, and the third table contains the DOM node types.

Primitive data types are those types identified in the XML 1.0 specification. These basic data types are used to identify different "pieces" of an XML document, and are not the data types you would typically find in a traditional programming language or database management system (DBMS). For example, the type *entity* identifies to the processor that the object is an entity and must therefore follow certain rules. But specifying this type doesn't indicate whether the data is text, a number, or a date, for example, because according to the XML 1.0 specification, all text that is not markup constitutes the character data of the document. So you can think of the primitive data types as different varieties of character data, or text. More information on how primitive types are used can be found in Chapter 4.

Rich data types are referenced in the XML-Data specification and are used within the *datatypes* namespace. These data types are more typical of those found in a programming language or DBMS, and include types such as *int, char,* and *date.* More on rich data types can be found in Chapters 6 and 10.

DOM provides support for typing nodes of the document tree. Many of these types map to the primitive XML data types, but others are included as well. A DOM node type identifies the type of node being worked with and might indicate the type of data contained in the node. For example, *NODE_COMMENT* indicates that the node in question is a comment. DOM identifies each node type by a numerical value. More information on DOM node types can be found in Chapter 9.

Primitive Types (Available for Attributes Only)

Data Type Name	Example of Attribute Value	Parse Type
entity	entity1	*ENTITY*
entities	entity1 entity2	*ENTITIES*
enumeration	one	*ENUMERATION*
id	a	*ID*
idref	a	*IDREF*
idrefs	a b c	*IDREFS*
nmtoken	name1	*NMTOKEN*
nmtokens	name1 name2	*NMTOKENS*
notation	GIF	*NOTATION*
string	This is a string.	*PCDATA*

Rich Data Types (Available for Elements and Attributes)

Data Type Name	Examples of Element/ Attribute Values	Parse Type
bin.base64		MIME-style Base64 encoded binary chunk.
bin.hex		Hexadecimal digits representing octets.
boolean	0, 1 (0 equals *false*, 1 equals *true*)	"0" or "1"
char	x	*string*
date	1994-11-05	A date in a subset of the ISO 8601 format with no time.
dateTime	1988-04-07T18:39:09	A date in a subset of the ISO 8601 format with optional time and no optional zone. Fractional seconds may be as precise as nanoseconds.
dateTime.tz	1988-04-07T18:39:09-08:00	A date in a subset of the ISO 8601 format with optional time and optional zone. Fractional seconds may be as precise as nanoseconds.
fixed.14.4	12.0044	Same as *number* but no more than 14 digits to the left of the decimal point, and no more than 4 digits to the right.
i1	1, 127, −128	A number with optional sign, no fractions, and no exponent.
i2	1, 703, −32768	A number with optional sign, no fractions, and no exponent.
i4	1, 703, −32768, 148343, −1000000000	A number with optional sign, no fractions, and no exponent.
i8	1, 703, −32768, 1483433434334, −1000000000000000	A number with optional sign, no fractions, and no exponent.
int	1, 58502, −13	A number with optional sign, no fractions, and no exponents.

(continued)

Data Type Name	Examples of Element/ Attribute Values	Parse Type
number	15, 3.14, –123.456E+10	A number with essentially no limit on the number of digits. May potentially have a leading sign, fractional digits, and, optionally, an exponent. Punctuation as in U.S. English.
r4	.3141592E+1	Same parse type as *number*, but with approximate minimum value 1.17549435E–38F and approximate maximum value 3.40282347E+38F.
r8	.314159265358979E+1	Same parse type as *number*, but with approximate minimum value 2.2250738585072014E–308 and approximate maximum value 1.7976931348623157E+308.
string	This is a string.	*PCDATA*
time	08:15:27	A time in a subset of the ISO 8601 format with no date and no zone.
time.tz	08:1527-05:00	A time in a subset of the ISO 8601 format with no date but optional zone.
ui1	1, 255	An unsigned number with no fractions and no exponent.
ui2	1, 255, 65535	An unsigned number with no fractions and no exponent.
ui4	1, 703, 3000000000	An unsigned number with no fractions and no exponent.
ui8	1483433434334	An unsigned number with no fractions and no exponent.
uri	urn:schemas-microsoft-com	Universal Resource Identifier
user-defined type		*VT_UNKNOWN*
uuid	333C7BC4-460F-11D0-BC04-0080C7055A83	Hexadecimal digits representing octets, with optional embedded hyphens that should be ignored.

DOM Node Types

Node Type Name	Value
NODE_ELEMENT	1
NODE_ATTRIBUTE	2
NODE_TEXT	3
NODE_CDATA_SECTION	4
NODE_ENTITY_REFERENCE	5
NODE_ENTITY	6
NODE_PROCESSING_INSTRUCTION	7
NODE_COMMENT	8
NODE_DOCUMENT	9
NODE_DOCUMENT_TYPE	10
NODE_DOCUMENT_FRAGMENT	11
NODE_NOTATION	12

Appendix C
Related Topics

This appendix provides a list of topics, organized by chapter, that contain additional information regarding XML. This information is part of the Microsoft Site Builder Network (SBN) and the Microsoft Developer Network (MSDN). The topics can be accessed on the companion CD or on the Internet. To access a topic on the CD, open the file *Workshop XML Reference.htm* to reach the XML Table of Contents (XML TOC on SBN), and then navigate as described to the link for that particular topic. For example, to find the topic **XML Tutorial Lesson 1: Authoring XML Elements**, open *Workshop XML Reference.htm,* expand *XML Tutorial* in the left-hand frame, and then click *Authoring Elements.*

This information is also available on the Internet. To get to the online version of our example, visit the MSDN Online Resource page at *http://msdn.microsoft.com/resources/ pardixml.htm,* or open the file named *MSDN_OL.htm* on the companion CD, and choose *Authoring Elements.*

Chapter 1: Understanding Markup Languages

For more information about the technical side of XML, see the topic **XML: A Technical Perspective.** Go to *General Information,* and choose *Technical Perspective.*

Chapter 2: Enter XML

For more details about the basics of XML, see the following topics:

◆ **XML: Enabling Next-Generation Web Applications.**   Go to *General Information,* and choose *Overview.*

◆ **Frequently Asked Questions About XML.**   Go to *General Information,* and choose *FAQ.*

Chapter 3: XML Structure and Syntax

To access the W3C XML 1.0 Recommendation on the Internet, go to *W3C XML Documentation,* and choose *XML Recommendation.*

Chapter 4: Playing by the Rules—The DTD

For more information about working with a DTD, access the W3C XML 1.0 Recommendation on the Internet by going to *W3C XML Documentation* and choosing *XML Recommendation,* or see the following topics:

◆ **Frequently Asked Questions About XML.**   Go to *General Information,* and choose *FAQ.* In the right-hand frame, select the question, *What are XML schemas? How are they different from DTDs?*

◆ **XML, Validation, and Extra Cheese.** Go to *Extreme XML Columns*, and choose *XML & DTD*.

Chapter 5: Scripting XML

For information about scripting and the XML object model, see the following topics:

◆ **XML Tutorial Lesson 5: Using the XML Object Model.** Go to *XML Tutorial*, and choose *Using the Object Model*.

◆ **XML DOM Reference.** On the CD, go to *XML Support in IE 5 Beta*, and then select *XML DOM Reference*. On the Internet, go to *XML Support in IE 5.0*, and then select *XML DOM Reference*.

Chapter 6: XML As Data

For additional information about using XML as a data source, access the Namespaces in XML specification on the Internet by going to *W3C XML Documentation* and choosing *XML Namespaces Spec,* or see the following topics:

◆ **XML Tutorial Lesson 11: Using the C++ XML DSO.** Go to *XML Tutorial*, and choose *Using the C++ XML DSO*.

◆ **XML Tutorial Lesson 6: Using Data Types Within XML Documents.** Go to *XML Tutorial,* and choose *Using Data Types*.

◆ **XML Tutorial Lesson 7: Accessing Typed XML Values.** Go to *XML Tutorial,* and choose *Accessing Typed Values*.

◆ **Get Your Data on Board: Creating XML Data Sources from Relational Databases.** Go to *Extreme XML Columns,* and choose *Creating XML Data Sources*.

◆ **XML 1.0 and Namespace Support.** On the CD, go to XML Support In IE 5 Beta, and choose XML 1.0 and Namespace Support. On the Internet, go to XML Support In IE 5.0, and choose XML 1.0 and Namespace Support.

Chapter 7: Linking with XML

For additional information on XLink and XPointer, see the following Web sites. Note that these Web sites are not included on the CD that accompanies this book and are not a part of Microsoft Site Builder Network (SBN) or Microsoft Developer Network (MSDN).

◆ **XLink Working Draft.** *http://www.w3.org/TR/WD-xlink*

◆ **XPointer Working Draft.** *http://www.w3.org/TR/WD-xptr*

◆ **XLink Design Principles.** *http://www.w3.org/TR/NOTE-xlink-principles*

Chapter 8: XSL: XML with Style

For additional information about using Extensible Stylesheet Language (XSL), access the XSL working draft on the Internet by going to *W3C XML Documentation* and choosing *XSL Working Draft,* or see the following topics:

- **XML Tutorial Lesson 14: Handling XSL Errors.**   Go to *XML Tutorial,* and choose *Handling XSL Errors.*

- **XML Tutorial Lesson 15: Using Script in XSL.**   Go to *XML Tutorial,* and choose *Using Script in XSL.*

- **XML Tutorial Lesson 16: Handling Irregular Data in XSL.**   Go to *XML Tutorial,* and choose *Handling Irregular Data in XSL.*

- **XSL Reference.**   On the CD, go to *XML Support In IE 5 Beta,* and choose *XSL Reference.* On the Internet, go to *XML Support In IE 5.0,* and choose *XSL Reference.*

Chapter 9: Addressing Data with XSL Patterns

For more information about working with XSL Patterns, see the following topics:

- **XML Tutorial Lesson 9: Using XSL Patterns to Retrieve Nodes.**   Go to *XML Tutorial,* and choose *Using XSL Patterns.*

- **XML Tutorial Lesson 13: Using XSL to Generate XML.**   Go to *XML Tutorial,* and choose *Using XSL to Generate XML.*

Chapter 10: XML-Data

For information about the XML-Data specification, access the XML-Data specification on the Internet by going to *W3C XML Documentation* and choosing *XML-Data Spec,* or see the following topics:

- **XML Tutorial Lesson 8: Authoring XML Schemas.**   Go to *XML Tutorial,* and choose *Authoring XML Schemas.*

- **XML Schema and Data Types Preview.**   On the CD, go to *XML Support In IE 5 Beta*, and choose *XML Schema and Data Types Preview.* On the Internet, go to *XML Support In IE 5.0,* and choose *XML Schema and Data Types Preview.*

Chapter 11: XML Today and Tomorrow

For information about other XML developments, refer to the following:

- **Java Parser.**   Go to *General Information,* and choose *Microsoft/DataChannel Parser Announcement.*

- **Applying XML to various scenarios.**   Go to *XML Scenarios,* and choose any of the available topics.

- **Document Content Description for XML.**   Go to *W3C XML Documentation,* and choose *DCD for XML.*

Index

Note: Italicized page references indicate figures, tables, or code listings.

Special Characters

E

element declarations, *continued*
    data types, 53–54
    empty-element declaration, 53
    introduced, 52
    mixed content, 53
Element element, 232, *232*
elementIndexList method, *191, 221*
element method, *222*
elements
    Anchor, 139, *139, 140, 140–41,* 141
    AttributeType, 233
    Document, 34–35
    Element, 232, *232*
    ElementType, 230–32
    Extends, 246–47
    Group, 231–32, *232*
    H1, 163, *164,* 165
    Link, 142–43, *142*
    Schema, 228–29
    subclassing, 246–47
    Table, 119, 120
    Xml, 257–58
    XSL, 189, *189–90*
ElementType element, 230–32
element value queries, 182–83, *182–83, 183*
empty-element tag, 39–40
EMPTY keyword, 53
encoding declaration, 34
encoding scheme, 227
end method, 220, *221, 222*
entities
    defined, 13, 35
    external, 37–39, 60–62
    general, 60
    internal, 37–39, 60
    introduced, 60
    parameter, 64–65
    parsed, 35, 36
    predefined, 37, *37*
    unparsed (binary), 35, 36–37
    in XML-data, 241
ENTITIES attribute, *56, 102*
entities data type, *235, 304*
ENTITY attribute, *56, 102*
entity data type, *235, 304*
entity references, 36, 62–64, *63, 64*
enumerated attributes, *57, 103*
enumeration data type, *235,* 236, *304*
–*eq*– expression, 215

equality, 215–16
errorCode property, 300
error handling, *parseError* property for, 100, 281
event handlers, 78–79
events
    onclick, 78
    ondataavailable, 292–93
    onload, 85
    onreadystatechange, 293
Extends element, 246–47
extensible computer languages, 32
Extensible Linking Language (XLL), 16
Extensible Markup Language (XML)
    acceptance of, 270
    additional information, 310, 312
    advantages over SGML, 16–17
    as application data, 136
    cross-platform, 268–70
    as data, 17–18, 311 (*see also* Data Source Object (DSO); data types; namespaces)
    defined, 16
    document for memo data, 19–20, *20*
    goals
        implementing, 25
        introduced, 23
        list of, 23–25
    HTML and, 19, 22–23
    introduced, 4
    logical structure
        Document element, 34–35
        introduced, 32, *32,* 33
        prolog, 33–34
    object model for (*see* XML object model)
    object persistence with, 252–53
    physical structure
        internal and external entities, 37–39
        introduced, 32, *32,* 35
        parsed and unparsed entities, 35–37
        predefined entities, 37, *37*
    scripting in (*see* scripting in XML)
    separating data from display, 22
    SGML and, 18–19
    success of, 270
    syntax
        additional information, 310
        attributes, 40
        introduced, 39
        opening and closing tags, 39–40

methods, *continued*
   alert, 89–90
   ancestor, 222
   ancestorChildNumber, 190, 221
   appendChild, 284
   attribute, 222
   childNumber, 190, 221
   cloneNode, 284
   collection, *222*
   comment, 222
   createAttribute, 285
   createCDATASection, 285
   createComment, 285
   createDocumentFragment, 285–86
   createElement, 286
   createEntityReference, 286
   createNode, 286–87
   createProcessingInstruction, 287
   createTextNode, 287–88
   date, 222
   defined, 46, 77
   depth, 191, 221
   document object, 283–92
   element, 222
   elementIndexList, 191, 221
   end, 220, *221, 222*
   formatDate, 191, 221
   formatIndex, 191, 221
   formatNumber, 191, 221
   formatTime, 191, 221
   getElementsByTagName, 288
   hasChildNodes, 288, 297
   index, 220, *220, 222*
   information, *222*
   insertBefore, 288–89
   item, 298
   load, 289
   loadXML, 289
   movenext, 119
   moveprevious, 119
   nextNode, 298
   node, 222
   nodeFromID, 290
   nodeList object, 298–99
   nodeName, 219, *222*
   node object, 297
   nodeType, 219, *219, 222*
   parsed, 290
   pi, 222
   removeChild, 290

methods, *continued*
   replaceChild, 291
   reset, 298–99
   selectNodes, 223, 223–24, 224, 291
   selectSingleNode, 224, 291–92
   text, 218–19, *218, 222*
   textnode, 222
   transformNode, 174, 292
   uniqueID, 191, 221
   value, 219, *222*
   XSL, 190, *190–91, 221*
   XSL Patterns, 221, *221, 222*
Microsoft XML (Msxml) processor, 81
min attribute, 236
minOccurs attribute, 232, *232,* 242
model attribute, 246
mouseHover function, 133
movenext method, 119
moveprevious method, 119
Msxml. *See* Microsoft XML (Msxml) processor
multimedia description languages
   HTML Timed Interactive Multimedia
      Extensions (HTML+TIME), 260–61
   introduced, 258
   Synchronized Multimedia Integration
      Language (SMIL), 258–60

N

NAME attribute, 141, 150, 158
namespace declarations, 104, 112–13
namespace names, 112–13
namespace prefixes, 112–13
nameSpace property, 295
namespaces
   additional information, 311
   creating unique names via
      attribute namespaces, 116
      declaring namespaces as URL or URN,
         115–16
      default namespaces, 114
      introduced, 112
      namespace scope, 113–14
      qualified names, 112–13
      unqualified names, 113
   datatypes, 104, 113, 117, 234
   including other schemas by using, 248
   introduced, 104, 111–12

scripting in XML, from XML to HTML,
continued
    introduced, 84
    measuring costs and benefits, 93–94
scripting in XSL, 187–89, *187–88, 188*
SCRIPT tag, 76, 77
select attribute, 178
selection operators, 211–13, *212*
selectNodes method, 223, *223–24, 224,* 291
selectSingleNode method, 224, 291–92
self-describing documents, 12, 17
serialization, 252–53
SGML. *See* Standard Generalized Markup
    Language (SGML)
SGML Editorial Review Board (SGML ERB),
    18–19
SGML Working Group, 18–19
SHOW attribute, 147–48
showList function, 134, 135–36
single-value elements, 118
SkipLit keyword, 159
SMIL. *See* Synchronized Multimedia
    Integration Language (SMIL)
sorting in XSL, 181–82, *181, 182*
source code, 5
spanning location terms, 158
specificity test, 191–92
specified property, 296
SRC attribute, 79, 142
srcText property, 301
stand-alone document declaration, 34
Standard Generalized Markup Language
    (SGML)
    advantages of XML over, 16–17
    HTML versus, 13–14
    overview, 12–13
    XML and, 18–19
start function, 86, 89–90, 95, 96–97, 201, 209
STEPS attribute, 155
store. *See* online store
string data type, *104, 235, 304, 306*
string location terms, 159
strong typing, 103
structure symbols, 54, *54–55, 55*
style sheets. *See also* Cascading Style Sheets
    (CSS); Extensible Style Language (XSL)
    online store, 133
subclasses, 47, *47,* 69
subclassing, 246–47
subqueries, 214

Synchronized Multimedia Integration
    Language (SMIL), 27, 258–60
syntax
    attributes, 40
    introduced, 39
    opening and closing tags, 39–40
SYSTEM keyword, 61

T

Table element, 119, 120
tags
    !ATTLIST, 56
    closing, 39–40
    comment, 67
    empty-element, 39–40
    HTML, 9
    opening, 39–40
    P, 39
    SCRIPT, 76, 77
    TITLE, 10
TARGET attribute, 147–48, 150
templates in XSL
    anatomy of, 168–70
    built-in, 191
    introduced, 166–67
    multiple templates structure, 170–73, *171,*
        172–73
    patterns, 167–68
    single template structure, 170
text method, 218–19, *218, 222*
textnode method, *222*
text property, 296
time data type, *110, 306*
time.tz data type, *110, 306*
TITLE attribute, 147, 149
TITLE tag, 10
todata object, 90
tokens. *See* tags
transformNode method, 174, 292
type attribute, 234

U

ui1 data type, *111, 306*
ui2 data type, *111, 306*
ui4 data type, *111, 306*

Bill Pardi

After completing a bachelor's degree in broadcast production at Cedarville College in Ohio, Bill earned a master's in Television/Radio/Film at Syracuse University. He decided on a career in multimedia software development after his first encounter with the subject in a course at Syracuse. Following his work as a developer on several multimedia reference titles with Multicom Publishing in Seattle, Bill accepted a position with Microsoft as a program manager. He is now lead program manager and works with a talented team of people creating interactive training software. Bill's after-work activities include writing about technology and playing with his two boys. Originally from New York, he currently lives in Edgewood, Washington, with his wife, Jodie, and their two sons, Cody and Ryan.

The manuscript for this book was prepared and submitted to Microsoft Press in electronic form. Text files were prepared using Microsoft Word 97. Pages were composed by Microsoft Press using Adobe PageMaker 6.52 for Windows, with text in Stone Serif and display type in Univers. Composed pages were delivered to the printer as electronic prepress files.

Cover Design
Tim Girvin Design, Inc.

Cover Illustrator
Tom Draper Design

Electronic Artist
Alton Lawson

Desktop Publisher
Paula Gorelick

Principal Proofreader/Copy Editor
Roger LeBlanc

Indexer
Hugh Maddocks

Microsoft press online

press**On!**

mspress.microsoft.com

Microsoft Press Online is your road map to the best available print and multimedia materials— resources that will help you maximize the effectiveness of Microsoft® software products. Our goal is making it easy and convenient for you to find exactly the Microsoft Press® book or interactive product you need, as well as bringing you the latest in training and certification materials from Microsoft Press.

Where do you want to go today?®

Microsoft®

http://mspress.microsoft.com/reslink/

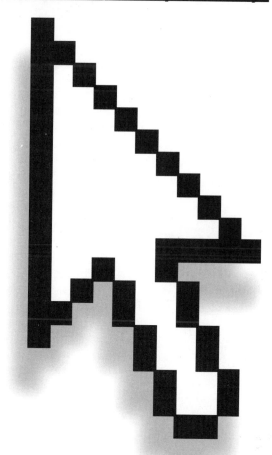

Look
beyond
the kits!

If you deploy, manage, or support Microsoft® products and technologies, here's a hot link to the hottest IT resources available—http://mspress.microsoft.com/reslink/. Microsoft Press® ResourceLink is an essential online information resource for IT professionals—the most complete source of technical information about Microsoft technologies available anywhere. Tap into ResourceLink for direct access to the latest technical updates, tools, and utilities—straight from Microsoft—and help maximize the productivity of your IT investment.

For a **complimentary 30-day trial CD** packed with Microsoft Press IT products, order via our Web site at http://mspress.microsoft.com/reslink/.

mspress.microsoft.com

MICROSOFT LICENSE AGREEMENT

Book Companion CD

IMPORTANT—READ CAREFULLY: This Microsoft End-User License Agreement ("EULA") is a legal agreement between you (either an individual or an entity) and Microsoft Corporation for the Microsoft product identified above, which includes computer software and may include associated media, printed materials, and "on-line" or electronic documentation ("SOFTWARE PRODUCT"). Any component included within the SOFTWARE PRODUCT that is accompanied by a separate End-User License Agreement shall be governed by such agreement and not the terms set forth below. By installing, copying, or otherwise using the SOFTWARE PRODUCT, you agree to be bound by the terms of this EULA. If you do not agree to the terms of this EULA, you are not authorized to install, copy, or otherwise use the SOFTWARE PRODUCT; you may, however, return the SOFTWARE PRODUCT, along with all printed materials and other items that form a part of the Microsoft product that includes the SOFTWARE PRODUCT, to the place you obtained them for a full refund.

SOFTWARE PRODUCT LICENSE

The SOFTWARE PRODUCT is protected by United States copyright laws and international copyright treaties, as well as other intellectual property laws and treaties. The SOFTWARE PRODUCT is licensed, not sold.

1. GRANT OF LICENSE. This EULA grants you the following rights:

a. Software Product. You may install and use one copy of the SOFTWARE PRODUCT on a single computer. The primary user of the computer on which the SOFTWARE PRODUCT is installed may make a second copy for his or her exclusive use on a portable computer.

b. Storage/Network Use. You may also store or install a copy of the SOFTWARE PRODUCT on a storage device, such as a network server, used only to install or run the SOFTWARE PRODUCT on your other computers over an internal network; however, you must acquire and dedicate a license for each separate computer on which the SOFTWARE PRODUCT is installed or run from the storage device. A license for the SOFTWARE PRODUCT may not be shared or used concurrently on different computers.

c. License Pak. If you have acquired this EULA in a Microsoft License Pak, you may make the number of additional copies of the computer software portion of the SOFTWARE PRODUCT authorized on the printed copy of this EULA, and you may use each copy in the manner specified above. You are also entitled to make a corresponding number of secondary copies for portable computer use as specified above.

d. Sample Code. Solely with respect to portions, if any, of the SOFTWARE PRODUCT that are identified within the SOFTWARE PRODUCT as sample code (the "SAMPLE CODE"):

  i. Use and Modification. Microsoft grants you the right to use and modify the source code version of the SAMPLE CODE, *provided* you comply with subsection (d)(iii) below. You may not distribute the SAMPLE CODE, or any modified version of the SAMPLE CODE, in source code form.

  ii. Redistributable Files. Provided you comply with subsection (d)(iii) below, Microsoft grants you a nonexclusive, royalty-free right to reproduce and distribute the object code version of the SAMPLE CODE and of any modified SAMPLE CODE, other than SAMPLE CODE (or any modified version thereof) designated as not redistributable in the Readme file that forms a part of the SOFTWARE PRODUCT (the "Non-Redistributable Sample Code"). All SAMPLE CODE other than the Non-Redistributable Sample Code is collectively referred to as the "REDISTRIBUTABLES."

  iii. Redistribution Requirements. If you redistribute the REDISTRIBUTABLES, you agree to: (i) distribute the REDISTRIBUTABLES in object code form only in conjunction with and as a part of your software application product; (ii) not use Microsoft's name, logo, or trademarks to market your software application product; (iii) include a valid copyright notice on your software application product; (iv) indemnify, hold harmless, and defend Microsoft from and against any claims or lawsuits, including attorney's fees, that arise or result from the use or distribution of your software application product; and (v) not permit further distribution of the REDISTRIBUTABLES by your end user. Contact Microsoft for the applicable royalties due and other licensing terms for all other uses and/or distribution of the REDISTRIBUTABLES.

2. DESCRIPTION OF OTHER RIGHTS AND LIMITATIONS.

- **Limitations on Reverse Engineering, Decompilation, and Disassembly.** You may not reverse engineer, decompile, or disassemble the SOFTWARE PRODUCT, except and only to the extent that such activity is expressly permitted by applicable law notwithstanding this limitation.

- **Separation of Components.** The SOFTWARE PRODUCT is licensed as a single product. Its component parts may not be separated for use on more than one computer.

- **Rental.** You may not rent, lease, or lend the SOFTWARE PRODUCT.

- **Support Services.** Microsoft may, but is not obligated to, provide you with support services related to the SOFTWARE PRODUCT ("Support Services"). Use of Support Services is governed by the Microsoft policies and programs described in the user manual, in "on-line" documentation, and/or in other Microsoft-provided materials. Any supplemental software code provided to you as part of the Support Services shall be considered part of the SOFTWARE PRODUCT and subject to the terms and conditions of this EULA. With respect to technical information you provide to Microsoft as part of the Support Services, Microsoft may use such information for its business purposes, including for product support and development. Microsoft will not utilize such technical information in a form that personally identifies you.

- **Software Transfer.** You may permanently transfer all of your rights under this EULA, provided you retain no copies, you transfer all of the SOFTWARE PRODUCT (including all component parts, the media and printed materials, any upgrades, this EULA, and, if applicable, the Certificate of Authenticity), **and** the recipient agrees to the terms of this EULA.

- **Termination.** Without prejudice to any other rights, Microsoft may terminate this EULA if you fail to comply with the terms and conditions of this EULA. In such event, you must destroy all copies of the SOFTWARE PRODUCT and all of its component parts.

3. **COPYRIGHT.** All title and copyrights in and to the SOFTWARE PRODUCT (including but not limited to any images, photographs, animations, video, audio, music, text, SAMPLE CODE, REDISTRIBUTABLES, and "applets" incorporated into the SOFTWARE PRODUCT) and any copies of the SOFTWARE PRODUCT are owned by Microsoft or its suppliers. The SOFTWARE PRODUCT is protected by copyright laws and international treaty provisions. Therefore, you must treat the SOFTWARE PRODUCT like any other copyrighted material **except** that you may install the SOFTWARE PRODUCT on a single computer provided you keep the original solely for backup or archival purposes. You may not copy the printed materials accompanying the SOFTWARE PRODUCT.

4. **U.S. GOVERNMENT RESTRICTED RIGHTS.** The SOFTWARE PRODUCT and documentation are provided with RESTRICTED RIGHTS. Use, duplication, or disclosure by the Government is subject to restrictions as set forth in subparagraph (c)(1)(ii) of the Rights in Technical Data and Computer Software clause at DFARS 252.227-7013 or subparagraphs (c)(1) and (2) of the Commercial Computer Software—Restricted Rights at 48 CFR 52.227-19, as applicable. Manufacturer is Microsoft Corporation/One Microsoft Way/Redmond, WA 98052-6399.

5. **EXPORT RESTRICTIONS.** You agree that you will not export or re-export the SOFTWARE PRODUCT, any part thereof, or any process or service that is the direct product of the SOFTWARE PRODUCT (the foregoing collectively referred to as the "Restricted Components"), to any country, person, entity, or end user subject to U.S. export restrictions. You specifically agree not to export or re-export any of the Restricted Components (i) to any country to which the U.S. has embargoed or restricted the export of goods or services, which currently include, but are not necessarily limited to, Cuba, Iran, Iraq, Libya, North Korea, Sudan, and Syria, or to any national of any such country, wherever located, who intends to transmit or transport the Restricted Components back to such country; (ii) to any end user who you know or have reason to know will utilize the Restricted Components in the design, development, or production of nuclear, chemical, or biological weapons; or (iii) to any end user who has been prohibited from participating in U.S. export transactions by any federal agency of the U.S. government. You warrant and represent that neither the BXA nor any other U.S. federal agency has suspended, revoked, or denied your export privileges.

6. **NOTE ON JAVA SUPPORT.** THE SOFTWARE PRODUCT MAY CONTAIN SUPPORT FOR PROGRAMS WRITTEN IN JAVA. JAVA TECHNOLOGY IS NOT FAULT TOLERANT AND IS NOT DESIGNED, MANUFACTURED, OR INTENDED FOR USE OR RESALE AS ON-LINE CONTROL EQUIPMENT IN HAZARDOUS ENVIRONMENTS REQUIRING FAIL-SAFE PERFORMANCE, SUCH AS IN THE OPERATION OF NUCLEAR FACILITIES, AIRCRAFT NAVIGATION OR COMMUNICATION SYSTEMS, AIR TRAFFIC CONTROL, DIRECT LIFE SUPPORT MACHINES, OR WEAPONS SYSTEMS, IN WHICH THE FAILURE OF JAVA TECHNOLOGY COULD LEAD DIRECTLY TO DEATH, PERSONAL INJURY, OR SEVERE PHYSICAL OR ENVIRONMENTAL DAMAGE.

DISCLAIMER OF WARRANTY

NO WARRANTIES OR CONDITIONS. MICROSOFT EXPRESSLY DISCLAIMS ANY WARRANTY OR CONDITION FOR THE SOFTWARE PRODUCT. THE SOFTWARE PRODUCT AND ANY RELATED DOCUMENTATION IS PROVIDED "AS IS" WITHOUT WARRANTY OR CONDITION OF ANY KIND, EITHER EXPRESS OR IMPLIED, INCLUDING, WITHOUT LIMITATION, THE IMPLIED WARRANTIES OF MERCHANTABILITY, FITNESS FOR A PARTICULAR PURPOSE, OR NONINFRINGEMENT. THE ENTIRE RISK ARISING OUT OF USE OR PERFORMANCE OF THE SOFTWARE PRODUCT REMAINS WITH YOU.

LIMITATION OF LIABILITY. TO THE MAXIMUM EXTENT PERMITTED BY APPLICABLE LAW, IN NO EVENT SHALL MICROSOFT OR ITS SUPPLIERS BE LIABLE FOR ANY SPECIAL, INCIDENTAL, INDIRECT, OR CONSEQUENTIAL DAMAGES WHATSOEVER (INCLUDING, WITHOUT LIMITATION, DAMAGES FOR LOSS OF BUSINESS PROFITS, BUSINESS INTERRUPTION, LOSS OF BUSINESS INFORMATION, OR ANY OTHER PECUNIARY LOSS) ARISING OUT OF THE USE OF OR INABILITY TO USE THE SOFTWARE PRODUCT OR THE PROVISION OF OR FAILURE TO PROVIDE SUPPORT SERVICES, EVEN IF MICROSOFT HAS BEEN ADVISED OF THE POSSIBILITY OF SUCH DAMAGES. IN ANY CASE, MICROSOFT'S ENTIRE LIABILITY UNDER ANY PROVISION OF THIS EULA SHALL BE LIMITED TO THE GREATER OF THE AMOUNT ACTUALLY PAID BY YOU FOR THE SOFTWARE PRODUCT OR US$5.00; PROVIDED, HOWEVER, IF YOU HAVE ENTERED INTO A MICROSOFT SUPPORT SERVICES AGREEMENT, MICROSOFT'S ENTIRE LIABILITY REGARDING SUPPORT SERVICES SHALL BE GOVERNED BY THE TERMS OF THAT AGREEMENT. BECAUSE SOME STATES AND JURISDICTIONS DO NOT ALLOW THE EXCLUSION OR LIMITATION OF LIABILITY, THE ABOVE LIMITATION MAY NOT APPLY TO YOU.

MISCELLANEOUS

This EULA is governed by the laws of the State of Washington USA, except and only to the extent that applicable law mandates governing law of a different jurisdiction.

Should you have any questions concerning this EULA, or if you desire to contact Microsoft for any reason, please contact the Microsoft subsidiary serving your country, or write: Microsoft Sales Information Center/One Microsoft Way/Redmond, WA 98052-6399.